VALUES, RATIONALITY, AND POWER

CRITICAL MANAGEMENT STUDIES

Series Editor: Albert J. Mills

VALUES, RATIONALITY, AND POWER: DEVELOPING ORGANIZATIONAL WISDOM

A Case Study of a Canadian Healthcare Authority

BY

BRAD C. ANDERSON
Kwantlen Polytechnic University, Canada

United Kingdom – North America – Japan – India – Malaysia – China

Emerald Publishing Limited
Howard House, Wagon Lane, Bingley BD16 1WA, UK

First edition 2019

British Library Cataloguing in Publication Data
A catalogue record for this book is available from the British Library

ISBN: 978-1-83867-942-2 (Print)
ISBN: 978-1-83867-941-5 (Online)
ISBN: 978-1-83909-091-2 (EPub)

ISSN: 2059-6561

INVESTOR IN PEOPLE

Contents

List of Figures

List of Tables

About the Author

Dr Brad C. Anderson teaches business at Kwantlen Polytechnic University, focusing on operations management as well as business analysis and decision-making. Prior to that, he worked as a scientist in the biotech industry where he made drugs for a living (legally!). In addition to his teaching and research interests, he is a published science fiction author. Learn more about him and his work at www.bradanderson2000.com.

Acknowledgements

There are many people to whom I owe a debt of gratitude. Dr. Gabrielle Durepos devoted a tremendous amount of time, effort, and thought into helping me shape this book into what it is. This work would be a mere shadow of itself without her guidance and support. Likewise, Dr. Janice Thomas made the time to take me on as a graduate student despite an already vast array of responsibilities. It was she who introduced me to Bent Flyvbjerg's book *Making Social Science Matter: Why Social Inquiry Fails and How It Can Succeed Again*. There are books that change lives, and this book changed mine. I also wish to thank Drs. Gloria Filax, Gina Grandy, and Jim Grant, who took the time to review and provide feedback on my research. Their insights and challenging questions only made this work stronger.

There are many within my research setting to whom I owe thanks. To maintain their confidentiality, however, I can only refer to them by their code names. The Mentor was the first person in the BC Health Authority to introduce me to the Seniors Programme. From day one, she showed interest and passion for my research. Similarly, the Site Director was incredibly supportive, giving me access to a treasure trove of documents. These two plus my other interviewees, the MD Lead, Head Coach, Senior Improvement Lead, CEO1 and CEO2, gave generously their time participating in my interviews. Associated with many of these individuals and the research ethics boards I interacted with are unsung heroes: executive assistants and administrators with whom I worked to arrange meetings, organize interviews, and guide paperwork through the labyrinthine complexity of bureaucracy. Without the generosity and support of these people, this research would not exist.

Chapter 1

Study Overview

How do we create organizations that act wisely? Can we even put 'organization' and 'wise' in the same sentence without irony? Through this study, I hope to demonstrate that organizations can act wisely, and more importantly, we can help them do so. In this investigation, I performed an embedded, single case study (Yin, 2014) within the British Columbia (BC) Health Authority, a regional health authority situated in a major metropolitan area of BC, Canada. The specific case was the implementation of the Seniors Programme, a pilot project for the community-based care of seniors who are not yet frail but are at risk of becoming so.[1] This single case study drew on a narrative analysis of interviews I had with programme stakeholders as well as a textual analysis of documents produced through the programme's implementation.

Why the focus on a Canadian Health Authority? Canadian spending on healthcare is one of the highest in the Organization for Economic Co-operation and Development (OECD), yet its performance outcomes on many measures are worse than OECD averages (Conference Board of Canada, 2012; 'OECD Health Data 2014', 2014). The causes of this are complex and multifactorial. One piece of the puzzle, however, is the healthcare system is composed of multiple groups, each in possession of considerable power, each representing different value positions and self-interests, and each of whom must work together and implement decisions for the betterment of patient care and society (Simpson, 2012). Decision-making in such pluralistic organizations can be complicated and fraught with political strife, making wise decisions challenging to implement (Bucher & Stelling, 1969; Scott, 1982). According to Simpson (2012), Canadian healthcare costs with their current growth trajectories challenge the sustainability of the system. Since other countries can achieve more value for their healthcare dollar than Canada, there is a need to develop our understanding of how to facilitate wise decision-making to enable a financially viable healthcare system meeting the values espoused in the Canada Health Act.

In the following sections, I lay out an overview of this study and its findings. I open with an introduction to organizational wisdom and my main constructs of values, rationality, and power. Then, I summarize the theoretical frameworks on

---

[1]To maintain confidentiality of my interview subjects, I have changed the names of all organizations and programmes.

which I built this study and my methods, followed by an overview of my results. I close this chapter with a preview of the key learning uncovered in this study.

1.1. Introduction to Organizational Wisdom, Values, Rationality, and Power

What does wisdom mean? How do we study it? How do we develop the wisdom of our society's establishments? I explore answers to these questions in Chapter 2. In brief, wisdom is a social construct, which leads to diverse conceptualizations of it (McNamee, 1998; Pitsis & Clegg, 2007; Sampson, 1998). We see wisdom in those capable of balancing many forms of knowledge and values to reach a common good over the long- and short-term (Jordan & Sternberg, 2007). Organizations are collections of individuals working together, creating additional challenges to wise action. Overcoming these challenges, however, gives individuals useful tools to navigate the wild complexity of organizational reality (Vaill, 1998, 2007), avoid costs of foolish mistakes (Beyer & Nino, 1998), and capture unique opportunities (Chia & Holt, 2007).

Kessler and Bailey (2007a) stratified organizational wisdom along four levels of analysis: individual, teams, organizations, and strategy. Individually, people exhibit practical wisdom by focusing on contexts rather than applying general rules. They use multiple forms of rationality and values to navigate complexity (Flyvbjerg, 2001). In teams, wise groups bring a diversity of opinions and values into dialogue to create effective action (Boyatzis, 2007). Organizationally, wise leaders develop the ability to learn on the fly (Vaill, 1998, 2007) and improve long-term viability by balancing the needs of the broadest range of stakeholders (Conger & Hooijberg, 2007). Strategically, wisdom is the use of knowledge and experience to act in a manner appealing to different environmental stakeholders (De Meyer, 2007). Three themes of wisdom arose from the literature: (1) values guide wise action, (2) knowledge is required, but insufficient for wise action, and (3) wisdom is action-oriented, requiring individuals to exercise power in order to act.

In Chapter 3, I review the literature on two of these three themes: values and rationality. Values are the ends we find worth achieving and inform the means we are willing to employ to achieve those ends (Townley, 2008b). Beck Jørgensen and Sørensen (2013) have classified several value constellations expressed in the public sector. They show that Canada has emphasized several of these values in its 'Values and Ethics Code for the Public Service', and the Canada Health Act embodies a number of these values. These values are diverse and are at times incompatible, if not incommensurable with each other (De Graff, Huberts, & Smulders, 2014). Workers in the public sector use several tactics to address these value conflicts (De Graff et al., 2014; Oldenhof, Postma, & Putters, 2014).

Rationality is the basis of social coordination and provides the foundation, defence, and explanation of action (Townley, 2008b). Its relation to action intertwines it with power (Flyvbjerg, 1998). Townley (2008b) identified three faces of rationality. *Disembedded rationality* assumes the existence of objective knowledge that is discoverable through the application of several techniques. *Embedded rationality* argues that an observer can only consider rationality from the context of the situation. *Embodied rationality* maintains that rationality is experienced viscerally through our bodies, emotions, and psyche. When individuals work together, they engage in forms of collective rationality. When individuals and groups bring multiple rationalities to bear on a subject, using disembedded rationality to inform embedded and embodied rationality, practical reason becomes achievable.

The third theme of wisdom is its action-oriented nature. Acting requires the exercise of power. Chapter 4 presents my review of power research. Hardy and Clegg (1996) identified two categories of power research. The first took a critical view of power that considered power from the perspective of classes. This view evolved into the four dimensions of power conceptualized by Lukes (2005). The first dimension considered how to get others to do what you want. The second explored how power suppressed conflict by preventing discussion on specific topics. Power's third dimension explained how it prevented conflict through the legitimation of authority. The fourth dimension viewed power as social networks and discourses encompassing all members of society. Hardy and Clegg's (1996) second branch of power research took a structural functionalist direction observed through a managerial perspective. Researchers working on this branch saw power as hierarchical in that the organization allocated power according to one's position. Workers, however, maintained the capacity to resist this hierarchical order through various means. Fleming and Spicer (2014) presented an organizing framework for power research. They mapped power along two axes. The first axis listed the faces of power. These included episodic uses of power such as coercion and manipulation and systematic power such as domination and subjectification. The second axis identified sites of power. These sites included power in, through, over, and against organizations.

Power is intertwined with values and rationality. I argue that systematic power influences the values people hold. Moreover, I further hypothesize that when values conflict, individuals exercise power to promote the values they pursue. Power exhibits its relation to rationality through influencing what individuals debate and how they construct their arguments (Townley, 2008b). Additionally, power structures adopt the rationalities that support them (Flyvbjerg, 1998; Townley, 2008b).

My research setting is a healthcare organization. Such organizations are pluralistic (Bucher & Stelling, 1969; Scott, 1982). Pluralistic organizations consist of specialized, highly trained groups with different objectives and complex power relations between them. Though this organizational structure effectively deals with work that is complex, uncertain, and important, it can lead to environments where political infighting dominates (Scott, 1982). The complexity of pluralistic organizations makes them a great test bed to study the dynamics of values, rationality, and power.

1.2.   Introduction of Theoretical Frameworks
and Research Questions

I have embedded this study in the philosophical school of critical realism. As I describe in Chapter 5, critical realism possesses a stratified ontology wherein social structures, such as power relations, simultaneously constrain and enable individuals' actions. These actions produce and reproduce social structures and, if these actions are observed, create experiences (Bhaskar, 1978). In this book, I classify values, rationality, and power as relevant social structures for study. I apply a research approach developed by Flyvbjerg (2001) called 'phronetic research' (PR). Though I explore PR deeply in Chapter 5, I will briefly introduce it here.

As Flyvbjerg (2001) described it, PR is an approach aimed at developing the practical wisdom of society's institutions. Its underlying assumption is that through an understanding of how rationality and power influence each other, actors can increase the capacity for value-rationality in institutions (Flyvbjerg, 2001). Through the application of a PR approach, this study contributes to our understanding of how to develop organizational value-rationality. PR focuses on power because power influences the creation of knowledge to justify its actions and mechanisms of control (Flyvbjerg, 1998). Moreover, PR emphasizes creating knowledge that allows people to facilitate change (Flyvbjerg, Landman, & Schram, 2012; Schram, 2012). With this understanding, Flyvbjerg (2001) listed four questions for researchers to use when applying a PR approach: (1) Where are we going? (2) Is this desirable? (3) With each decision, who gains, who loses, and through what power mechanisms? (4) What should be done? I have developed my study's research questions, shown in Table 1.1, around these four questions.

Table 1.1. Research Questions.

PR Questions Addressed by the Research Question	Research Questions
(1) Where are we going? (3) With each decision, who gains, who loses, and through what power mechanisms?	How did power affect the process of developing and implementing the Seniors Programme in the BC Health Authority?
(2) Is this desirable?	Did power wielded by stakeholders of the Seniors Programme result in organizational actions in keeping with the values of Canada's healthcare system?
(4) What should be done?	No research question *per se*, but recommendations at the end address the final PR question.

You will notice that I have introduced a value judgment in my second research question: 'Did power wielded by stakeholders of the Seniors Programme result in organizational actions in keeping with the values of Canada's healthcare system?' I have prioritized the values of Canada's healthcare system and set them as the litmus test for wise action. Is this appropriate? As I will discuss when reviewing the literature on organizational wisdom, what people consider wise is embedded in systems of power – that is, whether someone judges an act as wise depends on who is doing the judging (McNamee, 1998; Pitsis & Clegg, 2007; Sampson, 1998). Flyvbjerg (2001) recognized this, arguing there exists no objective definition of which acts are wise. Instead, individuals act 'wisely' by determining what is ethically practical within a social context. The social context of my research setting is a Canadian healthcare system. Following this logic, then, the litmus test of wise action for stakeholders of the Canadian healthcare system are the values of the Canadian healthcare system.

1.3. Summary of Methodology

In Chapter 6, I describe my methodology. I performed an embedded case study on the implementation of the Seniors Programme. The Seniors Programme was a pilot project implemented through a collaboration between health authorities in BC and Nova Scotia (NS) and the Foundation, a not-for-profit organization focused on the development and spread of innovative healthcare solutions. The purpose of the Seniors Programme was to develop an intervention that paired seniors with appropriate community resources to facilitate lifestyle choices that delayed the progression of frailty. To implement the Seniors Programme, the BC and NS health authorities sent individuals to participate in a training programme the Foundation ran to teach administrators how to develop, apply, and spread innovations. Compounding the difficulty of developing an intervention to delay frailty, the BC Health Authority experienced turnover at the level of the chief executive officer (CEO) that threatened organizational commitment to the programme.

My data included texts and semi-structured, open-ended interviews of key individuals involved in developing and implementing the Seniors Programme. On this data, I performed a narrative analysis as per Feldman, Sködberg, Brown, and Homer (2004). I coded the data for values, rationality, and power. PR research justified a qualitative approach such as the ones I used (Flyvbjerg, 2001). These methods can provide detailed situational information needed to understand the interplay of values, rationality, and power within my research setting (Flyvbjerg, 2001). Case studies allow the researcher to observe human behaviour and values within social contexts (Flyvbjerg, 2001, 2004, 2006a, 2006b). Narrative analyses are an effective means to understand the underlying meaning of discourses (Eriksson & Kovalainen, 2008; Flyvbjerg, 2001, 2004, 2006b) and provide the same data individuals operating within organizations use to evaluate their own reality (Pentland, 1999).

1.4.   Overview of Results

Chapter 7 presents my analysis of the values the developers of the Seniors Programme pursued. These included public interest, sustainability, innovation, effectiveness, self-development of employees, accountability, dialogue, user orientation, and spread of innovation. My data showed that not all values were equal: some were what Dahl and Lindblom (1953) called 'prime values' (ends in themselves), while others were instrumental values (means to achieve those ends). These values were consistent with the values espoused in the Canada Health Act, demonstrating that the development of the programme was within the remit of the healthcare system. The data showed the link between values, rationality, and power. My interviewees often noted how vital it was that the programme was 'evidence-based'. That is, they joined the programme not only because it pursued relevant values but because it did so using a form of rationality they venerated. Moreover, the programme only gained organizational reality through individuals' exercise of power.

Despite the alignment of values between the Seniors Programme and the Canada Health Act, I show in Chapter 8 that some vice presidents (VPs) within the BC Health Authority resisted the development of this programme. Interestingly, these VPs seemed to share prime values with the developers of the Seniors Programme. Why, then, were they unsupportive of it? Conflicts across two parameters caused their resistance. First, though they shared prime values, instrumental values differed. VPs pursued public interest through the value robustness (i.e. managing acute care and decongestion of hospitals), whereas the programme developers pursued public interest through innovation (i.e. creating the Seniors Programme to reduce frailty). Second, though they shared the prime value of public interest, the time frame VPs operated in differed from the programme developers: VPs managed acute care in the present; the programme developers were seeking long-term solutions. The VPs did not disagree with the aims of the Seniors Programme. Instead, they were hesitant to devote resources to a programme utilizing different instrumental values and operating in different time frames.

VPs exercised their resistance through use of episodic power, most notably manipulation. For example, they discouraged their staff from working on the Seniors Programme and kept the programme from appearing on meeting agendas where developers could present their work. Nonetheless, developers found ways to exercise their power in the organization to meet with VPs. Through the emphasis of shared prime values and effective use of multiple forms of rationality, they got senior managers interested and supportive of the programme. They built on this support throughout the life of the Seniors Programme by presenting positive results and by carefully managing communication within the BC Health Authority to embed their programme within an incumbent community of senior care initiatives. Later, programme developers leveraged this support to protect the programme during periods of CEO turnover.

The CEO of the BC Health Authority initiated the Seniors Program. He left the organization partway through the program's implementation. Despite his departure, the Seniors Programme survived, and a subsequent CEO became its new executive champion. This did not happen by accident. As I describe in Chapter 9, from the program's earliest conception, the first CEO acted to bind his organization to the Seniors Programme despite initial resistance from his VPs. These actions included recruiting project champions who possessed passion, drive, and political savvy to move the project. He then used a variety of bureaucratic structures to protect those champions from the politics of the organization. He further used various forms of bureaucratic rationality to commit his organization to a national collaboration to develop the program, which subsequently created external allies fostering the Seniors Program's survival.

Chapter 10 presents my analysis of the different forms of rationality individuals used throughout the Senior Program's life. A specific form of disembedded rationality, named technocratic rationality, dominated. This rationality assumes there is a best way of accomplishing a task revealed through application of the scientific method. Though technocratic rationality dominated, individuals used various forms of rationality. Sometimes the use of multiple rationalities added benefits. For example, when designing the intervention the Seniors Programme would implement, programme developers combined technocratic rationality with contextual (i.e. cultural) rationality, an embedded rationality. Technocratic rationality informed what the science said about how to prevent frailty, whereas contextual rationality informed how best to engage seniors to partake in those activities.

Different rationalities did not always complement each other. Recall that the Seniors Programme was a collaboration between BC and NS health authorities. These regions possessed differences in population and healthcare administration. That is, contextual rationalities differed between the regions. These differences prevented a single approach to the Seniors Program, thus undermining pure technocratic rationality. The developers attempted to reconcile this conflict by establishing high-level principles for the intervention (i.e. technocratic rationality) while allowing each region to modify the implementation of those principles (i.e. contextual rationality). Likewise, the BC working group undertook a similar reconciliation when applying the intervention to BC-based seniors. They had coaches apply an evidence-based intervention (technocratic rationality), which coaches then modified to the individual needs, limitations, and comfort level of senior participants. This individualization represented body rationality, which is a form of embodied rationality.

The developers also engaged in acts of defining rationality, a form of episodic power. For example, they defined the patient population the Seniors Programme targeted. This act pitted technocratic rationality against body, emotional, and contextual rationalities. In short, the scientific literature led to a name that seniors found negative and distasteful. Likewise, they created the program's vision statement, 'Age well, die fit'. Though this vision captured what the literature said was possible, it conflicted with contextual and emotional rationalities because it broke the taboo of healthcare professionals speaking about death. Throughout the life of the Seniors Program, technocratic rationality was a dominant rationality, and it bumped heads with several other rationalities. In each case, the rationality of the group that held power in a particular context prevailed.

In Chapter 11, I analyse how individuals reified power through the Seniors Program's life. I demonstrate how shared values motivated people to overcome structures constraining action. Importantly, my data showed how individuals used bureaucratic rationality to give power structure and reality. I also assessed how individuals exercised empowerment using contextual and body rationalities. The data demonstrated that a critical action the developers took to avoid conflict and build power relations was the careful management of communication. Finally, I explored how managers created organizational structures that protected workers from political turmoil, allowing them to focus on the work needed to bring the Seniors Programme to life.

In Chapter 12, I explore the developer's intentions to spread the Seniors Programme nationally. I assessed how important the intent to spread was to the people involved in the Seniors Programme and consider why individuals employed to administer healthcare to a localized region were interested in national spread. The data showed that my interviewees only viewed the Seniors Programme as a qualified success. They felt their results were positive – their intervention meaningfully delayed the onset of frailty. My interviewees also felt they learned much from the experience of participating in a multi-institution collaboration to create the program. National spread, however, was not happening at the time I wrote this book. Instead, spread was limited to the region administered by the BC Health Authority. The programme was alive, but more limited than they had hoped.

Thus, I explored the structures constraining spread of the Seniors Program. I learned that health authorities were risk-averse. They were responsible for managing acute care, often under conditions of strained resources. This created an environment of risk aversion. When the health authority made a mistake, people may die. Consequently, health authorities were hesitant to experiment with innovations. Structural constraints also hampered spread. For example, fee codes failed to compensate for some of the activities required of physicians implementing the Seniors Program. In the absence of a fee code, doctors were unable to bill for the work they needed to do to implement the Seniors Program's intervention, thus constraining spread. Similarly, if other healthcare professionals, such as nurses and physiotherapists, could offload some of the work from physicians, the issue of fee codes would become moot. The way BC structured primary care, however, precluded such tight integration of healthcare professionals. These constraints worsened as individuals sought to spread the programme nationally because each province delivered healthcare differently, meaning the challenges would-be spreaders faced differed across the country. Moreover, my interviewees identified that the difficulty of managing a healthcare region pulled at managers' attention, strained their resources, and sapped their energy. Sites may simply lack the resources of time, personnel, funding, and passion to take on something new due to the daily pressures they faced. The intensity of managing over-crowded hospitals day after day led to fatigue and an inability to absorb new programs.

All was not lost, however. In spreading the Seniors Programme through their region, my interviewees demonstrated there are actions individuals and organizations can take to overcome these constraints. I describe these actions in Chapter 13. Enabling structures included action-oriented leaders who recognized the importance of innovations and used their power to foster adoption. Critically, recruiting programme champions who were passionate about the programme to drive adoption was important. The passion champions brought was instrumental in inspiring others to act and imbued people with the endurance needed to push against constraints. The nature of the programme itself was an essential facet of whether it could spread – programs with generalizable interventions were more easily spread than those that only worked in specific contexts. Effective use of bureaucratic rationalities also facilitated adoption by overcoming structural constraints. For example, the developers created electronic forms automating many of the physicians' activities, reducing the barriers posed by lack of fee codes and staff. Finally, waiting until managers are ready to take on a new programme facilitated spread better than trying to foist it on regions.

1.5. Summary of Discussion

What can we learn from these results? I begin exploring this in Chapter 14. Here, I discuss what my results demonstrated about the role of values, rationality, and power in organizational action. Values enabled certain actions. For example, the ability of the CEO to commit the BC Health Authority to a multi-institutional collaboration to develop the Seniors Programme was enabled because Canada's healthcare system embodied the values of dialogue and collaboration. Conversely, values also constrained action. For example, several managers exhibited the value of accountability – they perceived themselves accountable to administer healthcare within the boundaries prescribed by their organization's mandate. This value led some VPs to resist collaborating with other organizations. It also lowered the priority to spread the Seniors Programme nationally. Developers of the Seniors Programme had to exercise power to overcome the constraining effect of this value.

Similarly, rationality enabled and constrained action. Effective exercise of bureaucratic rationality facilitated the implementation of the Seniors Programme in multiple ways. The Project Charter reified the collaboration, defined responsibilities and processes, and established the project's scope. On the other hand, economic rationality, which is a form of disembedded rationality where individuals make utility-maximizing decisions, constrained physicians from adopting the Seniors Programme due to a lack of fee codes. As with values, individuals acted to overcome these constraints by, for example, automating specific functions to minimize the impact of no fee code.

How did power affect the process of developing and implementing the Seniors Programme in the BC Health Authority? Values need rationality and power. Though values need power to have effect, power needs values to have direction. It was only through power structures that values enabled and constrained action, and it was through subsequent exercises of power that individuals overcame constraining effects. Regarding rationality, my data showed that bureaucratic rationality reified power. Moreover, when different rationalities brought different groups into a disagreement, the power dynamics between the groups influenced which rationality prevailed.

Did power wielded by stakeholders of the Seniors Programme result in organizational actions in keeping with the values of Canada's healthcare system? This question was trickier than it appeared. Chapter 15 explores my answer to it. The complexity of Canada's healthcare system contributed to this question's difficulty. I saw in this study, however, that developers of the Seniors Programme recognized the importance of the values other individuals pursued, even when those values led them to resist the Seniors Program. They sought ways to reconcile those values so that the programme advanced without compromising the system's ability to administer healthcare elsewhere. Likewise, even though the developers venerated technocratic rationality, they understood its limitations and respected the forms of rationality other stakeholders used. Overall, they sought to advance the Seniors Programme in a manner that maintained stability and added to the healthcare system's capacity. Though this led to the slower spread of the program, it built a web of support within the community that kept the programme alive.

In Chapter 16, I summarize several propositions from this study and present recommendations to develop organizational wisdom. Values guide wise action. This study demonstrated that values give direction to episodic uses of power. They drove project champions who then drove action, and when personal values aligned with organizational values, synergies happened. Thus, I recommend that organizations pursuing wise action incorporate value alignment in their recruitment processes. The results also showed that even when groups shared prime values, conflicts may occur along instrumental or temporal lines, and these conflicts can form points of resistance. To manage this, individuals must develop their capacity to recognize and reconcile value conflicts.

The results of this study also confirmed that knowledge is required but insufficient for wise action. To address this, individuals tapped into the power of collective reasoning where groups blended multiple rationalities to create a fuller picture of the environment they faced. Moreover, knowledge's limitations required individuals to engage in experimentation with an appreciative enquiry mindset. The existence of multiple forms of rationality, however, could lead to conflict. Part of wisdom is recognizing which rationality has power in a specific context. Individuals can enhance their ability to recognize this through developing their bureaucratic, institutional, and contextual rationalities through experience, self-reflectivity, and mentoring.

Wisdom is action-oriented. It is not *knowing* the right thing but *doing* it. Action requires an exercise of power, and this study showed that bureaucratic rationality was essential to translating power into action. Though effective bureaucratic rationality enabled action, ineffective bureaucratic rationality constrained it. It was institutional and contextual rationalities that informed the creation of effective bureaucratic rationalities. Thus, individuals need to strengthen their mastery of these forms of rationality to drive organizational action. This study also demonstrated that organizational action was a group activity. Developing organizations capable of wise action, therefore, requires the development of teams capable of implementing the precepts of wise action identified in this book. It then behooves leaders to act to protect those teams from the political dynamics of the organization to allow them to focus on the task at hand. Finally, producing power relations with other groups was critical to the Seniors Program's success. Individuals and groups should, therefore, choose their partners thoughtfully. This study demonstrated that defining rationality, an episodic use of power, was an effective means to forge these power relations. Developing effective negotiation skills was instrumental in enhancing one's capacity to forge these supportive relations.

I believe we can grow wiser. There are actions I present in Chapter 17 to further develop our capacity for wise organizational action. Though we may not be able to teach wisdom per se, there are actions educators, trainers, mentors, and coaches can take to create fertile soil in which it can flourish. This requires use of pedagogical tools to develop personal, social, and emotional intelligence developed through techniques such as experiential learning. Further research is also required to deepen our understanding of organizational wisdom. I believe enriching our understanding of values in organizational contexts is an essential first step to this end. Moreover, performing studies like this one at different levels within the organization and with organizations under varying degrees of duress will further add to our understanding of organizational wisdom.

Overall, through the application of a phronetic research approach as developed by Flyvbjerg (2001), this study advanced our understanding of organizational wisdom and provides actionable recommendations to develop it. It added to the literature on phronetic research by putting values on equal footing with rationality and power. This revealed values' capacity to drive action as well as identified how conflicts create points of resistance. Through applying Townley's (2008b) framework of rationality, this study demonstrated how different ways of understanding the environment influenced action. Though differing rationalities led to conflict, blending different rationalities yielded innovative solutions to sticky problems. This study also demonstrated how individuals within an organization wielded power positively to drive wise action. As you can see, we have an exciting road ahead. Let us now dive into this study by first establishing an understanding of what I mean by the phrase 'organizational wisdom'.

Chapter 2

Overview of Organizational Wisdom

Since my research focused on organizational wisdom, this raised a more foundational question: What is wisdom? Countless are the thinkers who have contemplated what it means to be wise and no wonder. Wisdom is critical (Kessler & Bailey, 2007b). Whereas knowledge is the application of information (Bierly, Kessler, & Christensen, 2000), mere possession of knowledge seldom informs us of how we should apply it, or when, or whose knowledge is pertinent for any given circumstance. Seldom do we have all the facts we feel we need to make the decisions facing us. Real life is messy. We are surrounded by people and groups who have different values, different interests, different types of knowledge, and different levels of mastery of their knowledge. The problems we face are rarely as simplistic as textbooks portray. The brilliant bit of knowledge we gain from reading a report that makes us go 'Ah-ha!' somehow never seems as elegant when we try to apply that knowledge to our actual lives, as if applying theoretical knowledge to the real world somehow sullies it. It is chaos out there (Vaill, 1998). Out of this chaos, we must forge order to progress. It is the faculty of wisdom we use to navigate this turbulent sea and chart a path forward (Weick, 2007).

What, however, is wisdom? Can we measure it? Can we teach it? How does one become wise? Is wisdom something organizations can possess? If they can, is it worth the bother? It is through wisdom we struggle to master a chaotic world (Kessler & Bailey, 2007b; Weick, 2007). It should be no surprise, then, to find the tool we use to manage complexity defies simple categorization.

For thousands of years, thinkers have written on the topic of wisdom, and it has meant many different things through time and across cultures (Chia & Holt, 2007; Kessler & Bailey, 2007b). Summarizing this vast body of literature in a concise and digestible way is problematic. For that reason, I will focus my review on the literature pertinent to organizational wisdom. I will start my review with a brief overview of what wisdom is, especially in organizational contexts. I will then evaluate whether wisdom is an attribute that we can apply to organizations. After this, I will present arguments for and against whether organizations should strive for wisdom. Then, I will review the literature on wisdom manifest at the individual, interpersonal, organizational, and strategic levels of analysis.

2.1. Wisdom: What Is It?

Wisdom is a social construct, and so those who have power embed it in their value system (McNamee, 1998; Pitsis & Clegg, 2007; Sampson, 1998). This leads to diverse conceptualizations of wisdom. For example, though Earley and Offermann (2007) found that even though the structures of wisdom were universal, including an appreciation for cognitive capabilities, applied knowledge, interpersonal intelligence, and personal demeanour, the specific attributes within each of those categories, and relative importance of each category, differed across cultures. In Canada, for example, Holliday and Chandler (1986) noted that general cognitive capacity was assessed based on an exceptional understanding of phenomena and general competency. Among Tibetan Buddhist monks, however, Levitt (1999) showed they measured it by the ability to perceive Buddhist truths about reality. Thus, the definition of wisdom depends on who is defining it. Naturally, the same is true of my study. In the spirit of full disclosure, I will identify the perspective from which I approach the definition of wisdom. My interests lie in organizational action, specifically how organizations may act in a value-rational manner. That is the lens through which I present this literature review. With that in mind, let us now consider some views on wisdom.

Kessler and Bailey (2007b) discussed three wisdom frameworks: integrative, developmental, and balance. The *integrative* framework results from the integration of cognitive, reflective, and affective aspects (Ardelt, 2000, 2004). Weick (2007) explained that though a critical element of wisdom is the possession of knowledge, an equally important element is understanding knowledge may have its flaws. Thus, wisdom integrates many ways of knowing to chart a course through complex situations. These ways of knowing may include emotion, will, and intellect (Birren & Fisher, 1990), technical know-how and theory (Pitsis & Clegg, 2007), scholarly knowledge, historical wisdom traditions, and experience (Adler, 2007), among others.

The *developmental* framework, conceptualized by Baltes and Kunzmann (2004) and Baltes and Staudinger (2000), asserted that wisdom was a developmental process. It grows from personal, domain-specific, and contextual factors. These factors manifest in a progression and thus improve through experience and targeted interventions. Conversely, Sternberg (1990, 1998, 2003a, 2003b, 2005b) formulated a *balanced* framework of wisdom. In this framework, those exhibiting wisdom balance multiple cognitive domains, such as values, social, and temporal, against one another to select actions. In brief:

> [W]isdom is the ability to use one's successful intelligence, creativity, and knowledge, as mediated by personal values, to reach a common good by balancing intrapersonal, interpersonal, and extrapersonal interests over the short and long terms to adapt to, shape, and select environments. (Jordan & Sternberg, 2007, p. 6)

As introduced in the above description of wisdom, many scholars see values as an integral component of wisdom. Value-rationality and instrumental-rationality are the Weberian concepts of *Wertrational* and *Zweckrational* action, respectively (Flyvbjerg, 2001, p. 176). Instrumental-rationality are means-ends calculations (Weber, 1978, p. 26) whereby actors make rational calculations to efficiently advance goals of either self-interest or rules and laws without regard for other persons (Kalberg, 1980). This form of rationality draws from Aristotelean concepts of *techne* (technical know-how) and *episteme* (scientific knowledge). Despite its strengths in finding ways to achieve ends, instrumental-rationality is weak at choosing which ends to pursue. Here, value-rationality is strong (Weber, 1978, p. 26). Whereas instrumental-rationality is means-focused, value-rationality is ends-focused (Kalberg, 1980). Under value-rationality, rather than rely on self-interest or impersonal rules, actors' values guide the actions of individuals (Kalberg, 1980).

An essential facet of wisdom is action. Whereas knowledge is *knowing* something, wisdom is *doing* the right thing (Bierly et al., 2000; Kessler & Bailey, 2007b). Consequently, wisdom requires the courage to act (Beyer & Nino, 1998). Even then, action may not be enough. Actors need to carry out the act in a wise manner to achieve success (Statler & Roos, 2006).

This call to action, combined with the above attributes of wisdom, focuses on the characteristics and actions of individuals. Organizations are not individuals, however; they are collections of individuals working in concert. They face different forces and constraints. It is, thus, worth asking if it is possible for organizations to act wisely. I turn to this question now.

2.2.   Can Organizations Act Wisely?

Conger and Hooijberg (2007) identified several forces conspiring against organizations' ability to act wisely. They argued that organizational activity is rife with ethical dilemmas, an increasing number of active stakeholders, and the constant tension between short-term and long-term goals, each of which undermines the ability to act wisely. They also explored the 'tyranny of small steps', where managers continually choose short-term actions with small costs that meet immediate needs at the cost of long-term negative consequences. In addition to the 'tyranny of small steps', Sternberg (2002) identified five fallacies managers frequently succumb to that prevent wise organizational action. These fallacies include the unrealistic optimism fallacy (decision-makers see themselves as smarter than others), egocentrism fallacy (individuals believe the world revolves around them, or at least it should), omniscience fallacy (decision-makers believe they know all they need to know), omnipotence fallacy (decision-makers believe they are all powerful), and the invulnerability fallacy (the belief nothing terrible can happen to you). Janis (1972) also observed the tendency of groups to fall prey to groupthink, where people agree for the sake of agreeing without critical thought, leading to sometimes disastrous decisions. Compounding this is a dearth of tools that facilitate the development of wisdom (Conger & Hooijberg, 2007).

Despite all these challenges, Kessler and Bailey (2007b) presented evidence that organizations can act wisely and may be capable of greater wisdom than individuals. Groups and organizations are composed of multiple individuals who bring a diversity of ideas, knowledge, competencies, and perspectives that, if managed well, lead to performance superior to the individual (Hackman,

2002; Katzenbach & Smith, 2015). Moreover, I see the challenges to organizational wisdom described above not as barriers to wisdom but rather as problems that require wisdom to overcome. These problems are complex and defy easy solution. One might, therefore, ask if it is worth the organization's effort to seek wisdom. I turn to that question now.

2.3.   Do Organizations Need to Act Wisely?

In this section, I will first present three categories of arguments *against* fostering organizational wisdom. The first category considers the benefits of striving for organizational simplicity rather than wisdom. The second reflects on the incentives many managers face that contraindicate wisdom. The third explores the political dangers of wise action. Following that, I will present a general argument supporting the pursuit of organizational wisdom.

Sternberg (2005a) argued that the opposite of wisdom is not 'foolish'. It is 'simple'. That is, people do not require wisdom for simple decisions. They need it for the sticky, complicated ones at the limits of our knowledge where we must think and decide (Pitsis & Clegg, 2007). Operating at the limits of our knowledge has dangers. Mistakes will happen and showing the limits of our knowledge allows those who claim certainty to damn us (Pitsis & Clegg, 2007). It is not surprising, then, that many organizations strive to simplify by implementing routines and systems to decrease thinking and decision-making (Pitsis & Clegg, 2007; Weick, 2007). Rather than develop wisdom, they seek to eliminate the need for it.

Moreover, developing the capacity for organizational wisdom takes time and resources for non-revenue-generating work (Burke, 2007), which can put the drive for short-term profit maximization at odds with wisdom (Nicholson, 2007). Behaving ethically, a key facet of wise action, often puts individuals at a disadvantage in negotiations, which further erodes short-term profit maximization (Barry, Fulmer, & Long, 2000; Lewicki & Robinson, 1998). Organizations reward and venerate managers for decisive action, not contemplation, and for prioritizing financial stakeholders over all others, even at the expense of the long-term health of the organization (Conger & Hooijberg, 2007). There are, therefore, strong incentives to avoid the pursuit of wisdom.

Wise action can also possess political risks within an organization. When the 'wise action' challenges established power structures, individuals within those power structures may try to stop what you are doing (Schön, 1983), discredit your work (Flyvbjerg, 2001), or threaten your career (Flyvbjerg, 2012). Within the bureaucratic hierarchies characterizing North American corporations, managers often find success is founded on pleasing the boss, maintaining the appearance of certainty and control, and avoiding blame rather than questioning the status quo and standing by principles (Beyer & Nino, 1998). Oftentimes, what managers want is confirmation of their beliefs rather than wisdom (De Meyer, 2007; Pitsis & Clegg, 2007). Even if managers are in favour of developing a 'wise' course of action, if the change to the organization is too disruptive, the organization can shut down that change (De Meyer, 2007).

The above presents compelling reasons why organizations may wish to avoid the pursuit of wisdom. Let us now explore the merits of developing organizational wisdom. I organize these supporting arguments into two categories: the reality of organizational life and profitability through cost avoidance and opportunity capture. The arguments for organizational wisdom presented here are brief, but as I delve into components of organizational wisdom in the following sections, further reasons for pursuing organizational wisdom will become evident.

Regarding the nature of organizational reality, management is action-oriented. So is wisdom. If wisdom is the capacity to act rightly, then it stands to reason that this is an attribute we would want managers to have (Kessler & Bailey, 2007b). Though managers may wish to simplify systems and routines to eliminate the need for decision-making in the face of complexity, this is not the reality of organizational life (Vaill, 1998, 2007). Organizational life is a fast-paced, ever-changing environment where managers seldom have complete information to inform these decisions. It is precisely these environments that call for wisdom (Vaill, 1998, 2007).

Moreover, wise organizational action can lead to superior profitability through cost avoidance and opportunity generation. On the cost side, there are potentially significant costs to unwise action. Beyer and Nino (1998) presented examples of these costs. For example, in the Barings Bank fiasco, poor hiring practices led to the loss of $1.4 billion (Lewis, 1996). In the *Challenger* space shuttle disaster of 1986, NASA, despite being aware of a flaw, cleared the launch of the space shuttle, resulting in its destruction (Vaughan, 1990). Cameron, Freeman, and Mishra (1993) recorded acts of short-sighted downsizing where corporations attempted to cut costs through layoffs, only to have to hire back personnel as consultants, often at multiples of their original salary. As the above demonstrates, short-sighted actions may result in severe performance penalties (Beyer & Nino, 1998). Beyond cost avoidance, wisdom is key to opportunity generation. Chia and Holt (2007) argued that focus on short-term profit and key performance indicators leads to incremental innovations but does not lead to what they called 'performative extravagance'. They further proposed that innovations come from unlearning orthodoxy and becoming ignorant of constraints, which are states of mindfulness facilitated through wisdom. Further to that, Adler (2007) noted that wisdom supports organizational processes capable of responding to societal challenges by allowing managers to see possibilities where others cannot.

Thus far, I have introduced the concept of wisdom and presented an overview of the literature describing what wisdom is in relation to my study. I have presented arguments as to why organizational wisdom may not be possible. Further to this, I explored literature demonstrating that despite these challenges, organizations can, indeed, act wisely. Then, I explored the literature that considered whether it is worth the organization's efforts to act wisely. With this background established, I will now explore elements of organizational wisdom described in the literature.

2.4. Elements of Organizational Wisdom

In my consideration of organizational wisdom, I will present the literature organized along different levels of analysis as informed by Kessler and Bailey (2007a). Organizations are composed of people working individually, so I will start with elements of personal wisdom. People in organizations often work in teams, and so I will follow with a discussion of interpersonal wisdom. Organizations often encompass the coordinated activity of multiple groups, so I will then explore elements of wisdom at the level of the whole organization. Organizations interact with other organizations in society as they implement their strategies, and so I will conclude with a summary of the literature addressing wisdom at this strategic level. In each of these sections, I will start with a discussion of the importance of wisdom at each level of analysis and then proceed with the elements of wise action at each level.

2.4.1. Individual Attributes of Wisdom

Individuals in organizations have to deal with a competitive landscape where self-seeking individuals and groups often undermine good intentions (Badaracco, 1997; Cropanzano, Stein, & Goldman, 2007). Nicholson (2007) maintained that wisdom gives individuals the foresight needed to deal with this environment effectively. He further identified that we could observe the foresight wisdom gives across three realms: human affairs (the ability to guide and lead others' opinion), relationships (the ability to correctly identify and deal with the emotions of others), and self-control. The presence of wisdom gives individuals the ability to realize the full potential of their intelligence and creativity (Sternberg, 2005a, 2005b). The absence of wisdom, however, leads to five cognitive fallacies according to Jordan and Sternberg (2007): (1) fallacy of egocentrism (the belief that one should be the centre of attention), (2) fallacy of omnipotence (the belief that one can make others follow your every wish), (3) fallacy of omniscience (the belief that one knows everything they need to know), (4) fallacy of invulnerability (the belief that no harm will come to you), and (5) fallacy of unrealistic optimism (the belief that everything will work out all right). Gioia (2006) further added that we create the worlds in which we live. Wisdom lies in creating individual, organizational, societal situations that are workable and responsible for the consequences (Gioia, 2007).

At the individual level, many of our stickiest problems incorporate moral dilemmas (Bartunek & Trullen, 2007). How are those best addressed? As noted by Cropanzano et al. (2007), self-interest is a prime motivator individuals rely on when navigating such problems (see, for e.g., Badaracco, 1997; Holmes, Miller, & Lerner, 2002; Marwell & Ames, 1981). That said, human behaviour is complex, and many examples exist of individuals sacrificing self-interest to pursue other ends. These examples include sanctioning people who act unfairly

(Camerer & Thaler, 1995; Güth, Schmittberger, & Schwarze, 1982; Henrich et al., 2001; Kahneman, Knetsch, & Thaler, 1986; Ostrom, 1998), rendering assistance to those in need (for a review, see Eisenberg & Miller, 1987), or adhering to a code of conduct (Kahneman et al., 1986; Turillo, Folger, Lavelle, Umphress, & Gee, 2002; van Dijk & Tenbrunsel, 2005).

To navigate these complex, morally charged problems, practical wisdom (*phronesis*) is a useful tool (Bartunek & Trullen, 2007; Flyvbjerg, 2001; Statler & Roos, 2006). *Phronesis* exists where intellectual and moral domains meet and is a means of doing what is worthwhile in a specific context (Bartunek & Trullen, 2007; Peterson & Seligman, 2004). What are the attributes of someone exhibiting *phronesis*? Such a person can extrapolate from experience and help others understand their contexts in a way that leads to practical action (Gioia, 2007). Such a person also exhibits a mix of humility, open-mindedness, and decision-making that leads to the ability to make sound judgements in complex and ambiguous environments that benefit in the short- and long-term (Nicholson, 2007).

Bartunek and Trullen (2007) identified four characteristics of individuals who exhibit *phronesis*. (1) They focus on a specific context rather than general laws, with the ability to flip between the requirements for the situation and more general laws (Flyvbjerg, 2001). (2) They possess the ability to attend to different, complex, contradictory considerations when there is no clear right decision (Durand & Calori, 2006; Hariman, 2003; Sternberg, 1998). (3) They confront complexity as a whole person, bringing emotions, actions, and character to bear while simultaneously recognizing the distinct nature of other people involved in the situation (Durand & Calori, 2006; Fowers, 2003; Orwoll & Perlmutter, 1990; Townley, 2008b). (4) They learn from experience by engaging in self-reflectivity (Fowers, 2003), mentoring (Baltes & Kunzmann, 2004), and studying stories accompanied with guiding principles (McCloskey, 2007; Oliver & Roos, 2005). As I mentioned earlier, individuals seldom work alone in organizations. Instead, they work in teams. I now turn to interpersonal attributes of wisdom active in group action.

2.4.2. *Interpersonal Attributes of Wisdom*

Through the above collection of attributes, individuals exhibiting *phronesis* possess the ability to navigate complex, morally challenging situations where information may be incomplete and no ideal solution is evident. Organizations, however, often require the coordinated activity of groups of individuals. Indeed, Vaill (2007) argued that wisdom is a social phenomenon, rather than an individual trait. Attributes that lead to individual wisdom may be insufficient to create wise group action. Nielsen, Edmondson, and Sundstrom (2007) demonstrated that wise teams are more likely to be effective and that those lacking wisdom tend to focus on what is urgent rather than what is essential. Group action adds to the complexity of the context in which individuals operate. For example, people within the group may not agree on the right action, may have different morals and ideals, and may have conflicting personal interests (Lewicki, 2007). Thus, agreeing on group action requires negotiation, which Lewicki (2007) identified creates conditions of opportunity, desperation, lack of trust, and expectation that others will not play fair, which may undermine the group's ability to act wisely. Given these complexities, what additional attributes lead to wise group action?

Nielsen et al. (2007) identified how team members might overcome tensions occurring in team settings. These tensions include individuals' needs conflicting with those of the team's, external demands on the team conflicting with the team's internal demands, short-term goals conflicting with long-term, and multiple priorities conflicting with each other. Boyatzis (2007) argued that managing these tensions requires team members to exhibit an awareness of the emotions of themselves and others, as well as to possess the ability to manage these emotions. That is, to achieve wise team action, team members must develop what Salovey and Mayer (1990) called 'emotional and social intelligence'. Moreover, team wisdom is context dependent as different types of teams in different situations experience a different mix of tensions, and so team members must possess the flexibility to deal with this (Nielsen et al., 2007).

In an ethnically diverse workforce, Earley and Offermann (2007) suggested that leaders of wise teams exhibit cultural intelligence. As defined by Earley and Ang (2003), cultural intelligence is the ability of individuals to adapt to different cultural contexts. As I mentioned earlier, Earley and Offermann (2007) demonstrated that the structures of wisdom are universal, including an appreciation for cognitive capabilities, applied knowledge, interpersonal intelligence, and personal demeanour. The specific attributes within each of those categories, however, differ across cultures. People expect leaders to act wisely (Offermann, Kennedy, & Wirtz, 1994), but actions that may define one as wise in one culture may not suffice in another (Earley & Offermann, 2007). Such differences may negatively impact employee satisfaction and respect for team leads (Chong & Thomas, 1997; Tsui & O'Reilly, 1989). To develop cultural intelligence, Offermann and Phan (2002) suggested leaders seek to understand the impact their own culture has on their biases and values, understand how other people's cultures impact their biases and values, and then match appropriate behaviour to expectations when working in cross-cultural settings.

2.4.3. Organizational Attributes of Wisdom

The above section identified attributes needed to overcome the barriers to wise team action. Those barriers in team action are magnified at the organizational level, as many organizations involve the activities of multiple teams functioning in concert. Conger and Hooijberg (2007) defined the goal of wise organizational leadership as improving the long-term viability of the organization in a way that balances the needs of the broadest range of stakeholders possible. Burke (2007) demonstrated that in the absence of wisdom, organizations fail to address the causes of problems, ignore data and theory, and do not relate organizational development to business issues. He further established that unwise organizations tolerate arbitrary uses of power, impose values on its staff, and ignore the impact that power and politics have on organizational decisions. Lawrence

(2007) made the case that the absence of appropriate checks and balances on power subsequently leads to abuse of employees, small stakeholders, consumers, suppliers, and the environment, as well as facilitates corruption.

Beyer and Nino (1998) further argued wisdom at the organizational level is needed to overcome a bias in management culture towards radical change. They argued that this bias for radical change often results in actions that harm long-term organizational performance. They attributed this bias to four factors. (1) Managers want to exercise control to make a difference. Driving change creates the appearance of a dashing executive bravely foraging into uncharted lands. (2) Managers want promotions, and driving change gives advantages to achieve this. (3) Stock markets reward signs of change over continuity. (4) Institutional isomorphism (DiMaggio and Powell, 1983) — managers feel they need to do what other businesses are doing, lest they are left behind.

Vaill (1998) maintained that the nature of organizational life challenges our attempts at organizational wisdom. He characterized organizational life as being in a state of 'permanent white water', which he defined as '... the nonstop cascade of surprising, novel, obtrusive events that pepper (and sometimes bombard) all managers, events that often cannot be foreseen or planned away' (p. 31). Compounding this chaos is the temporal aspect of management. Managers cannot step outside of their time pressures to learn or think because the act of management is temporal — that is, managing requires managers to think and act on the fly. Simplistic management models fail to work in these environments because they are often developed in isolation or in a detemporized environment (Vaill, 1998).

Given the above challenges, how can one lead an organization to wise action? Vaill (1998, 2007) argued managers must exhibit 'process wisdom'. He specified that process wisdom is not a stock of knowledge. Instead, it is an ability to learn as you go. It is not learned, it is *learning*. Vaill (1998) identified attributes of process wisdom managers might develop within themselves. These include (1) rethinking the nature and limits of managerial control — learn to let go of what you cannot control; (2) maintaining fundamental values and priorities; (3) not sacrificing principles for processes, but instead expressing principles in processes; (4) living a value system rather than holding one; (5) finding the ongoing meaning of principles over time; (6) recognizing that many principles are always in play rather than one overriding principle; (7) weaving principles and priorities together to generate insights about courses of action. Later, Vaill (2007) maintained that wisdom is dual-sourced: It is exhibited in the choice of what people discuss (identifying and framing problems effectively), and the quality of communication (facilitating effective communication among multi-disciplinary groups). He again described attributes managers might develop within themselves to achieve this. These attributes include (1) understanding how they use power to disempower others in their organization; (2) identifying and developing possibilities offered by their staff; (3) stepping back from organizational turbulence to become aware of the paradigm in which they are trying to solve problems; (4) exhibiting paradigm leadership that helps their staff think of problems in a new way; (5) letting go of what they cannot control; (6) understanding that wisdom has a spiritual foundation of values and meanings; and (7) being a continual learner.

Lawrence (2007) took inspiration from neuroscience in devising a conceptualization of organizational wisdom. He suggested that the prefrontal cortex in the human brain mediates between four unconscious motives when making complex decisions: the desire to acquire, to bond, to comprehend, and to defend (Lawrence & Nohira, 2002). Each drive serves as a check on the other, and when in proper balance, people can make wise choices. Corporations that build similar checks and balances into their structures likewise become capable of acting wisely (Lawrence, 2007). He then used the American constitution as an exemplar of an organizing structure that provides checks and balances against these motives to ensure wise action.

Beyer and Nino (1998) further argued that organizations could develop wisdom by honouring the past and fostering leadership continuity. Regarding honouring the past, managers can gain useful insights from how the organization solved historical problems that they can then apply to current and future problems (Wilkins, 1989). Similarly, Hamel and Prahalad (1994) demonstrated that developing organizational competency takes years and succeeds only if the organizations apply a consistent effort throughout that time. They stated organizations could facilitate this through the continuity of management. Longitudinal studies support the claim that leadership continuity leads to superior organizational performance (Collins & Porras, 1997).

2.4.4.   *Strategic Attributes of Wisdom*

Organizations do not act in isolation. They exist in networks of other organizations, including competitors, government, customers, and so on. These relationships further add to the complexity individuals within an organization must contend with when striving to act wisely. To contend with this level of complexity, Freeman, Dunham, and McVea (2007) suggested the attribute of *phronesis* becomes increasingly essential. They explain *phronesis* is the ability to act on what is right and realistic for you and others, is adaptable and responsive to different contexts, requires an understanding of what is ethical in each situation, and has a commitment to action to achieve those ethical ends.

There exist other views on strategy that do not rely on wisdom. For example, the Kantian view argues the leader should focus on doing what is right rather than what is good (Bowie, 1999; Freeman et al., 2007; Phillips, 1997). Doing what is right, however, requires the leader to know what is right before making the decision, which leads to abstraction and discourages use of practical intuition (Freeman et al., 2007). Moreover, even if managers did know what is right, knowledge is not enough — you need to know what to do with that knowledge and when it is appropriate to apply rules (Fukami, 2007). Freeman et al. (2007) also identified utilitarianism as an alternative to wisdom. They argued that utilitarianism is compatible with many management tools (e.g. cost-benefit, return-on-investment). They concluded, however, that utilitarianism alone does not cause leaders to focus on what is valuable. Instead, it leads them to focus on what is measured. Moreover, Freeman et al. (2007) further maintained that not everything of value could be quantified, and different stakeholders may pursue incommensurable benefits, defying simple cost-benefit analysis. Instead, we need to approach strategy as a way of 'constructing the good' (p. 159), where multiple values are harmonized and blended in any decision – the focus is on harmony rather than maximization (Freeman et al., 2007).

Bierly and Kolodinsky (2007) identified three limitations to current approaches to strategic research that do not consider wisdom. First, researchers simplify multiple purposes of the firm to merely one of profit maximization (Grant, 2005), even though this is not meaningful to US workers, who find more value in autonomy, family time, and recognition (de Graaf, 2004; Giacalone & Jurkiewicz, 2003). There is a link between employee performance and firm performance, and so organizations capable of balancing the business's goals with employees' goals can become high performing (DeNisi & Belsito, 2007). Moreover, the focus on profit maximization ignores other responsibilities such as the firm's impact on society, corporate social responsibility, its responsibility to work for the common good, and the positive impacts that result from these elements (Bierly & Kolodinsky, 2007). Second, current research into corporate strategy ignores the role of judgement, intuition, and complexity (Bierly & Kolodinsky, 2007). Third, current strategic research focuses on the firm as the level of analysis, ignoring that it is individuals and small groups that often make strategic decisions. A wisdom-based approach to strategy solves these shortcomings (Bierly & Kolodinsky, 2007).

Wisdom at the strategic level is the use of knowledge and experience to make choices of long-term appeal to different stakeholders (De Meyer, 2007). How then do we give strategy a wisdom-based structure and direction? *Phronesis*, Freeman et al. (2007) answered. *Phronesis* places ethics centrally, embraces uncertainty, is flexible and adaptable to the situation, addresses the incommensurability of values, and enables our sense of good to come forth (Freeman et al., 2007). If managers apply a stakeholder approach (Freeman, 2010) supplemented with *phronesis*, they will see means and ends as co-dependent and reciprocal. That is, we understand how much we value an end when we reflect on the means and consequences needed to achieve it (Freeman et al., 2007). Once managers see the co-dependency of means and ends, they can begin to consider what ends are valuable in light of all stakeholder means (Freeman et al., 2007). Adopting *phronesis* allows managers to integrate ethics into decision-making, moves them past means-end dichotomies, and embraces the messy complexity of real life (Flyvbjerg, 2001; Freeman et al., 2007; Sternberg, 2003b).

Bierly and Kolodinsky (2007) identified characteristics of wise executives. They posited that executive wisdom is composed of a combination of knowledge, experience, and spirituality. *Knowledge* refers to knowing how and knowing about (Grant, 1996a, 1996b). Though it is necessary for wisdom, it is not sufficient on its own (Sternberg, 2003b), partly because knowledge is always limited and fallible (Weick, 1998). *Experience*, Bierly and Kolodinsky (2007) argued, is key to understanding the broader context of issues. Experience facilitates executives' ability to integrate new knowledge into current knowledge, and how to access and weave different types of wisdom together. It improves executives' ability to assess the importance of events, detect changing patterns, and judge the importance of new developments (Bierly & Kolodinsky, 2007). Moreover, experience develops executives' understanding of how to apply tacit knowledge to a given situation (Nonaka, 1994; Polanyi, 1966; Spender, 1996). Experience gives executives confidence in making decisions when they have incomplete information and facilitates the development of effective intuition (Bierly & Kolodinsky, 2007). Bierly and Kolodinsky (2007) related *spirituality* to moral maturity. Morality is the ability to justify one's actions in terms of universal principles (Dreyfus, 1990). These universal principles include characteristics such as integrity, compassion, responsibility, forgiveness, honesty, justice, and trust (Covey, 1990; Lennick & Kiel, 2008). Wisdom shifts focus from self-interests to others' needs (Mathieson & Miree, 2003).

In the above sections, I have introduced the concept of wisdom in an organizational context. I have reviewed literature questioning whether organizations can and should act wisely. Following this, I explored the literature on organizational wisdom stratified along several levels of analysis, including individual, team, organizational, and strategic. There are three general themes I would like to pull out to establish the context for the remainder of this book. Though I draw these themes from the above review, Flyvbjerg (1998, 2001) strongly influenced my conceptualization of these themes.

The first theme is that values guide wise action. As per my discussion on value-rationality, values identify the goals we find worth pursuing and the means we are willing to employ to achieve them. In organizational contexts, the values of multiple stakeholders interact and, at times, conflict. Wise action requires individuals to navigate this web of values. Second, knowledge is required but insufficient on its own for wisdom. By exercising our knowledge and rationality, we may plan how best to achieve an end. Our knowledge is often flawed and incomplete, however. Therefore, those acting wisely include different types of knowledge in their decision-making calculus and seek to expand their base of knowledge by drawing on the insights of other stakeholders in the process. Third, wisdom is action-oriented. Wisdom is more than knowing the right thing. It is *doing* the right thing. Acting requires individuals and groups to exercise power.

These themes have led me to structure the remainder of my literature review as follows. In Chapter 3, I review the literature on organizational values. Because my research setting is a healthcare environment, which, in Canada, is part of the public sector, I focus on public sector values. Then, I review the literature on rationality. Following this, I review the literature on power in Chapter 4. Power is the foundation of action, and, as I will show below, is deeply intertwined with values and rationality. I, therefore, explore the connection power has with values and rationality. With this foundation, I will then consider pluralistic organizations, focusing on the healthcare industry as much as possible, and the challenges they face when striving for wise action.

Chapter 3

Values and Rationality

In this chapter, I review the literature for two of the three constructs of my study: values and rationality. I explore power and the functioning of pluralistic organizations in Chapter 4. With values, I review literature pertaining to the public sector. I further explore ways values may conflict within a single organization and strategies individuals use to manage those conflicts. Regarding rationality, I present an organizing framework developed by Townley (2008b) that categorizes different ways of knowing.

3.1. Conceptualizations of Values in Public Sector Organizations

Values inform the ends we find worthy of achieving (Townley, 2008b). Just as values may guide an individual, they may also guide groups and organizations. As described in Chapter 6, the setting for this proposed research project is a Canadian healthcare institution, which is a public sector entity. This book, therefore, focuses on values as they pertain to the public sector. Public values are '[…] the ideals, articulated as principles, to be followed when producing a public service or regulating citizens' behaviour, thus providing direction to the behaviour of public servants' (Beck Jørgensen & Sørensen, 2013, p. 72). Beck Jørgensen and Sørensen (2013) reviewed the codes of governance for 14 nations to identify which public values each prioritized. They organized these values under a series of value constellations developed by Beck Jørgensen and Bozeman (2007). Table 3.1 summarizes Beck Jørgensen and Sørensen's (2013) findings for Canada. In brief, the values they found emphasized by Canada's public sector include *public interest, regime dignity, political loyalty, openness, neutrality, effectiveness*, and *accountability*. Since my research setting, specifically the BC Health Authority, is a part of the Canadian healthcare system, I will next identify the values espoused in the Canada Health Act and the BC Health Authority's mission statement. Following this, I will review the literature on how public sector organizations manage the conflict between incompatible and incommensurate values. In the following chapter, I will review the interplay between values and power.

Public values underpin the Canada Health Act. Though not explicitly referred to as values, the preamble to the Canada Health Act outlines objectives that embody specific values. In brief, these objectives include disease prevention/health promotion, future improvements through cooperation between governments, health professionals, voluntary organizations and individuals, and,

Table 3.1. Public Values Emphasized in Canada's 2003 Values and Ethics Code for the Public Service as Identified by Beck Jørgensen and Sørensen (2013).

Constellations of Public Values	Discrete Values within Constellations	Emphasis on the Values in Canada's 2003 'Values and Ethics Code for the Public Service'
Public sector's contribution to society	Public interest	**Significant**
	Altruism	Somewhat
	Sustainability	Negligible
	Regime dignity	**Significant**
Transformation of interests to decisions	Majority rule	Somewhat
	User democracy	Negligible
	Protection of minorities	Negligible
The relationship between administrators and politicians	Political loyalty	**Significant**
The relationship between public administrators and their environment	Openness	**Significant**
	Neutrality	**Significant**
Intraorganizational aspects of public administration	Competitiveness	Negligible
	Robustness	Somewhat
	Innovation	Somewhat
	Effectiveness	**Significant**
	Self-development of employees	Negligible
The behaviour of public sector employees	Accountability	**Significant**
The relationship between public administrators and citizens	The rule of law	Somewhat
	Equity	Somewhat
	Dialogue	Somewhat
	User orientation	Somewhat

finally, access to quality healthcare without barriers, financial or otherwise (Government of Canada, 2014). In Table 3.2, I cross-reference these objectives with the public values listed in Table 3.1. I used these values as a starting point for identifying the values different actors in my research setting were pursuing.

Table 3.2. Cross-reference of Canada Health Act Objectives with Public Values.

Objectives Listed in the Preamble of Canada Health Act	Corresponding Public Values
Disease prevention and health promotion	Public interest
Future improvement through cooperation between governments, health professionals, voluntary organizations and individuals	Innovation, dialogue
Access to quality healthcare without barriers, financial or otherwise	Equity, altruism, neutrality

Table 3.3. Cross-reference of the BC Health Authority's Vision, Purpose, and Values with Public Values.

Vision, Purpose, and Values Espoused by the BC Health Authority	Corresponding Public Values
Better health. Best in healthcare.	Public interest, competitiveness
To improve the health of the population and the quality of life of the people we serve.	Public interest, user orientation
Respect, caring and trust characterize our relationships.	User orientation, public interest

The Province of BC established the BC Health Authority as one of five regional health authorities to implement healthcare ('About [BC Health Authority]', 2018). According to their website ('About [BC Health Authority]', 2018), its vision was 'Better health. Best in healthcare'. Its purpose was 'To improve the health of the population and the quality of life of the people we serve'. The following statement described its values: 'Respect, caring and trust characterize our relationships'. In Table 3.3, I cross-reference the BC Health Authority's vision, purpose, and values with the public values listed in Table 3.1.

From Tables 3.1 to 3.3, you can already see these public values are diverse and differ between different levels of the organization. Some values may be incompatible, if not incommensurable with each other (De Graff et al., 2014). Indeed, meeting different, often opposing public values is a challenge for governments (Kettl, 1993). De Graff et al. (2014) explored how public servants coped with conflicting values through two exploratory case studies: one in a municipality and the other in a hospital, both in the Netherlands. Data collection consisted of a series of semi-structured interviews with 19 people in the municipality and 16 individuals in the hospital occupying several roles within different functional areas. Researchers determined the value profile of respondents using Q-methodology.[1] Also, they listed six traditional coping strategies typically observed when values conflict in the public sphere, and through their interview process, they attempted to identify the coping mechanisms used. The first three traditional coping strategies, identified initially by Thacher and Rein (2004), included firewalls, cycling, and casuistry, and the following three, identified by Stewart (2006), included bias, hybridization, and incrementalism. As De Graaf et al. (2014) explained, *firewalls* consist of different departments or groups having responsibility for achieving different values. *Cycling* consists of one set of values achieving pre-eminence for a time until resistance grows and new values rise to dominance (De Graff et al., 2014). *Casuistry* occurs when officials resolve value conflicts by relying on their experience with similar conflicts (De Graff et al., 2014). De Graaf et al. (2014) explained *bias* occurs when one set of values falls out of favour. *Hybridization*, on the other hand, occurs when officials attempt to reconcile conflicting values (De Graff et al., 2014). Other times, officials may slowly emphasize one value over time in a process called *incrementalism* (De Graff et al., 2014).

De Graff et al. (2014) demonstrated that respondents' organization and job influenced the values they prioritized. They also identified several value conflicts respondents typically faced. For example, in the hospital setting, middle managers and nurses often faced conflicts between efficiency and efficacy. All hospital respondents (physicians, nurses, and managers) faced a conflict between the values of transparency and effectiveness. Physicians and nurses also felt a conflict between the values of patient participation and their professionalism. To deal with these conflicts, De Graff et al. (2014) observed various coping strategies. For example, nurses exhibited a bias towards following the rules, which, in turn, compromised effectiveness. Physicians, on the other hand, relied on casuistry, seeking to rely on their judgement to find the best solution on a case-by-case basis. This study demonstrated that actors in public sector settings may operate from different value positions and may use different mechanisms to move forward when the choices facing them create value conflicts.

Oldenhof et al. (2014) studied the role of compromises and justifications in dealing with conflicting values that middle managers and executives faced in small care homes in the Netherlands. They performed semi-structured interviews with 16 middle managers and 13 executives, as well as 11 months of ethnographic observation of seven middle managers. Their analysis consisted of two phases: an inductive phase, where the researchers identified value conflicts the respondents faced, and a deductive phase, where they sought to link those conflicts to justifications. They relied on justification categories developed by Boltanski and Thévenot (1991), which included market (what is profitable), industry (what is functional), civic (what improves public welfare), domestic

---

[1]Q-methodology uses factoring as a means of determining respondents' viewpoint. For applications of this method to public sector values, see Selden, Brewer, and Brudney (1999) and De Graaf & Van Exel (2009).

(what is traditional), inspired (what is unique), and fame (what enhances our image). Due to recent changes in health administration, the Netherlands went to a model of small care homes for long-term care patients. Oldenhof et al. (2014) reported this change as a compromise between civic and domestic justifications. Managers found themselves having to justify this compromise in their daily activities, and this justification consisted of three elements: rhetoric (what they said), behaviour (working processes), and materials (layout and types of buildings/equipment). According to Oldenhof et al. (2014), this compromise was subject to two types of criticism. The first was external, where actors favouring other values criticized the compromise. The other was internal, where advocates of either pure civic or pure domestic justifications attacked the compromise. In the face of these critiques, managers engaged in two types of justification work. First, they attempted to justify the current compromise by taking arguments from the civic and domestic justifications and reiterating internally and externally. Second, when managers viewed the value conflict as unsolvable, they attempted to construct a new compromise. To create this, managers had to stress the weaknesses of the current compromise, and then create a new compromise that they then needed to justify to critical stakeholders. Oldenhof et al. (2014) found justification work was an ongoing process of recrafting compromises, justifying them, and then recrafting again when they became untenable. This study thereby adds *compromise* as a tactic for individuals to manage value conflicts and explores the process of justification in establishing and maintaining compromises. Like the previous study, it showed the propensity of value conflicts in public sectors like healthcare and added to our knowledge of how actors in these fields manage value conflicts. This concludes, for now, my review of public sector values. In Chapter 4, I will return to values when I evaluate them in the context of power. For now, I turn to a review of rationality.

3.2. Conceptualizations of Rationality in Organizations

Townley (2008b) sought to provide an answer to the question, 'how do we make wise decisions?' (p. 213) at an organizational level of analysis. To answer this, she began with an exploration of three faces of rationality: disembedded, embedded, and embodied rationality. She then explored differences between collective action and collective reasoning. Finally, she added to our conceptualizations of rationality by forwarding her concept of practical reason, which she equated to *phronesis*. Townley's (2008b) review presented a framework of understanding rationality that I have adopted. Thus, a summary of her framework follows. Later, I explore research studying the interplay between rationality and power in organizational settings.

Disembedded rationality refers to objective knowledge (Townley, 2008b). As Townley described, disembedded rationality takes three forms: economic, bureaucratic, and technocratic. She described *economic rationality* as a form of instrumental-rationality where individuals seek to maximize their utility. It is a means to an end, though as to which ends are appropriate, reason is silent

(Townley, 2008b). Townley (2008b) established that this form of rationality became a founding principle upon which modern concepts of the organization rest. She explained many researchers and managers see organizations as utility-maximizing structures with clear goals and structures designed to achieve those goals.

Early criticisms of economic rationality's assumptions (such as humans act rationally, have access to complete information, and make probability-based cost-benefit analyses) led to concepts of bounded rationality and satisficing, where human actors with limited information use decision-making systems that are sensible given their constraints (Simon, 1959). Even with concepts of bounded rationality and satisficing, however, some of economic rationality's assumptions remain problematic (Townley, 2008b). As Perrow (1986) explained, economic rationality assumes individuals are utility maximizing, yet utilities are often vague and undefinable. He further added individuals often make decisions in the absence of the information required to make reasonable cost-benefit analyses and often possess a poor understanding of the relation between cause and effect. Moreover, he demonstrated an individual's self-interested behaviour varies depending on context. In situations where work and rewards are individualized, self-interested behaviour rises. However, in situations where people work collaboratively, other-regarding behaviour takes the fore (Perrow, 1986).

Townley's (2008b) second form of disembedded rationality was *bureaucratic rationality*. She explained Weber's intent with his work on bureaucracies was not to create an operationally efficient structure, but rather '[…] rational bureaucracy is formally rational because it provides the calculability of means and procedures. Bureaucracy allows administration to be discharged precisely and unambiguously […]' (Townley, 2008b, p. 49). That is, bureaucratic rationality is not about efficiency. It is about control. Townley (2008b) stated bureaucracies achieve this control by dominating through knowledge, enacted through the following five mechanisms. (1) Bureaucracies use documentation as a means of defining and classifying objects, activities, and people. (2) Bureaucracies define boundaries to circumscribe '[…] jurisdictional areas and spheres of competence […]' (Townley, 2008b, p. 55). (3) Bureaucracies use rules of conduct to guide behaviour and eliminate the unpredictability of human discretion. (4) Bureaucracies create processes and standardization to achieve predictability. (5) Bureaucracies further eliminate the unpredictability of human discretion by creating impersonal procedures and roles. 'Organizations are not an aggregate of individuals, but of roles and patterns as the result of an interdependence of roles' (Townley, 2008b, p. 64).

Technocratic rationality is Townley's (2008b) final form of disembedded rationality. As she described, technocratic rationality assumes rational action consists of desires and beliefs leading to actions, which lead to intended outcomes. It seeks to translate means-ends relations into reality under the assumption there exists one best technique to achieve a particular end, and that technique is knowable through the application of the scientific method (Townley, 2008b). She explained, since the organization is a means-end structure, the organization becomes a form of technology that is subject to scientific improvement. In this setting, management is a causal factor that implements scientifically derived techniques. She added that technique relies on modelling reality, which gives it the characteristics of transportability, comparability, and standardization, which in turn leads to objectivity. This, in turn, introduces power dynamics into the organization.

> [T]he objective privileges the universal over the local. It invests power in techniques not in people. The 'objective' not only delineates the observer and the observed, but it also introduces hierarchy: the hierarchy of the active recording subject and the relatively passive recorded object. (Townley, 2008b, p. 70)

Technocratic rationality's quest to find the one best way of achieving ends overrides politics and interests and, given its assumption that all problems have technical solutions, devalues non-scientific thought. Townley (2008b), however, identified that science could only be decisive in two situations: when there exist unambiguous ends and where people can unambiguously compare means. 'Most problems involve clashes about values or ends and as such are not solvable in an 'objectively' rational manner' (Townley, 2008b, p. 78). Applying scientific methods to inappropriate situations introduces the type of politics technocratic rationality seeks to avoid, because what, how, and when to measure are subjective choices that influence what people perceive as legitimate and are thus a subject of contention between competing values (Townley, 2008b).

With this background of disembedded rationality, Townley (2008b) turned to explore *embedded* rationalities. As she reported, embedded rationality problematizes disembedded rationality's presumption of the existence of external, objective truth. Embedded rationality presumes knowledge is embedded in a perspective. Thus, actors must consider rationality in the context of the situation (Townley, 2008b). Townley (2008b) presented three forms of embedded rationality: *institutional, contextual*, and *situational*.

Townley (2008b) explained *institutional rationality* assumes that institutions reflect multiple spheres of society, such as government, church, family, law, and so on. These spheres may conflict along the lines of conduct, values, and norms. What is rational varies by the sphere, and an individual may face multiple rationalities as they move from one sphere to another throughout their day. Institutional rationality is the name given to the rationality guiding the actions within a sphere. Townley (2008b) explained a body of practitioners establish each sphere's rationalities, and then through the process of centralized education, these rationalities spread amongst practitioners. Over time, structures and activities become institutionalized, and their logics taken-for-granted and unquestioned – they become rationalized myths. Adoption of these rationalized myths becomes the key to the legitimacy of organizations operating within a sphere. Additionally, Friedland and Alford (1991) identified that institutional logics take hold, which are the rationales behind institutional actions, and these logics may conflict with those of other spheres (Townley, 2008b). As a result, the sphere from which an organization is operating determines what appropriate ends are and the rational means to achieve those ends (Townley, 2008b).

As Townley (2008b) explained, *contextual rationality* is cultural rationality. She argued a culture possesses values, is shared amongst members, has hidden layers, and uses symbols to communicate meaning. A culture is a community; it is what people within a group hold in common. Cultures can exist in workplaces, industries, occupations, and communities of practice. Cultures are a means of coordinating behaviour, which requires a shared understanding of values, understandings, and assumptions. In this way, Townley (2008b) concluded competent action is culturally based. That is, what is rational can only be judged from within a culture.

Situational rationality challenges the notion that rationality occurs in advance of a behaviour (Townley, 2008b). Weick (2001) claimed we presume people act rationally and that their actions will have made sense. Participants, thus, supply a meaning that renders an action rational (Townley, 2008b). Townley (2008b) further added the sources of knowledge participants use to supply meaning comes from two sources. The first is 'everyday knowledge' (p. 138) consisting of learned experiences of what is probable or typical in a specific situation. The second is 'common sense' (p. 139), which is unexamined, institutionalized knowledge held in common with others. Thus, what is rational is socially determined by observers and participants (Townley, 2008b).

The previous two categories of rationality — disembedded and embedded — view rationality as something separate from the self. Disembedded rationality seeks grand truths independent of human activity or thought. Embedded rationality is context-dependent, something ascribed to actions based on the social situation in which the action occurred. Townley (2008b) then considered rationality derived from the self — *embodied* rationality. She explained that, historically, literature views rationality as the purview of the mind and irrationality, or passion, the purview of the body. She argued, however, it is through our bodies that we know the world.

> It is the lived, embodied, corporeal experience of being in the world that functions to give access to knowledge of the world. It is only through an embodied self that a self, others, and the world can be known. (Townley, 2008b, p. 156)

Her explorations of embodied rationality included the role of the *body, emotions,* and the *irrational subconscious*.

The *body* as a source of rationality encompassed the belief that our senses are our source of knowledge (Townley, 2008b). Experience, Townley added, is a form of tacit knowledge.

> As we become familiar with something, an object or a scientific theory, we interiorize it, and attend to things using it [...] The quality of tacit knowledge is influenced by the variety of

individual experience and 'knowledge of experience', the latter involving its absorption as a bodily experience. Thus, the body is thus fundamental to our knowledge of the world. (Townley, 2008b, p. 163)

Tacit knowledge gained through experience and interiorized by our body gives us a broader picture of a situation that drives our actions. This tacit knowledge forms the basis of what Barnard (1962) referred to as non-logical thought. The non-logical thought is the basis of intuition and is not to be confused with illogical thought (Barnard, 1962; Townley, 2008b). Intuition is a powerful source of knowledge: It is a fast-act of logical reasoning (Townley, 2008b). It is a process of reasoning:

> [...] not capable of being expressed in words or as reasoning [...]
> This may be because the processes are unconscious, or because they are so complex and so rapid, often approaching the instantaneous, that they could not be analyzed by the person within whose brain they take place. (Barnard, 1962, p. 302)

It is through our intuition obtained through our physical experience that we gain the ability to take action in situations that are too complex given the available time to process information consciously in a logical manner. (Barnard, 1962; Townley, 2008b)

Contrary to popular belief, Townley (2008b) argued *emotions* were another source of rationality. Our emotions straddle the individual (what we feel) with the social (what we express). That is, they are relational. In that capacity, observers may judge an emotion reasonable or unreasonable. 'A failure to respond with a predictable emotional response, to feel outrage when faced with gross injustice, to be afraid when faced with danger, etc. is deemed 'irrational' and requires explanation [...] The absence of emotion can be as disruptive as too much emotion' (Townley, 2008b, pp. 177–178). Emotions are a source of knowledge of our presence in the world (Crossley, 1998). Townley (2008b) explained that our emotions move us to action. They dictate our preferences, informing the ends we desire and the means we find appropriate to achieve them. In our effort to achieve those ends, reason serves our passion.

Finally, Townley (2008b) considered the *irrational unconscious* as a form of embodied rationality. It is our psychic, rather than objective, reality. As she explained, the 'irrational' unconscious consists of

> [...] that which is known at some level but which has not been put into words, whose manifestations appear as 'irrational'. Thus, responses in adult life to new situations will be based not just on the 'reality' of the new situation but also, in part, on an internal repertoire of responses based on earlier experiences. Shared and projected emotions, especially in hierarchical

relationships, provide the dynamics of the enfolding organizational relationship. (2008b, p. 179)

In organizational contexts, Townley (2008b) maintained the 'irrational' unconscious manifests in the form of myths, rituals, and unquestioned beliefs. Individuals in organizations base these seemingly irrational actions on experiences that have created a more profound, unconscious rationality that informs behaviour.

With this background of disembedded, embedded, and embodied rationality, let us now consider *collective rationality*. Townley (2008b) distinguished between collective action and collective reasoning. She explained *collective action* occurs when individuals in groups make self-interested choices, and the sum of these individual choices creates group action. That is, the actions of individuals in a group result in a group action. The assumptions of collective action are (1) individuals seek to maximize self-interest and (2) if individuals are a member of a group, and their fortunes rise and fall with those of the group, then individuals will make choices that benefit the group (Townley, 2008b). Townley (2008b) noted, however, that what may make sense at an individual level may not always result in what is in the best interests of the group, and she cites several game theory scenarios as examples (e.g. Prisoner's Dilemma, Tragedy of the Commons, and Arrow's Impossibility Theorem).[2] *Collective reasoning*, on the other hand, employs group rationality that is different from individual rationality. Townley (2008b) presented the concept of deliberative democracy, which occurs when individuals put forward ideas for public debate. This process creates a shared pool of rationality from which citizens may draw (Townley, 2008b). Whereas *individuals* make a collective decision through collective action, collective rationality consists of a *collective entity* making a decision (Townley, 2008b). Through this public debate, citizens scrutinize ideas, proponents sharpen arguments, people judge the reasonableness of reasons, and the public sideline unsustainable positions while retaining defensible ones. Townley (2008b) concluded that for these reasons, collective reasoning leads to better decisions. Collective reasoning has not been well studied in businesses because, as Townley (2008b) pointed out, businesses are not democratic. Instead, they are private

---

[2]*Prisoner's Dilemma* — Two criminals are arrested for suspicion of a crime. Well-being of the group occurs if the two criminals collude and neither informs the police. Self-interest is achieved if they inform on their partner (see Tucker, 1983, p. 228). *Tragedy of the Commons* — If collective self-discipline is required for group welfare (say, in preserving grazing land, or fishing stocks), individuals achieve self-interest by applying less individual discipline (i.e. grazing or fishing more than allowed), benefiting from the discipline others in the group exhibit (see Hardin, 1968). *Arrow's Impossibility Theorem* — situations where groups of three or more people are attempting to aggregate preferences, and each have two alternatives then this creates a situation where it is impossible to achieve everyone's preferences (see Arrow, 1992).

property, and in private property, Townley (2008b) argued, individual rationality dominates.

To wrap up this discussion on rationality, Townley (2008b) argued irrational outcomes often result from an exclusive focus on disembedded rationality. She cited by way of example literature reporting unintended outcomes from the implementation of performance metrics (see Carter, Klein, & Doey, 1992; Meyer, 2002; National Audit Office, 2001; Paton, 2003; Smith, 1993; Townley, 2008a). Rationality is a social process, people ascribe it to behaviours, and this judgement of an act's rationality is dependent upon the situation in which observers witness it (Townley, 2008b). So then, how do we make wise decisions? Townley (2008b) argued we achieve this through *practical reason*, a construct analogous to the Aristotelian concept of *phronesis*. To achieve practical reason, individuals use disembedded rationality as a tool to inform embedded and embodied rationality. 'Each form of rationality informs what is legitimate and appropriate; rational, within its own sphere' (Townley, 2008b, p. 207).

It is important to remember that reason is not the same as morality (Townley, 2008b). 'Reason is "goal" directed not "truth" directed' (Townley, 2008b, p. 213). Even though rationality does not equal morality, nor can we resolve the choice between values rationally, we can frame moral questions rationally through the application of practical reason (Townley, 2008b). Individuals and organizations develop practical reason through experience (embedded and embodied rationality) and then use theory (disembedded rationality) to focus on the means to achieve socially determined moral ends (Townley, 2008b).

> A practical reason is the ability to retain the disembedded, embedded, and embodied dimensions of rationality and to incorporate or distil them into a unified understanding or picture. It is to be able to hold and see the interrelationships between all the dimensions of that with which there is engagement, the ability to see in the abstract the concrete and vice versa. It is informed by the knowledge of all subject positions, the disembedded, embedded, and embodied, to give a fully rounded interpretation of what suitable action should be. [...] It is to be able to make a judgement on a case using concrete, practical context-dependent knowledge informed by general principles. In this sense, it is allied to 'reason' as 'really knowing something'. (Townley, 2008b, p. 216)

This concludes my review of the literature on rationality. I explore the relation between rationality and power in the following chapter. Now, let us turn to contemplate power.

Chapter 4

Power and the Nature of Pluralistic Organizations

In this chapter, I review the literature on power and pluralistic organizations. When discussing power, I present a high-level overview of different branches of research in the area and then present an organizing framework developed by Fleming and Spicer (2014). As I will discuss, power is a pervasive structure weaving through every facet of social life. Thus, I review the connection between power and values as well as the relation between power and rationality. I finish this chapter with a review of research investigating these constructs within pluralistic organizations. Pluralistic organizations contain multiple groups of specialized, highly trained individuals, each pursuing different organizational objectives, each with complex power relations to the others. My interest in this stems from the fact that healthcare organizations, such as the one that is the research setting of this study, are pluralistic (Bucher & Stelling, 1969; Scott, 1982). With that overview, let us explore power.

4.1. Conceptualizations of Power

4.1.1. *Overview of Power Research*

There are those who have described power as the ability to get someone to do something they otherwise would not, against their will if necessary (Hardy & Clegg, 1996). The negative tone of this definition has tainted the concept of power with cynicism, focusing our attention mainly on power's abuses, even though it is through power that human societies organize themselves to survive and prosper (Foucault, 1977). Regardless, scholars and practitioners alike recognize the reality that to get something done in an organizational setting, one must understand power. Hardy and Clegg (1996) presented an overview of power. They observed early power research as falling into two categories: critical and structural functionalist views. Karl Marx and Max Weber laid down the foundation for the critical view. This branch of research considered power from the perspective of classes, especially owners/managers versus workers. As Grandy (2011) described, this critical perspective studied the political and economic contexts of power, and viewed power through a 'sovereign model', where someone or some group possessed power and dominated those who did not. Much of this work focused on exploring tools the dominated could use to free themselves or, when it was observed people seldom resist their oppressors, exploring why the dominated accept their position (Hardy & Clegg, 1996).

This work evolved into what scholars commonly refer to as the four dimensions of power (Lukes, 2005). The first dimension is the ability of people to use power to get others to do what they want. The second considers how people use power to suppress conflict, preventing contentious topics from becoming a topic of discussion. The third dimension considers how use of power prevents conflict from occurring by leading people to accept their domination by defining a reality that legitimates authority. The fourth dimension, discussed in detail later, views power as a social network of relations and discourses encompassing all members of society (Lukes, 2005).

The second branch of power research discussed by Hardy and Clegg (1996) took a structural functionalist approach as observed through a managerialist perspective. Under this perspective, power possessed two aspects. The first was hierarchical – that is, the level you occupied in an organization afforded you a certain amount of authority (see, e.g., Mechanic, 1962). Hardy and Clegg (1996) reported that researchers of this branch did not view this aspect as a form of 'power' per se, but rather as the natural order of things. The power possessed by managers and owners, thus, remained unquestioned and unproblematized. The second aspect of power included the ability of workers to resist this hierarchical order. These abilities to resist derived from workers' ability to control organizational uncertainty (i.e. strategic contingency theory; e.g. Crozier, 1964; Hickson, Hinings, Lee, Schneck, & Pennings, 1971) or critical resources (i.e. resource dependency theory; e.g. Pfeffer & Salanick, 1974). As these forms of power rested outside the organizational hierarchy, Hardy and Clegg (1996) identified that managers and researchers alike perceived them as illegitimate, and scholarly work focused on helping managers reduce and eliminate them.

As power research evolved, Hardy and Clegg (1996) reported some scholars began exploring tools of legitimation and their role in reducing resistance (see, e.g., Astley & Sachdeva, 1984). These studies took an interpretivist approach, observing processes of power as negotiations of meaning, which established the legitimacy of the power structure in the minds of stakeholders. Hardy and Clegg (1996) also explored the role of power and identity. They observed extra-organizational as well as organizational group affiliation contributed to the construction of an individual's identity. Extra-organizational identities, such as gender or ethnic background, created a mechanism of resistance to organizational power by controlling how different groups could treat others. Within organizations, individuals were grouped and departmentalized, creating loci of control, contestation, and negotiation between groups, the outcomes of which were divisions of labour (Hardy & Clegg, 1996).

Foucault was instrumental in conceptualizing the fourth dimension of power (Hardy & Clegg, 1996). Foucault (1977) observed power as a dense web of relations in which everyone was immersed. He argued against the idea of sovereign points of power. Instead, he advocated that ruler and ruled alike were themselves embedded in society's network of power, which is continuously negotiated and renegotiated. In modern times, society exerts its power through applications of discipline and surveillance (Foucault, 1977). According to Foucault (1977), *discipline* is achieved through four acts: spatial segregation of individuals, controlling activities through partitioning of time and action, segmenting and documenting training, and coordination of activities to create integrated group action. *Surveillance* is the means through which institutions maintain discipline. The awareness that your work is subject to surveillance creates a form of self-discipline, resulting in all members performing their roles. Importantly, Foucault viewed power as a productive and positive force, for it is through power that we create reality and truth (Foucault, 1977).

Other researchers looked at resistance as a form of power. Power involves delegation, delegation requires rules, applying rules requires individual discretion, and it is through this discretion that individuals may resist power (Hardy & Clegg, 1996). If resistance is a natural by-product of power, however, how then do stable power structures persist? Part of the answer to this is the observation that discourses organizations use to construct reality become perceived as fact, and so become difficult to challenge (see, e.g., Knights & Morgan, 1991). Furthermore, the production of identities from group affiliations creates a positive experience for individuals, further strengthening the power relations supporting those identities (e.g. Knights & Morgan, 1991). Moreover, those in power are best able to defend the current power structure (Hardy & Clegg, 1996).

Hardy and Clegg (1996) argued contemporary power research leans heavily on poststructuralism, assuming the socially constructed nature of reality, and thus such research is itself a product of power. This has important implications for power research. Hardy and Clegg (1996) cautioned that scholars are not neutral observers, but rather active members of a web of power relations. Therefore, a theory of power cannot exist because researchers create and accept theories within the dynamics of power structures they find themselves a part of (Hardy & Clegg, 1996). Thus, power research has its own double hermeneutic: Rather than the traditional researchers interpreting other people's interpretations (Giddens, 1982), power research has researchers using tactics of power to create the truth of how other people use tactics of power (Hardy & Clegg, 1996).

4.1.2.   An Organizing Framework of Power Research

Fleming and Spicer (2014) presented a framework for organizing power in management research. They mapped power research along two axes. Their first axis consisted of *faces* of power. These included episodic exercises of power, including coercion and manipulation, as well as systematic expressions of power, such as domination and subjectification. Their second axis included the *sites* of power. These included power in, through, over, and against organizations. I will describe these axes in more detail, present a summary of where broad themes in organizational power research fit into Fleming and Spicer's (2014) framework, and then conclude with how this framework applied to this study.

4.1.2.1. Faces of Power
Fleming and Spicer (2014) divide the faces of power into two categories. *Episodic* power refers to 'the direct exercise of power' (p. 240) and includes

coercion and manipulation. *Systematic* power, conversely, includes 'power that is congealed into more enduring institutional structures' (p. 240) such as domination and subjectification. *Coercion*, as Fleming and Spicer (2014) explained, is the direct use of power to compel another to perform an action they otherwise would not. They identify sources of coercive power, such as bureaucratic authority (e.g. Merton, 1968), psychological propensity to coerce (e.g. House, 1968), a capability to reduce uncertainty (e.g. Crozier, 1964), and possession of valuable resources (e.g. Pfeffer & Salanick, 1974). *Manipulation* involves actors taking action to control the agenda of what people discuss or to frame issues within desired boundaries (Fleming & Spicer, 2014). Fleming and Spicer (2014) identified sources of this include manipulation of rules (e.g. Slaznick, 1949), shaping the outcomes individuals anticipate (e.g. Gouldner, 1970), mobilization of bias (e.g. Alexander, 1979), and influencing the process of how people make decisions (e.g. Burt, 1995).

As Fleming and Spicer (2014) explained, *domination* is the process where individuals construct hegemonic ideologies that shape peoples' preferences and limit their wants. They report on a number of techniques used to accomplish this, including corporate culture (e.g. Kunda, 1992), the creation of assumptions in fields and society (e.g. Alvesson, 1987; Simons & Ingram, 1997), institutionalization (e.g. Lawrence & Suddaby, 2006), and as a means to obtain organizational legitimacy (e.g. Meyer & Rowan, 1977). Fleming and Spicer's (2014) final face of power is *subjectification*, which explores how individuals obtain their sense of identity within a social order. Studies have explored how organizations achieve this, including teams and surveillance (e.g. Barker, 1993; Sewell & Wilkinson, 1992), strategy (e.g. Knights & Morgan, 1991), and managerial discourses (e.g. Townley, 1993). Researchers have demonstrated the importance of discourses as a tool to construct identities and guide behaviour (Phillips & Oswick, 2012), which powerful actors can then use to achieve political ends (Holmqvist & Maravalias, 2011).

4.1.2.2. Sites of Power

Fleming and Spicer (2014) identified four sites of power. These included power in, through, over, and against organizations. Power *in* organizations are those efforts within institutional boundaries to affect current hierarchies. Examples cited by Fleming and Spicer (2014) included resistance to change, employer/ employee conflict, command structures, and treatment of whistleblowers. Power *through* organizations include actions taken by an organization (Fleming & Spicer, 2014). These actions may include exerting influence to improve the operating environment, but it may also include third parties such as governments or non-governmental organizations partnering with organizations to achieve a social or political end (Fleming & Spicer, 2014). Fleming and Spicer (2014) consider power *over* organizations as actions taken by elites to influence and control an organization. These actions include takeovers, shareholder activism, government intervention, and lobbying by third parties to change corporate business practices (Fleming & Spicer, 2014). Power *against* the organization are those acts undertaken by extra-organizational parties to create a change within the organization, such as social movements (Fleming & Spicer, 2014).

In closing this section, we can see power research is a diverse area of study. Earlier, I alluded to the idea that power influences values and rationality. I now return to those constructs to consider how power shapes them and is shaped by them. I start considering the interplay between power and values followed by power and rationality. After that, I will turn to review research on how all these constructs operate in pluralistic organizations.

4.1.3. Power and Values

The studies I presented in the previous chapter showed values as something influencing the preferred objectives of different actors. These values, however, were static and unchanging. As we will see below, studies show tactics of power may influence what people perceive as the 'rational argument', but they do not show how tactics of power influence what people perceive as the desired 'moral outcome'. Moreover, they do not consider how actors use power to advance their values over those of others. Indeed, Oldenhof et al. (2014) assumed in their work exploring justification processes that all actors were equivalent and desired resolution between conflicting values without resorting to power. This seems unlikely. If, as Fleming and Spicer (2014) explained, domination creates ideologies shaping peoples' preferences and subjectification forms peoples' sense of identity, then it follows that power influences the values people choose to pursue. Moreover, if different groups prioritize different values (De Graff et al., 2014), and if values influence the ends actors wish to achieve (Townley, 2008b), and if actors use power and rationality to achieve their desired ends (Flyvbjerg, 1998; Townley, 2008b), then it seems reasonable to conclude that when values conflict, actors will use power to assert the values they prioritize.

4.1.4. Power and Rationality

Power and rationality are linked (Flyvbjerg, 1998; Townley, 2008b). 'Forms of rationality operate as forms of power/knowledge. They have direct power/ knowledge effects and consequences' (Townley, 2008b, p. 211). This link between power and rationality occurs as power structures influence what individuals debate and how they construct their arguments (Townley, 2008b). Moreover, this linkage also occurs as different power structures adopt different rationalities to support them (Flyvbjerg, 1998; Townley, 2008b). To explore the interplay between rationality and power, I review several studies exploring this connection.

Of pertinence to the healthcare sector, Denis, Hébert, Langley, Lozeau, and Trottier (2002) evaluated the diffusion of medical innovations through a Canadian healthcare region, explicitly considering why some innovations with strong supporting evidence lag in adoption, while others with weaker data are accepted quickly. The authors looked at four cases of innovation, used statistics to measure diffusion patterns combined with interviews to understand the reasons behind choices to adopt the technology. They identified four patterns: (1) success (strong evidence for adoption combined with rapid adoption), (2) over adoption (weak evidence, rapid adoption), (3) under adoption (strong evidence, slow adoption), and (4) prudence (weak evidence, slow adoption).

These results suggested scientific evidence alone – that is, technocratic rationality in the parlance of Townley (2008b) – was not enough to drive adoption in all cases. Through their interviews, the authors identified that along with an innovation's supporting evidence, the characteristics of the innovation played a role, as did the values, interests, and power dependencies within the adopting system. Specific influencers included the distribution of risks and benefits, along with the power of actors within the system to influence adoption (examples of what Fleming and Spicer (2014) consider power in, through, and against groups). Additionally, differences in the values of actors in the system influenced willingness to adopt a technology.

Another key influence was the dynamics of the adoption process, such as whether a strong pro-adoption group existed (i.e. power through groups), or the need for adopters to learn new skills (i.e. acquire embodied rationalities). Moreover, innovations sometimes have aspects that are open to interpretation and discretion (embedded rationality) and are therefore negotiable. Some new technologies have variability in how practitioners implement them (embodied rationality), which may lead to a controversy that slows adoption. This study showed multiple types of rationality influencing the process of collective reasoning along with the influence of power. It also observed collective reasoning being subject to power acting in, through, and against groups and organizations.

In a similar vein to the above study, Langley and Denis (2011) considered the adoption of quality improvements by healthcare organizations. They argued that however reasonable and rational an improvement might appear, it will fail unless those championing their introduction take into consideration the patterns of values, interests, and power within the organization. Evidence alone (i.e. disembodied rationality) did not ensure implementation. Advocates needed to understand the specific context of the organization (i.e. embedded rationality) and take the micropolitics of the environment into account when advocating for the adoption of a new process.

Denis, Langley, and Rouleau (2006) looked at how senior leaders used rationality, specifically quantitative metrics, to drive strategy making. They performed a single case study of a significant strategic reform of a Canadian healthcare region involving the shutting down of some hospitals and reallocation of their budget to others. The board of the health authority based their decision on which hospitals to close on a set of performance metrics they developed.

Denis et al.'s (2006) study showed that developing a set of metrics (disembodied rationality) was not enough to legitimate change. Advocates had to establish the legitimacy of the number system, and this was a political process. The authors drew several propositions from their observations. First, in pluralistic settings, number systems gain power if their outcomes and use are consistent with the values and interests of a coalition of actors. In this case, once the metrics were made public, those hospitals who were to remain open had an immediate vested interested in supporting the number system for fear if the board introduced a new system, it might recommend closure of their hospital.

Second, Denis et al. (2006) demonstrated number systems gain power if agreements establishing a shared vision preceded them. For example, in this case, the board preceded the introduction of their metrics with a meeting where all parties affected by the reorganization agreed some hospitals had to close. This previous agreement lent legitimacy to the board as they made recommendations for closures. Third, number systems gain power if people present them consistently, transparently, objectively, and competently. In this case, hospitals targeted for closure argued tenaciously against the legitimacy of the metrics used by the board. Throughout this debate, all board members maintained discipline in how they described the metrics, showed a deep understanding of the measurements employed, shared how they constructed these metrics with all stakeholders, and consistently claimed their metrics were the only objective means of identifying hospitals for closure. Fourth, Denis et al. (2006) showed once all actors in a system agreed to the legitimacy and objectivity of a numbering system, that system then bound them, diminishing their scope for discretion and agency. In this case, once the board had established the metric system, it became tied to its conclusions and lost the ability to exercise personal judgement in the process.

Denis et al. (2006) concluded number systems (i.e. disembedded rationality) become powerful if those using them have a tacit understanding of the consequences and specificities of the industry (i.e. embedded rationality). In this study, the authors speculated the board knew which hospitals would be targets for closure with the metrics they chose. These hospitals were low performing, thus, perhaps, legitimating their number system and subsequent decisions based on them in the eyes of stakeholders. This study, thus, showed disembedded rationalities, such as number systems, require legitimization for them to have power. This legitimization process involved other forms of rationality (e.g. embedded rationality), as well as tactics of power.

Hamilton (2012) explored how physicians and veterinarians use language to establish the dominance of their truth when faced with patients who hold different perspectives. To uncover this, she performed a series of structured interviews and participant observation with three physicians and three veterinarians. Hamilton (2012) discovered both physicians and veterinarians were firm in their belief that through medical knowledge and scientific processes, they could transform what she called 'muck' – the sights, sounds, smells, and bodily manifestations of illness – into medical diagnoses and appropriate treatment. Consequently, her interviewees possessed strong positivist perspectives (i.e. disembedded rationalities). Throughout their professional activities, these professionals often encountered others possessing different perspectives. One interviewee raised the example of dealing with Hasidic Jews, who believe in the preservation of human life at all costs, whereas the interviewee maintained if a prognosis of death was likely, the physician should prescribe palliative care measures. In these instances, Hamilton (2012) observed interviewees relied on positivist language to justify their actions, implying that through the application of medical science, they were privy to objective truths that non-scientists were not. Through combinations of social and educational prestige, combined with the structural power afforded to physicians/veterinarians in healthcare institutions, they were able to assert the dominance of their perspective as *the* truth, over-riding the perspectives of others (Hamilton, 2012). According to Hamilton (2012), 'Some knowledges carry a powerful potential to become true when they are framed within dominant epistemologies' (p. 102). This study high-lighted how physicians (and possibly other healthcare providers) frame their reality, and how the power structures of the healthcare system enabled them to assert their knowledge as the truth.

Moving away from the healthcare sector, Kornberger and Clegg (2011) per-formed a case study on the City of Sydney and its creation of a municipal strat-egy over a two-year period. Their data analysed included interviews, direct observation, and document reviews. In this case, the public wanted the munici-pal strategy to concentrate first on the environment, then on transport, followed by economic concerns. The reality of what they got at the end of the process was a strategy that only prioritized the economy. The authors studied how project managers achieved this reversal.

In large part, Kornberger and Clegg (2011) showed the management team controlled the development of the strategy through the use of several tactics. For example, managers engaged in manipulation by distinguishing between strategic and non-strategic thinking, exhorting stakeholders to 'think strategically'. Managers defined strategic thinking as that possessing long-term economic con-sideration, thus ensuring the legitimation of only those projects with cost-benefit analyses (i.e. economic rationality). They also used public consultations, but rather than using them to gain new ideas or insights into stakeholder wants, they used them to provide legitimacy and perception of consensus to the project they were developing, even though consensus did not exist. Managers silenced dissenting voices by keeping conflicting groups separate. Doing so enabled man-agers to deal with each stakeholder group individually. This allowed them to control the debate, keeping contentious issues from public discourse. Managers also distracted the public from the details of their plan by relying on aesthetics, such as artist conceptions and models, rather than discussing concrete details in the media.

Kornberger and Clegg (2011) demonstrated the process of strategizing was linked with power, specifically acts of what Fleming and Spicer (2014) consid-ered manipulation. Kornberger and Clegg (2011) further concluded strategizing was performative in that discourse created reality and, thus, action. Additionally, strategizing was an aesthetic performance where rationality and values give power to the process. Finally, strategizing was a sociopolitical pro-cess aimed at moving people to action and legitimizing decisions (Kornberger & Clegg, 2011).

Gordon, Kornberger, and Clegg (2009) used an ethnographic approach over nine months to study the connection between power, rationality, and legitimacy in a police force undergoing organizational change. The police force in question had suffered several scandals due to corruption, and the current municipal authority was implementing a series of recommended changes to address this problem. Gordon et al. (2009) focused on three constructs for establishing legitimacy: structures of dominance, mobilization of bias, and structures of legitimacy. As Gordon et al. (2009) described, *structures of dominance* were those hierarchical structures imbued with organizational power. *Mobilization of bias* was the occurrence of taken-for-granted assumptions of how the organization makes decisions. A structure of dominance underpinned by prevailing authority created a *structure of legitimacy*. In their research setting, Gordon et al. (2009) observed mobilization of bias supported the status quo's structures of dominance. That is, members of the police force took for granted the traditional power held by members of the hierarchy and saw those power structures as natural and rational. Those higher up in the hierarchy reinforced this view through patterns of discipline and punishment (i.e. coercion), and, in turn, organizational members saw the use of punitive punishment as natural. The combination of mobilization of bias supporting structures of dominance created structures of legitimacy, which made it difficult for the organization to change. For example, Gordon et al. (2009) observed even though the organization introduced a merit-based promotion system supported by performance measures, the police force based promotions entirely on seniority. Members of the hierarchy manipulated the performance measures to ensure the promotion of senior staff over their junior counterparts. Regarding decision-making, those in authority perceived their decision-making processes as rational, and through the structures of dominance within the organization, compelled newer members lower down the hierarchy to comply.

> [N]ew recruits often found themselves in situations where they were dominated to the point where they either followed the irrationality of bad decisions, such as, in some instances, engaging in corruption, or sacrificed their career prospects. (Gordon et al., 2009, p. 26)

The police force under study attempted to change by modifying structures of dominance. The underlying mobilization of bias, however, continued to support the old system. Thus, the new system lacked structures of legitimacy, and, hence, the structures of the dominance of the old system remained, though in subtler or hidden forms (Gordon et al., 2009). Thus, in this study, we see an entrenched power system within an organization using tactics of coercion and domination to override the organization's attempt to change itself to operate more consistently with its values. We also see these power structures dominating staff to the point they see irrational actions (e.g. participating in corruption) as rational.

In his book *Rationality and Power: Democracy in Practice*, Flyvbjerg (1998) presented an in-depth case study of the City of Aalborg's process of revitalizing its downtown core. Throughout this process, Flyvbjerg (1998) recorded numerous instances of special interest groups acting to advance their best interests, frequently behind the scenes, and often through advancing their form of rationality and truth. From this study, Flyvbjerg (1998) drew several conclusions. First, throughout the revitalization project, formal policies and procedures of democratically elected bodies played only a minor role in the decisions of how to proceed. Behind-the-scenes political manoeuvring by special-interest groups played a much more prominent role in the evolution of the project. Institutions put in place to protect public interests were themselves embedded in and subject to these networks of power relations. These power relations often undermined their effectiveness at promoting the public's interests.

Second, Flyvbjerg (1998) demonstrated actors with power can define reality, and they do so by defining what is rational. Defining rationality is an example of agents reproducing and transforming the social structure of rationality within the social setting. Powerful actors can frame the debate in stakeholders' minds, influencing what they consider appropriate evidence for consideration and influencing how to interpret that evidence to justify action. Through studying how the Aalborg project unfolded, Flyvbjerg (1998) observed that rationality was seldom objective. It was, in fact, context-dependent, and the context in which it was often embedded was one of power. Rationality was a discourse of power, a tactic it may use as necessary, but when a powerful actor needed a rationalization (not rationality) to justify an action, then they produced a rationalization. Presenting a rationalization to the public under the guise of rationality was a common tactic of power (Flyvbjerg, 1998). Importantly, Flyvbjerg (1998) argued as an actor's power increases, rationality declines. 'Power, quite simply, often finds ignorance, deception, self-deception, rationalization, and lies more useful for its purposes than truth and rationality' (p. 230). Finally, Flyvbjerg (1998) also observed power relations were dynamic, requiring constant maintenance and cultivation, and usually existed in a stable, though not necessarily equal, equilibrium. Open conflicts were visual and tend to grab attention, but they were rare. When power and rationality came in conflict, rationality loses – naked power was stronger than calls to objectivity. Only when power relations were in a state of stability could rationality influence decision-making and action (Flyvbjerg, 1998).

Moving away from the Aalborg case to look at infrastructure projects in general, Flyvbjerg (2009) observed project costs were consistently underrepresented, and benefits overrepresented during the planning process. He found funding and approval processes created incentives for promoters to downplay costs and inflate benefits to win approval. Two mechanisms drove inaccurate cost-benefit projections. The first was optimism bias, where project promoters honestly over-estimated the ease with which they can complete a project. The second was strategic misrepresentation (a pleasant euphemism for lying), where promoters purposefully predicted lower costs and higher benefits than they knew were likely in order advance a project (Flyvbjerg, Garbuio, & Lovallo, 2009). Taken together, these works of Flyvbjerg (Flyvbjerg, 1998, 2009; Flyvbjerg et al., 2009) demonstrated the role of power to manipulate rationality as a tactic of control and domination. They showed that during periods of contestation, groups would advance threads of rationality supporting their objectives, and those with greater power were better able to assert their specific rationalities in the minds of stakeholders.

Townley (1993) presented a perspective on power and rationality in an organizational context premised on the works of Foucault. An essential connection between rationality and power, she stated, was that before something can be managed, it must first be known. Thus, understanding how the organization comes to know the individuals and activities within it is an important research endeavour. Townley (1993) looked at the activities of human resources management (HRM) by way of example. She explained in HRM, tools, such as employment contracts, job descriptions, and job analyses, identified geographic and temporal characteristics of the work, as well as identified the worker. HRM physically distributed individuals and equipment within a workspace and conceptually located workers in a hierarchy and job ladder. HRM identified tasks and assigned timetables for their completion. These became mechanisms of control, allowing the organization to know if the individual was present or not, what activities they could perform, and when they were to perform them (Townley, 1993). She added that through examinations (e.g. performance reviews) and confessions (e.g. self-evaluations), the organization's knowledge of their workers grew, allowing for better use of everyone's skill sets.

The above studies demonstrate the complex interplay between the structures of power and rationality. They show values, interests, and power often trump rationality or, at the very least, establish which rationality takes precedence. When using rationality to justify actions, the legitimacy of these rationalities is a negotiated process. We like to think we are rational beings and that we base our decisions on an understanding of the facts of a situation. The above studies show rationality is not an objective benchmark, but rather a negotiated concept, established as much, if not more, through tactics of power than the inherent strengths of the 'rational argument'. In a very real way, power is the ability to define what is rational in other people's mind and, thus, influences the actions they support. As Flyvbjerg (1998) concluded in his study of Aalborg:

> Power determines what counts as knowledge, what kind of interpretation attains authority as the dominant interpretation. Power procures the knowledge which supports its purpose, while it ignores or suppresses that knowledge which does not serve it. (p. 226)

He further concluded that for objective rationality to hold sway, actors must understand the power relations in which they are embedded and must build systems creating stable power relations while simultaneously constraining naked acts of power that promote self-interests. This concludes my review of the interplay between power and rationality. I now turn to review the literature of pluralistic organizations.

4.2. Pluralistic Organizations: How Wise Are They?

Healthcare institutions are pluralistic (Bucher & Stelling, 1969; Scott, 1982), and Canadian healthcare institutions are no exception (Denis, Lamothe, & Langley,

2001). Pluralistic organizations share similar traits to professional organizations, notably the presence of different groups of specialized, highly trained individuals (e.g. physicians, administrators, nurses), different objectives pursued by each group (e.g. patient care, cost-effectiveness, public health), and complex power relations between the groups (Bucher & Stelling, 1969; Scott, 1982). In this way, as Bucher and Stelling (1969) noted, professional organizations do not resemble the clear hierarchies and chains of command observed in traditional bureaucracies. Instead, role definition and negotiation among professionals is commonplace. These processes can lead to conflicts that are often resolved through political processes that usually involve coalition-building (Bucher & Stelling, 1969). According to Scott (1982), this organizational structure arose to deal with the unique nature of the work performed in these institutions, work that is 'unusually complex, uncertain, and of great social importance' (p. 214). This structure responds to these challenges by placing the most capable person closest to the problem situation and imbues within them the discretion to act in accordance to their professional judgement (Scott, 1982). Scott (1982) further noted this structure has the benefit of matching ultimate responsibility for outcomes to those with the greatest discretion, as well as prioritizing the individual needs of clients, even though this focus on individual needs contributes to cost pressures. Despite these benefits, the diversity of groups with a lack of clear hierarchy between them may create scenarios where politics trumps organizational values. Therefore, I review several studies exploring how pluralistic organizations, especially healthcare organizations, make and implement decisions. I will first consider studies that demonstrate challenges to effective decision-making followed by examples of pluralistic organizations functioning well.

Denis et al. (2001) studied the process of strategic change in a healthcare setting. Their investigation included two sets of case studies with embedded cases that transpired over an eight-year period in the Canadian healthcare sector. In one set of cases, the strategic change was limited to the redefinition of internal processes and missions. The second set focused on a merger between hospitals. The authors focused their evaluation on senior leadership processes for managing these changes.

Denis et al. (2001) observed that strong leadership coalitions marked periods where significant changes occurred. The authors grouped these coalitions into three categories: strategic coupling (between members of the leadership team), organizational coupling (between members of the leadership team and their organizational base), and environmental coupling (between members of the leadership team and the external environment). In the cases studied, these coalitions exhibited fragility, and as they collapsed, change processes stalled. This fragility stemmed from the reality that in pluralistic settings, leaders derive their legitimacy from different sources, which often results in trade-offs compromising one or more coupling. It is therefore difficult for senior leaders to maintain all three levels of coupling at once.

Consequently, Denis et al. (2001) observed change occurred in an episodic fashion. When all three levels of coupling were healthy, the change would proceed. Due to the fragile nature of these couplings, one or more level would eventually break down as different members acted to secure their political position at the expense of one or more levels of coupling, thus bringing the change process to a halt. A significant limitation of this study was its focus exclusively on senior leaders. As Flyvbjerg (1998) identified, stakeholder groups not formally a member of senior management may have considerable influence over strategic change initiatives. Though the actions of senior leaders are an essential piece, they are not the whole picture of what ultimately makes a change initiative successful.

Rodriguez, Langley, Beland, and Denis (2007) studied the process of strategic change in pluralistic settings when a supra-organizational entity mandated the change, forcing groups to collaborate. The authors performed a comparative longitudinal case analysis over four years of a situation where the board of a health-care region proposed a significant change involving the closing of some hospitals, increasing services provided by ambulatory care, reorganizing various partners around client segments, and enhancing the role of primary care providers. The authors observed the mix of powers, values, and interests of participating groups interacted with the governance structure of the mandated collaboration to create the outcomes observed. The governance structures they observed included clan-based (finding shared values), hierarchical (creating formalized rules), and market-based (using incentives to align interests). Those collaborations that relied solely on clan-based governance did not achieve the desired ends of the collaboration, whereas those employing all three were more successful (Rodriguez et al., 2007). The authors evaluated three explanations of why the regional board did not implement all three governance models consistently to ensure success in all its endeavours. A managerialist perspective suggested the board may have been incompetent. From a symbolic view, though, the researchers observed that in some situations there were secondary gains to 'going through the motions' while not implementing systems to drive success. For example, 'talk' around improving coordination, without really forcing any action, may have allowed the board to take coercive action to close hospitals. Rodriguez et al. (2007) also applied a political perspective to their findings and observed each group involved in the collaboration was embedded in a political field of power relations that constrained the actions available to them. For example, the board was timid in employing coercive power in the face of political influence held by physicians. This study demonstrated how the values, interests and power of various groups might place practical limitations on the actions groups can take, which ultimately influences the success or failure of mandated collaborations.

Denis, Dompierre, Langley, and Rouleau (2011) explored the phenomena whereby groups in pluralistic organizations may possess enough commitment to work on a project together but lack the commitment to bring the project to completion; a process they called *escalating indecision*. Escalating indecision is characterized by:

> [...] the perpetual reopening of decisions or a state of chronic collective ambivalence that prevents projects from moving forward while sustaining or even potentially widening the scope of decision-making activity as time goes on. (p. 227)

To study this, the authors used a single case study of a merger of three large teaching hospitals in Canada. The study was longitudinal, lasting from 1995 to 2002, and included direct observation, interviews, and document reviews.

The authors found escalating indecision resulted when actors became trapped in processes that kept a project alive, while simultaneously preventing its completion. This occurred when groups with disparate interests were forced to work together. To get each groups' support for the project, actors placed symbolic value on certain practices in a process the authors called 'reification'. For example, participants ascribed symbolic meaning to the merger protocol as the founding document of the proposed merger. Due to diverging interests, however, 'strategic ambiguity' — that is, leaving some processes undefined — was introduced to secure each group's buy-in. Project managers continually left these undefined processes for future discussions. This strategic ambiguity prevented groups from implementing the project. The symbolic nature of the founding document simultaneously kept groups from killing the project while preventing them from making radical changes to it that would have allowed them to move forward. Consequently, actors found themselves embedded in a 'network of indecision'.

The above collection of studies paints a bleak picture of decision-making in pluralistic organizations, one where tension between groups can keep the organization from enacting wise decisions — or any decision, for that matter. That, however, is not always the case. Kodeih and Greenwood (2013) presented a study of several universities in France that successfully reconciled competing institutional logics. Like healthcare organizations, universities also bear the hallmarks of pluralistic organizations (Scott, 1982). Kodeih and Greenwood (2013) performed a longitudinal case study of four business schools that included 41 semi-structured interviews and analysis of archival material. At the time of the study, the French government was requiring these business schools to reconcile two opposing institutional logics: maintaining traditional, domestic-based programme excellence while simultaneously evolving into internationally competitive universities. They found the keys to reconciling these logics were consistent support from field-level actors, such as government officials and influential members of the public. This support took the form of stressing the importance and compatibility of both institutional logics, as well as giving individual organizations discretion over how to reconcile both logics. Kodeih and Greenwood (2013) also noted differences in how each institution responded based on the aspired identities of each school. High-status schools chose to graft new programmes onto current ones to reconcile these competing institutional logics. Low-status schools, however, saw the new logic as an opportunity to restructure their entire programme to reconfigure their status (Kodeih & Greenwood, 2013). This study showed pluralistic organizations could effectively reconcile opposing objectives.

Researchers have also observed effective collaboration between opposing institutional logics in Canadian healthcare institutions. Reay and Hinings (2009) performed a study of how Alberta healthcare organizations reconciled their traditional institutional logic of medical professionalism (where physician–patient interactions guide all service processes) with the business-like healthcare logic (where efficiency is the dominant value). Their study consisted of archival analysis and interviews of 45 people across eight sights where doctors and representatives of the new business-like healthcare logic – the regional health authorities (RHA) – had to interact. They found physicians resisted the introduction of business-like healthcare. Despite this resistance, Reay and Hinings (2009) found both physicians and RHA developed a productive working relationship. They identified four practices enabling this working relationship. First, actors separated medical decisions from RHA decisions, allowing doctors to retain autonomy over patient treatment while RHA fulfilled its obligations. Second, Reay and Hinings (2009) noted RHA, even though not legally required, chose to seek input from physicians as part of their decision-making processes. Next, both physicians and RHA found common cause in opposing unpopular government decisions. Finally, physicians and RHA jointly collaborated on the development of new healthcare delivery innovations. This study showed groups operating from different value positions can retain those values and still collaborate. Reconciliation of values is not a prerequisite for effective working relations. Like the previous study in French business schools, this research presented an example of mechanisms through which pluralistic organizations may operate effectively.

The previous studies characterized how change occurs in pluralistic organizations. Successfully implementing change requires maintenance of coupling within the senior management team, as well as between that team and the external environment and its organizational base. Maintaining all three couplings is difficult, and, consequently, change proceeds in fits and starts (Denis et al., 2001). Even when higher authorities mandate collaboration, political interests of various groups can influence governance models used as well as the amount of coercive power different actors are willing to apply. These dynamics have a direct impact on the success of the collaboration (Rodriguez et al., 2007). Alternatively, even when disparate groups are bound together in a project, differences in interests can result in escalating indecision where participants continually expend energy on a project without achieving any resolution (Denis et al., 2011). That said, it is possible for pluralistic organizations to manage change. Doing so requires support from the external environment (Kodeih & Greenwood, 2013), as well as willingness to collaborate while respecting each other's values in the internal environment (Reay & Hinings, 2009).

In short, the interests of groups within pluralistic organizations directly influence the success of initiatives to implement change. Note that in the above studies set in healthcare organizations, an important stakeholder group was absent: the patient – the only stakeholder group for which these organizations exist to serve.

> Unfortunately, there is some truth to the idea that healthcare organizations sometimes seem to diffuse power among almost everyone, except the people for whom they exist—the patients needing care […] (Langley & Denis, 2011, p. i46)

Right now, society can only hope that the interplay between interests of those groups who are involved in these processes ultimately serve patients' best interests. Unfortunately, we have seen from Hamilton (2012) that physicians may use their positional power and training to prioritize their values over the patient's, which raises the question of whether this hope in the system is misplaced. It is the intention of this book to add to the dialogue around how healthcare institutions meet the interests of patients and society. To show how I approached this, I first turn to the theoretical frameworks of this study in the following chapter, followed by my research methods in Chapter 6.

Chapter 5

Theoretical Frameworks

I have embedded this study in the philosophical school of critical realism founded by Bhaskar (1978) and modelled it after the phronetic research (PR) approach developed by Flyvbjerg (2001). My intent with this research was to facilitate the development of the value-rationality, or practical wisdom, of organizations, and I found both theoretical frameworks helpful tools to that end. I feel the structured ontology of critical realism that I describe below gives practitioners an organizing framework to help guide their action in that it identifies societal structures that enable or constrain action, which may then inform them of actions they may take to achieve their goals. PR is a methodology specifically intended to develop *phronesis,* or practical wisdom, in organizational action. In the following sections, I present a review of critical realism and PR. In the next chapter, I then present the methodology I employed in this study.

5.1. Philosophical Framing: Critical Realism

This research takes a critical realist perspective. Developed by Bhaskar (1978), critical realism presents an alternative to positivism and poststructuralism (Ackroyd & Fleetwood, 2000). Whereas positivism assumes the social world mimics the natural world, critical realism recognizes the role of complex open systems and human perception in undermining this assumption (Ackroyd & Fleetwood, 2000). Whereas poststructuralism assumes the social world is discursively constructed, critical realism recognizes the presence of enduring social structures independent of any one actor (Ackroyd & Fleetwood, 2000). This section presents my overview of critical realism's central tenets. I then consider critical realism in the context of organizational studies. Next, I position critical realism against positivism and poststructuralism. I then explain why this perspective is appropriate for this investigation. I conclude with a discussion of the main structures of interest in this study.

5.1.1. What Is Critical Realism?

Ackroyd and Fleetwood (2000) posited the social world is different from the natural world. Most notably, the natural world does not require human action for its existence. The social world does. Even though the social world depends on human action, however, there exist social structures outside our awareness of them (Ackroyd & Fleetwood, 2000). By way of example, Ackroyd and

Fleetwood (2000) discussed class relations. They stated human activity mediates the constraints and resources afforded to different classes. Despite the requirement of human action to reproduce classes, class relations exist before an individual arrives on the social scene and persists after they leave. These class structures, thus, exist independently of any one person. Moreover, people may be unaware of the role their actions play in reproducing these relations (Ackroyd & Fleetwood, 2000). That is structures, even when unconceptualized, still have an effect. These observations led Bhaskar (1978) to develop a stratified ontology of social reality, summarized in Figure 5.1 and described below.

In Bhaskar's (1978) model, there exist three strata of social reality: the real, actual, and empirical domains. Structures in the real domain contain generative mechanisms, which may then create events in the actual domain. If individuals perceive these events, they create experiences in the empirical domain. (Ackroyd & Fleetwood, 2000; Bhaskar, 1978). I present an analogy of this in Figure 5.1. The hammer and nail are structures containing generative mechanisms. They simultaneously enable action (you can use the hammer to hit the nail) while constraining it (you cannot use the hammer to tighten a bolt). An actor swinging the hammer at the nail is an event, and if anyone witnesses the impact, striking the nail (or your thumb!) is an experience.

Analogies aside, what are social structures? In brief, they are '[...] constraining and enabling rules and resources which are implemented in human interaction' (Tsoukas, 1994, p. 292). Examples of structures include such things as the routines enacted by employees in their daily business (Costello, 2000) or the disposition of labour markets from which companies hire employees (Rubery, 1994). In open systems, in which the social world exists, the interactions within and between strata can be complex. Structures may contain contradictory elements of structuration (Ferguson, 1994). For example, structures mediating professional conduct may modify structures of racism in a work environment (Porter, 1993). Generative mechanisms within structures act transfactually, meaning that once set in motion, other countervailing powers may hide their effect (Ackroyd & Fleetwood, 2000). Time may separate causal powers and events, making it hard for researchers to

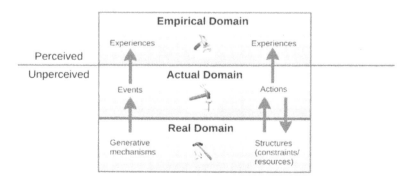

Figure 5.1. Critical Realism's Stratified Ontology.

establish causal links (Tsoukas, 1994). In short, '[...] events can occur without being experienced, causal mechanisms can counteract one another and there can be real mechanisms in nature which never have effects though they would under certain circumstances' (Pratten, 1993, p. 406).

A specific example will elaborate these strata further. Rubery (1994) took a critical realist perspective to assess the British production regime. She identified several structures in the real domain shaping British production systems. She noted the British labour pool lacked highly skilled workers. British employers, consequently, adjusted their organizations and wage systems to accommodate these low-skilled workers. She noted government policies and cultural attitudes towards education and employment reinforced training systems producing employees with low skills. These structures aside, she observed foreign invest-ment and trade relations (other social structures) brought new managerial ideas to Britain (events), which created a desire in some areas of the nation to shift towards high-skilled labour production (experiences). Stakeholders within the system attempted to change structures in the real domain to transition to a high-skilled labour production regime. Current structures, however, limited their abil-ity to do so. For example, Rubery (1994) noted British employers lacked the managerial expertise required to shift production to accommodate a high-skilled workforce, and the nation's training systems were unable to produce such a workforce. That is not to say these structures were immutable − Rubery (1994) noted the system was continually evolving and adapting − just that the con-straining effects of these structures were real and required effort to overcome.

The above example demonstrates the relation between structures and human agency is not one-way − structures constrain agency, but agency can modify struc-tures. This complex, back-and-forth relation is central to critical realism's stratified ontology. Reed (1997) stated social structures and agency are distinct but inter-dependent. Structures differentially distribute resources and constraints to indivi-duals depending on their position within a social system, which in turn impacts their ability to act (Whittington, 1989, p. 81). The transformational model of social action (TMSA) describes and builds on this relationship. As per the TMSA, every action an agent may take is shaped by the social structure, and every action serves to reproduce or change that structure (Ackroyd & Fleetwood, 2000; Bhaskar, 1986; Giddens, 1976, 1984; Manicas, 1980; Pratten, 1993). Thus, struc-ture and agency are irreducible to one another, yet exist in an interdependent relation (Reed, 1997). This model gives rise to the idea of emergence. The actions available to an individual emerge out of the setting's structures, and those struc-tures emerge out of agents' actions (Pratten, 1993; Tsoukas, 1994; Willmott, 1997). So, even though structure and agency emerge from one another, they are irreducible to each other (Pratten, 1993; Willmott, 1997). This allows critical rea-lists to assign structures ontological status without reifying them (Willmott, 1997).

5.1.2. Critical Realism in Organizational Studies

Ackroyd (2000) applied a critical realist approach to understanding organiza-tions. He maintained organizations are a central structure of modern society and argued that research aimed at understanding how individual action creates organizations is valuable. He maintained discourse was not all that went into constituting an organization, as poststructuralists argue. He made this claim based on the observation that discourse was also the means of opposition and dissent. Though organizations may fall from outside market influences, they seldom fall due to internal strife (Ackroyd, 2000). Thus, he concluded organizations possess structures contributing to their stability beyond mere discourse. These structures may include stable patterns of relationships and roles (Ackroyd, 2000), routines (Costello, 2000), and culture (Willmott, 1997). Once established, organizations resist change (Ackroyd, 2000). When they do change, new sets of rules and relations emerge quickly, solidifying new structures that future actors reproduce or transform through their actions (Coopey, Keegan, & Emler, 1998). Ackroyd (2000) added that though organizations are maintained by structures, they themselves are structures of broader society. Organizations mediate economic and social power, and through them, society's activities are perpetuated (Ackroyd, 2000). As structures of society, organizations have wide-ranging constraining and enabling effects. For example, as described above, Rubery (1994) showed industrial practices in the UK combined with international trade relations and social norms of labour force composition limited the nation's ability to shift from low-skilled manufacturing towards higher-skilled, value-added manufacturing.

Tsoukas (1994) looked within organizations to create a meta-theory of management using a critical realist perspective. He started with four prevailing perspectives on managerial actions: management controls, functions, task characteristics, and roles. He then established to which ontological strata each perspective belongs. He identified managerial controls are the generative mechanisms present in the real domain. These controls exist within the social and industrial matrix in which the manager operates. Managerial functions and task characteristics exist in the actual domain as events and actions taken by managers, which are then experienced in the form of management roles in the empirical domain (Tsoukas, 1994). Tsoukas (1994) identified three advantages of applying a critical realist perspective to management. First, he maintained such a perspective opens to the researcher the study of not just what managers do, but also what they are *capable* of doing. Second, Tsoukas (1994) stated a critical realist perspective allows researchers to evaluate other influences on management, such as gender or race (see, e.g., Whittington, 1992). Thirdly, this perspective allows researchers to understand management as a set of individual practices in the empirical domain as well as collective institutional resources and constraints in the real domain (Tsoukas, 1994).

5.1.3. *Critical Realism and Positivism*

Critical realism and positivism share the assumption there exists social truths separate from the perception of any one individual. For critical realists, these include structures embedded in the real domain. One of critical realism's critique of positivism, however, is positivist's need for closed systems to perform the scientific studies required to create predictive models (Ackroyd & Fleetwood,

2000). Positivist researchers use these closed systems to control all variables except the one under study, which they then manipulate to observe its effect (Ackroyd & Fleetwood, 2000). The social world, critical realists maintain, operates in an open system. In open systems, you cannot make one-to-one causal links between generative mechanisms and events due to the transfactual nature of generative mechanisms and complexity of interactions between structures, events, and experiences (Ackroyd & Fleetwood, 2000; Bhaskar, 1978; Harre, 1988; Harre & Madden, 1975; Sayer, 1992; Tsoukas, 1989). For example, the structure of labour markets is fundamentally shaped by a vast array of industrial and societal structures in a complex and reciprocal manner (Peck, 2000). Researchers lack the control over the real world to create closed systems for study, and even if they could, results would not yield models predictive of real-world complexities (Ackroyd & Fleetwood, 2000). Additionally, temporal dislocation between generative mechanisms, events, and experiences undermine our ability to create predictive models (Tsoukas, 1994). Moreover, if individuals do not perceive events when they occur, which is possible in open systems, they remain unaware generative mechanisms are even at play (Tsoukas, 1994).

So how is knowledge of the social world gained under critical realism? Ackroyd and Fleetwood (2000) maintained that despite these challenges, some forms of knowledge are better than others, and methods exist to produce better knowledge. Although researchers are themselves embedded in a social world and possess their own biases, they are usually independent of the social phenomena under study, which gives them some objectivity in identifying generative mechanisms (Sayer, 1992, p. 49). Moreover, recall the emergent nature of structures and agency discussed earlier. Though structures emerge from agency, they are irreducible to agency (Pratten, 1993; Willmott, 1997). Thus, reality is somewhat more than simply an account of reality – there are structures and generative mechanisms for researchers to identify and study (Ackroyd & Fleetwood, 2000). Ackroyd and Fleetwood (2000) maintained that under critical realism, research focuses on studying the conditions making action possible (or impossible). They further identified the goal of critical realist research is explanation rather than the positivist goal of prediction. Critical realists seek to understand what objects are capable of if contingent conditions are right (Harre & Madden, 1975; Harre & Secord, 1972), and to identify underlying generative mechanisms resulting in observable outcomes (Reed, 1997).

5.1.4. Critical Realism and Poststructuralism

Ackroyd and Fleetwood (2000) suggested critical realism shares with poststructuralism the understanding of the role discourse and sense-making play in our perception of reality. The difference, they claimed, lies in the degree to which each philosophy applies that assumption. Poststructuralists have a flat ontology – that is, reality is socially constructed, full stop. Ackroyd and Fleetwood (2000) further maintained that critical realists have a layered ontology – structures constrain and enable actions, leading to events experienced and interpreted by individuals. As they explained, whereas poststructuralists view social phenomena as socially *constructed*, critical realists see them as socially *dependent*. Whereas poststructuralist research focuses on events and discourses through which humans create their understanding of the world and their place in it, critical realism focuses on 'causal mechanisms, social structures, powers and relations that govern them' (Ackroyd & Fleetwood, 2000, p. 13).

5.1.5.   Why Is Critical Realism Appropriate for This Study?

This study sought to understand and facilitate wise decision-making in a real-world context. As such, the social environment under study was an open system with all the complexities that entails. Thus, scientific research in the positivist tradition with its necessity of studying artificially closed systems was unable to achieve the aims of this research. Moreover, this proposed study possessed a critical nature. It sought to identify obstacles to value-rational decision-making in the organization under study and to develop systems circumventing those obstacles. Critical realism is a practical framework for critical studies (Eriksson & Kovalainen, 2008; Reed, 1997).

That said, poststructuralism is also perceived as critical (Eriksson & Kovalainen, 2008, p. 267). Indeed, this research leaned on several poststructural theorists, especially in its conceptualization of power. I propose there is enough overlap between the two paradigms regarding individuals' interpretations of social experiences and sense-making that this was warranted. Reed (1997), however, points out that poststructuralism's refusal to accept the constraining/enabling nature of structures on agency limits its ability to change those structures. On the other hand, critical realism's concept of the emergent nature of structures and agency gives researchers and actors conceptual tools to understand and change those structures (Reed, 1997), which is more consistent with my research objectives.

5.1.6.   Structures of Interest in This Study

In this book, I assumed values, rationality, and power were essential structures in the real domain constraining and enabling actions of actors in the research setting I studied. As described in Chapter 3, values in the public sector are established before and persist after individuals arrive. They are thus irreducible to action. Individuals' activities, however, reproduce or transform values, and so they are emergent from action. Likewise, I assumed rationality was another structure. Through applying rationality, we obtain an understanding of the world. This understanding informs us of what actions are appropriate, what actions are possible, and how to perform those actions − that is, rationality enables and constrains actions. Through domination and subjectification as described in Chapter 4, actors assume the rationality dominant in the role they assume in their industry. Rationality is, thus, irreducible to action. Actors can, however, influence what stakeholders perceive as rational, and the greater power an actor has, the stronger their influence (Flyvbjerg, 1998, 2001, 2009; Flyvbjerg et al., 2009). Thus, rationality also emerges from action.

My proposed research leaned heavily on the fourth dimension of power, explicated by researchers such as Foucault and other poststructuralists. I assumed the web of power relations were another structure. For example, the power afforded to different groups in a social setting differentially enable and constrain the actions of different actors; thus, they are irreducible to action. I argue, however, they are emergent from action in that individuals' activities serve to maintain or transform those power relations. Moreover, as demonstrated by Flyvbjerg (1998), the *longue durée* of power persists beyond the arrival or departure of any one actor, again demonstrating the irreducibility of power relations to individual action.

5.2. Phronetic Research

PR, developed by Flyvbjerg (2001), focuses on the interplay between values, rationality, and power. It is a research approach aimed at developing *phronesis*, or practical wisdom, within institutions (Flyvbjerg, 2001). Researchers have applied PR to multiple levels of analysis, including at municipal, national, and international levels (Flyvbjerg, 2012). Topics have included how governments (mis)manage megaprojects[1] (Clegg & Pitsis, 2012; Flyvbjerg, 2012; Flyvbjerg, Bruzelius, & Rothengatter, 2003; Griggs & Howarth, 2012), urban development and planning (Basu, 2012; Flyvbjerg, 1998), social advocacy (Shdaimah & Stahl, 2012), racism and race relations (Sandercock & Attili, 2012), amnesty laws (Olsen, Payne, & Reiter, 2012), feminist scholarship (Eubanks, 2012), and teaching of social justice (Simmons, 2012). With its aim of improving institutional value-rationality, PR shares similarities with action research. Action research is an approach where researchers '[...] collaborate, actively engage with and work within businesses in order to help them solve specific problems' (Eriksson & Kovalainen, 2008, p. 193). There is a subtle difference, however. Whereas with action research, researchers adopt the goals of the subjects they are studying and use their research results to achieve those goals, the PR researcher maintains independence from their subjects and retains the right to problematize what they see (Flyvbjerg, 2004, 2006b).

Like critical realism, PR assumes the positivist traditions of theory development are not appropriate when studying human behaviour in natural settings. Rather than focusing on the development of theory, PR emphasizes observation with the intent to develop insight into the historical and narrative structure of people's reality (Clegg & Pitsis, 2012) to allow for the creation of solutions for action (Flyvbjerg, 2001; Schram, 2012). It is a prescriptive research approach.

---

[1]'Megaprojects are multibillion-dollar public infrastructure projects, each with the potential to transform cities, regions and the lives of millions' (Flyvbjerg, 2012, p. 98).

By way of counterpoint, though, Eubanks (2012) argued the needs and goals of PR need not run counter to the concepts of objectivity, generalizability, and theory building. Regarding objectivity, she stated feminist research managed to bridge the divide between neutral researcher and interested observer. It has done this by achieving *strong objectivity*, which is:

> [...] best achieved when a number of different standpoints are put in conversation with each other in the context of social justice-oriented research and action. This process develops oppositional consciousness, locatable political commitments, and strategies for alliance- and coalition-building [...] (Eubanks, 2012, p. 241)

She further argued that by integrating the points of view of several analysts and triangulating between standpoints of participants, it is possible to produce objective, rigorous, and generalizable knowledge. Eubanks (2012) also cautions against the focus on specific contexts to the exclusion of all else, stating, '[...] the reality of transnational politics and flows demands that we understand and account for both micro-level practices *and* the global processes and discourses that shape our experiences' (p. 243, emphasis in original). This sentiment was echoed by Flyvbjerg (1998), who stressed the importance of understanding the *longue durée*, or the historical evolution, of power relations predating and outside the focal research setting. Finally, Eubanks (2012) saw contribution to theory as an essential element of the action-reflection cycle of *praxis*. With this background, I now review how a PR approach understands the constructs of values, rationality, and power.

5.2.1.   *Phronetic Research and Values*

Flyvbjerg (2001) argued instrumental-rationality dominates the thinking of Western society, marked by veneration of those Aristotelian virtues of *episteme* (scientific knowledge) and *techne* (technical knowledge). Such emphasis has given us great knowledge and know-how, but it has left us wanting tools to enhance our society's value-rationality. It is through the virtue of *phronesis* (practical wisdom) that we may achieve value-rationality. As Schram (2012) explained, *phronesis* comes from understanding the social context intimately and knowing what is good to do in those specific settings. This is echoed by Flyvbjerg (2001):

> The person possessing practical wisdom (*phronimos*) has knowledge of how to behave in each particular circumstance that can never be equated with or reduced to knowledge of general truths. *Phronesis* is a sense of the ethically practical rather than a kind of science. (p. 57)

Because of the role of context in choosing the right action, one cannot implement *phronesis* as a science (*episteme*), nor can one develop absolute rules to guide action in every situation (*techne*). Instead, to exercise *phronesis*, one must possess experience and judgement (Flyvbjerg, 2001; Schram, 2012), or, as Townley (2008b) would put it, disembedded, embedded, and embodied rationality. It is the goal of PR to develop this capacity in our society and organizations by providing input into ongoing public discussions on issues we face and their solutions.

5.2.2. Phronetic Research and Rationality and Power

PR is an approach to power research (Flyvbjerg, 2002). It is thus vital to delineate how this research approach conceptualizes power. Flyvbjerg (1998) views rationality and power as deeply entwined. He (2001, 2002, 2004, 2006) takes elements from Foucault and Nietzsche to propose a conception of power possessing six characteristics:

(1) power is a positive and productive force;
(2) power manifests as a dense web of relations;
(3) power is dynamic;
(4) power produces knowledge, and knowledge produces power;
(5) how power is exercised is a more central question than who has power and why; and
(6) the point of departure for power studies are small questions.

Clegg and Pitsis (2012) expand on this. They identify power not as an outside force, but rather as how we structure our actions. Power does not have unique access to the truth, but rather it creates the truth and influences what knowledge people consider relevant for a given context. To understand current power relations, researchers must understand the history of how those relations came to be.[2] They view power as a dense network of relations, and so, to study power, one must 'work from the specificities of contexts outwards rather than assume that those sovereign points that dominate the landscape are necessarily the loci of power' (p. 73). Highlighting the importance of contexts, Rodriguez et al. (2007) confirmed this, noting that when studying the interactions between groups, the context in which they occur is critical to understanding how these interactions evolve. With this background of my theoretical framework, including critical realism and phronetic research, I now turn to discuss the methods I used to apply PR to my research setting in the following chapter.

---

[2]This focus on the history of power relations is consistent with critical realism's conceptualization of structures. Structures — such as these power relations — persist before and after an actor enters the social setting (Ackroyd & Fleetwood, 2000). Thus, as Clegg and Pitsis (2012) suggest, to understand this structure, one must understand the history of its development.

Chapter 6

Methods

For this project, I performed an embedded case study on the implementation of a pilot Seniors Programme performed by the BC Health Authority in conjunction with several other organizations. My data included texts and interviews of the key individuals involved in developing and implementing the Seniors Programme on which I performed a narrative analysis. In the following sections, I justify my use of qualitative methods for this study followed by an overview of the embedded case study that served as my research setting. This includes a detailed overview of the Seniors Programme, its goals, key organizations, and actors involved in its development and implementation, as well as the stages of its lifecycle. After this, I present my sources of data and conclude with a description of how I undertook my data analysis.

6.1. A Qualitative Approach

With its emphasis on understanding contexts, PR relies heavily (though not exclusively) on qualitative methods due to their ability to gain detailed situational information (Flyvbjerg, 2001; Schram, 2012). PR also requires a deep understanding of power relations and how different actors use rationality within the research setting. Townley (2008b) argued individuals rely on embedded (i.e. context-specific) forms of rationality as this allows them to '[...] grasp the modalities of power that they encounter' (p. 207). Positivist approaches fail to reflect the messiness of the reality in which individuals make value judgements, marginalizing subtle yet critical elements (Cicmil, 2006), and so, PR often relies on qualitative methods such as ethnographies and case studies (Flyvbjerg, 2001) as well as narrative analysis (Landman, 2012). The focus on developing action and creating change necessitates a relational scholarship of integration between researchers and practitioners and collaborative study designs (Bartunek, 2007; Shdaimah & Stahl, 2012). That said, PR is flexible and open to whichever methods are best able to address the four phronetic questions listed in Table 1.1 (page 4) (Flyvbjerg, 2001; Schram, 2012).

6.2. Case study: The Seniors Programme

I performed an embedded, single case study (Yin, 2014) within the BC Health Authority. As described earlier, the specific case was the initial testing of the Seniors Programme. The Seniors Programme was borne of the observation that in the area administered by the BC Health Authority, community-based support for the pre-frail elderly was fragmented, creating complexity for seniors navigating their health concerns ([The Foundation], 2015; [The Foundation]-[NS Health Authority]-[BC Health Authority] Collaborative, 2013). This increased the risk of premature admission to acute care facilities (e.g. emergency departments), which, in turn, increased the odds of the seniors experiencing negative health consequences compared to if they had been treated in the community ([The Foundation], 2015). This was an embedded case study since, as I describe below, I intended to interview members from different stakeholder groups involved with the implementation of the Seniors Programme. The following paragraphs first present a rationale for why a case study was appropriate followed by an explanation of why I chose this specific case setting. After that, I present a detailed overview of the Seniors Programme.

Flyvbjerg (2001, 2004, 2006) argued for the use of case study research in PR. He maintained researchers must observe human behaviour and values in relation to situational contexts. Moreover, PR focuses on individuals' actions, which only have relevance in the context of their circumstances. Furthermore, given the fourth PR question (What's to be done?), a principle aim of PR is to create change (Flyvbjerg, 2012). Siggelkow (2007) argued cases are an effective tool for showing causal mechanisms, suggesting their usefulness for motivating and guiding change. PR emphasizes generating thick, rich understandings of the context by uncovering situational details (Flyvbjerg, 2006b).

Furthermore, given the critical realist foundation of this study, I view the proposed case as an example of an open system where the transfactual nature of generative mechanisms and intricacy of interactions create a complexity challenging to understand (Ackroyd & Fleetwood, 2000; Bhaskar, 1978; Harre, 1988; Harre & Madden, 1975; Sayer, 1992; Tsoukas, 1989). As Yin (2014) suggested, case studies are an appropriate tool to capture a holistic perspective of real-world complexity. Yin (2014) further suggested case studies are appropriate when research questions focus on how and why types of questions. My research questions fell into this category (see Table 1.1, page 4). My research questions forced me to evaluate *how* power influences outcomes, *why* stakeholder groups take the positions they do, and ultimately *how* we can increase the value-rationality of organizations. A common challenge to case studies is their perceived lack of generalizability (Yin, 2014). Yin (2014), however, argued that though cases may not be *statistically* generalizable, they can be *analytically* generalizable. That is, they can build on a body of literature supporting a developing theory or paradigm. For example, there exists a growing body of PR work. This work is creating a burgeoning understanding of mechanisms affecting value-rationality. The results of this study add to that knowledge.

Siggelkow (2007) and Yin (2014) maintained that researchers do not select cases randomly. Instead, they look for those organizations with the potential to give insight into the phenomena under study. Regarding this specific case setting, it contained elements of values (numerous conflicting values within the BC Health Authority), rationality (evidence-based decision-making versus other types), and power (a collaboration between multiple stakeholder groups with varying interests). It proved a fertile field of data for this study. Now that I have introduced and justified the case for study, I will present a detailed overview of the Seniors Programme. After that, I will describe my sources of data and the narrative analysis I performed.

6.3. Overview of the Development and Implementation of the Seniors Programme

As introduced above, the research setting for this study was the development and implementation of a Seniors Programme within a health authority situated in a major metropolitan area in British Columbia, Canada. This programme had a complex structure involving collaborations between multiple organizations and possessed several key milestones during its life. To give the results of my research context, it is essential first to understand the details of how this programme unfolded. I will first describe the Seniors Programme. Then, I describe the structure of the programme, identifying the main organizations as well as the key individuals within those organizations responsible for the development of the Seniors Programme. Following this, I present a timeline identifying the significant events in the life of the Seniors Programme in the BC Health Authority. I conclude with a description of the scope of my study, identifying the boundaries of what was and what was not included in my analysis. Please note that to maintain the confidentiality of all participants in this study, I have replaced the names of all organizations, programmes, and individuals with generic descriptors where possible.

6.3.1. What Was the Seniors Programme?

The Seniors Programme was a research study developed through collaboration with several healthcare organizations. The goal of the programme was to determine whether physical activity could prevent frailty in seniors. Participating physicians assessed their senior patients using a frailty index adopted by the Seniors Programme. Physicians identified patients who, as indicated by this index, were at risk of becoming frail but were, nonetheless, not frail yet. They asked these pre-frail patients if they would like to participate in the Seniors Programme. Participating patients were assigned a physical activity coach. This coach met with the patient to discuss their fitness goals and then designed an individualized fitness programme for the patient. Throughout the study, the coach would contact the patient to assess their progress and adjust the fitness programme as appropriate. Patients participated in this programme for six months, after which their physician used the frailty index to assess their frailty to see if it had improved. Fifty-one patients enrolled in the study. Results demonstrated that for most patients, frailty scores improved throughout the study (Bedford et al., 2015; Park, Garm, Friesen, & Chu, 2015).

6.3.2. The Organizational Structure of the Seniors Programme

The development of the Seniors Programme was the product of a collaboration between three organizations, which then recruited two additional organizations

Table 6.1. Organizations Involved in the Seniors Programme.

Identifier	Description	Role
British Columbia (BC) Health Authority	A regional health authority located in a major metropolitan area in BC	Sponsor and contributor to the Training Fellowship that developed the Seniors Programme
Nova Scotia (NS) Health Authority	A regional health authority located in a major metropolitan area in NS	Sponsor and contributor to the Training Fellowship that developed the Seniors Programme
The Foundation	A federal, non-profit healthcare foundation that fostered the development and spread of healthcare innovations across Canada	Sponsor and mentor to the Training Fellowship that developed the Seniors Programme
BC Coaching Organization	A BC-based, non-profit organization that provided volunteer coaches who mentored seniors in physical fitness	Provided coaches to BC-based seniors enrolled in the Seniors Programme
NS Coaching Organization	A for-profit long-term care provider in Ontario and several Maritime provinces	Provided coaches to NS-based seniors enrolled in the Seniors Programme

to administer the programme (summarized in Table 6.1). The three organizations driving the development of the Seniors Programme included two health authorities, one in British Columbia (BC) and the other in Nova Scotia (NS) (herein called the BC and NS health authorities, respectively), along with a national, non-profit healthcare foundation (herein called the Foundation). The BC and NS health authorities were responsible for administering healthcare within a major metropolitan area of their province. The Foundation's mandate was to foster the development and spread of healthcare innovations across Canada ('About Us', 2018). To this end, the Foundation ran a yearly Training Programme whose intent was to train healthcare administrators to develop, apply, and spread innovations that address challenges affecting Canadian healthcare systems. Both the BC and NS health authorities participated in this Training Fellowship, and it was through this fellowship that they developed the Seniors Programme. As described above, a component of the Seniors Programme was pairing seniors with a coach. The BC and NS Coaching Organizations supplied coaches. In Table 6.2, I summarize the key personnel participating in the Training Fellowship and, subsequently, the Seniors Programme. In Figure 6.1, I display a visual representation of the organizational

Table 6.2. Key Individuals Involved in the Seniors Programme.

Identifier	Role
BC Health Authority	
CEO1[a]	CEO of the BC Health Authority at the start of the programme until June 2014
Interim CEO	CEO of BC Health Authority, June 2014 to January 2015
CEO2[a]	CEO of BC Health Authority, January 2015 to end of this study
Mentor[a]	Member of the BC working group; liaison between CEO's office and working group
MD Lead[a]	Member of the BC working group; as a practicing family physician, she was the lead physician in the working group
Site Director[a]	Member of the BC working group
Director 1	Member of the BC working group
Director 2	Member of the BC working group
Project Manager	Member of the BC working group; administrative coordinator
NS Health Authority	
NS CEO1	CEO of the NS Health Authority at the start of the programme to February 2015
NS CEO2	CEO of the NS Health Authority, February 2015 to the programme end
NS Senior Director	Senior Director of NS Health Authority
NS MD Lead	Member of the NS working group
NS Senior Manager	Member of the NS working group
NS Project Manager	Member of the NS working group; administrative coordinator
The Foundation	
Programme Lead, Education/Training	A senior executive overseeing the Training Fellowship
Director, Education & Evaluation	A senior executive overseeing the Training Fellowship; responsible for overseeing development of evaluation tools
Senior Director, Education/Training	A senior executive overseeing the Training Fellowship
VP, Programmes	A senior executive overseeing the Training Fellowship

Table 6.2. (*Continued*)

Identifier	Role
Senior Improvement Lead[a]	The manager brought in after the conclusion of the Training Fellowship to promote the spread of the Seniors Programme
BC Coaching Organization	
Executive Director	Senior manager of the BC Coaching Organization
Head Coach[a]	Lead coach responsible for training and coordinating volunteer coaches
NS Coaching Organization	
NS Coach CEO	Senior manager of the NS Coaching Organization

Note: [a]These individuals agreed to participate in interviews about their involvement in this project.

structure. The executive leadership of both health authorities as well as the Foundation sat on the Training Fellowship Steering Committee, which oversaw activities performed by the Training Fellows from the BC and NS health authorities.

6.3.3. *Timeline of the Seniors Programme*

Figure 6.2 summarizes the timeline of the Seniors Programme. During this period, turnover in executive leadership occurred in both the BC and NS health authorities. Since the scope of my research focused on the BC Health Authority, I have only shown the dates of transitions within that organization. I have divided the timeline into five stages. The first stage, *Assembling the training fellowship*, spanned the time from when CEO1 began contemplating innovative ways to significantly impact the care of the elderly to the signing of the *Project Charter: Collaborative Project to Improve Senior Care* on 2 December 2013 (herein called the Project Charter).[1] During this period, CEO1 began assembling a team that would eventually participate in the Training Programme and engaged the Foundation and NS Health Authority in collaboration. The *Seniors Programme development* phase spanned the time from the sign-off of the Project Charter in December 2013 to enrolment of the first patient in November 2014. During this stage, the Training Fellows performed extensive research and interviews with seniors' groups as they developed the Seniors Programme.

---

[1]This document was signed by CEOs of the BC and NS health authorities and the VP, Programmes, of the Foundation. The document indicated the intent of all three organizations to collaborate in the Training Fellowship, and outlined the project scope, approach, and organization of this collaboration.

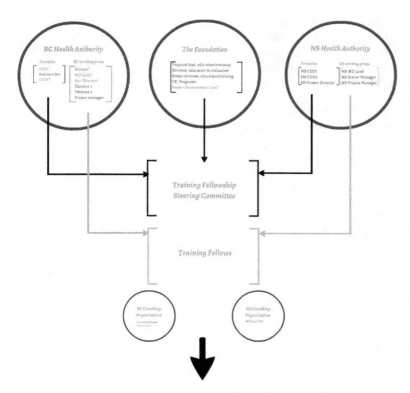

Figure 6.1. Organizational Structure of the Seniors Programme. *Note*: *These individuals agreed to participate in interviews about their involvement in this project.

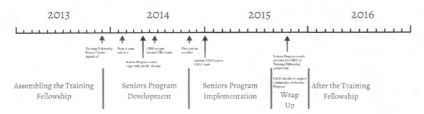

Figure 6.2. Timeline of the Seniors Programme.

Additionally, they partnered with coaching organizations willing to work on this project. The Training Fellows developed the public name of the Seniors Programme as well as its vision statement. Notably, CEO1 resigned from the BC Health Authority in June 2014, and Interim CEO replaced him.

The *Seniors Programme implementation* stage spanned the time from first patient enrolment in November 2014 to the end of Summer 2015 when patient follow-up ended. During this stage, the programme enrolled 51 patients, followed them for six months, collected health data, and analysed the data obtained from the study. Interim CEO left the BC Health Authority, replaced by CEO2 in January 2015. *The Wrap-Up* stage occurred in the Fall of 2015 and ended in October 2015 when CEO2 attended the Training Fellowship Symposium where the team presented the results of the Seniors Programme. A critical outcome of this symposium was the agreement of CEO2 to support the continuation of the Senior Programme beyond the completion of the Training Fellowship. The *after the Training Fellowship* stage commenced after CEO2 agreed to support the Seniors Programme once the Training Fellowship ended and continued up to the completion of my interviews and beyond. During this period, the formal collaboration between BC and NS health authorities ended and the BC Coaching Organization ceased operations. At the time of my interviews, the MD Lead and Site Director under the leadership of CEO2 were continuing the development and spread of the Seniors Programme throughout the local region administered by the BC Health Authority. The Foundation assigned the Senior Improvement Lead to work with the MD Lead and Site Director to assess the ability of the Seniors Programme to spread beyond the BC Health Authority to the rest of Canada.

6.3.4.   Scope of This Case Study

The above description of the Seniors Programme shows it had a complex organizational structure and involved many people spread across many organizations across the country. For practical purposes, I had to limit the scope of my study. I limited my scope temporally and organizationally. Temporally, my interview data covered the period from Assembling the Training Fellowship to the date when my interviews ended in the summer of 2017, well into the stage of After the Training Fellowship. The texts I obtained for analysis covered the Seniors Programme Development phase to the end of the Implementation phase. Organizationally, I limited my scope to the BC Health Authority, the Foundation, and the BC Coaching Organization. I excluded NS-based organizations from my study's scope. This was done for practical purposes. The organizational processes I analysed in the BC Health Authority were very complex. Adding to that a study of the NS Health Authority's processes would, in effect, double the size of this study. There is value in performing a future study on the NS Health Authority and comparing it to my findings from the BC Health Authority, but I chose not to do that here. Now that I have described the case study and identified my scope, I turn to the sources of the data I analysed.

6.4.   Data Sources

I obtained my data from three sources. First, my preliminary sources included public documents and meetings I had with members of the BC working group.

Second, I obtained text sources from the Site Director documenting the development and implementation of the Seniors Programme. Third, I conducted semi-structured, open-ended interviews with several individuals involved with the Seniors Programme. I turn now to a description of my preliminary sources.

6.4.1. Preliminary Data Sources

Prior to commencing analysis of the Training Fellowship's implementation of the Seniors Programme, I first had to familiarize myself with the programme's general outlines. I did this through several initial meetings with the Mentor in early 2014 where she gave me an overview of the project. On 19 June 2014, the Mentor invited me to a meeting of the BC Working Group to introduce me to the team. On 24 February 2016, I attended a conference where the MD Lead and Site Director presented the results of the Seniors Programme. As this was prior to obtaining research ethics board (REB) approval, I collected no data and performed no analysis of these meetings. My purposes, rather, were to familiarize myself with the Seniors Programme project to assess whether it suited my research needs as well as build a relationship with members of the BC Working Group to establish my access to the research site. Through this process, I gained a general understanding of the Seniors Programme's purpose and the collaborative nature of its development and implementation.

6.4.2. Text Sources

After I obtained REB approval in early 2016, the Site Director delivered electronic copies of all public documents they kept during the Training Fellowship. These documents included an exhaustive collection of meeting minutes and agendas, the Project Charter, multiple reports to various stakeholders, project plans, photos, and so on. During spring 2016, I performed a preliminary review of these documents to gain a deeper understanding of how the project unfolded and then used that insight to plan my research focus. My interests were not on the actual results of the Seniors Programme but rather how the individuals involved in its development and implementation navigated the webs of values, rationality, and power within their organizational context to move the project forward. Thus, I began a text analysis focusing on the Project Charter, the mission statements of the organizations collaborating on the Seniors Programme, the preamble to the Canada Health Act, and the meeting minutes, which I have summarized in Table 6.3. I chose the Project Charter for analysis as it captured the founding values of the programme, identified its broad plan of implementation, and documented the power structures upon which the Training Fellowship were founded. I chose the mission statements of the collaborating organizations and the preamble of the Canada Health Act to assess in general terms what value positions they were espousing. Finally, I chose the meeting minutes as they articulated who did what, when, along with the challenges and decisions they faced throughout the life of the Training Fellowship. I coded these documents using the coding system I describe below and constructed a detailed

Table 6.3. Summary of Documents Analysed.

Name	Description	# Documents
Project Charter (signed December 2013)	An agreement between the Foundation and the BC & NS health authorities to collaborate in the Training Fellowship	1
Canada Health Act (Preamble)[a]	The preamble to the Canada Health Act that identified the objectives the Act was intended to achieve	1
BC Health Authority mission statement[a]	A statement of the BC Health Authority's mission, vision, and values	1
The Foundation's mission statement[a]	A statement of the Foundation's mission, vision, and values	1
Meeting minutes of the BC Working Group (January 2014 to September 2015)	Meeting records for the BC Working Group	58
Meeting minutes of the Training Fellowship (March 2014 to September 2015)	Meeting records for the entire Training Fellowship	37
Meeting minutes of the steering committee (March 2014 to April 2015)	Meeting records for the Training Fellowship's steering committee	5

Note: [a]Online documents.

timeline of events and interactions. After this analysis, I performed my interviews, which I discuss next.

6.4.3.   *Semi-structured, Open-ended Interviews*

From my analysis of the above documents, I developed an interview guide (presented in "Appendix: Interview Questions") after which I approached members of the BC Working Group, the Foundation, and the BC Coaching Organization to ask if they would participate in approximately hour-long semi-structured, open-ended interviews (McCracken, 1988). I summarize those who agreed to participate in my interviews in Table 6.4. I interviewed CEO2 and the Head Coach in person. The remainder I interviewed over the phone. Interviews ranged from 15 to 71 minutes in length depending on how much time each person was willing to offer. It was not practical or relevant to ask each question in my interview guide to each participant. Instead, I selected questions from the guide based

Table 6.4. Summary of Interviews.

Interviewee	Organizational Affiliation	Date of Interview	Duration of the Interview (Minutes)	# Narratives Identified
CEO1	BC Health Authority	June 6, 2017	39	20
CEO2[a,b]	BC Health Authority	June 2, 2017	15	N/A[a]
Mentor	BC Health Authority	May 19, 2017	71	17
Site Director	BC Health Authority	May 12, 2017	55	24
MD Lead	BC Health Authority	August 8, 2017	55	22
Head Coach[b]	BC Coaching Organization	August 4, 2017	40	20
Senior Improvement Lead	The Foundation	June 13, 2017	33	10

Notes: [a]In the moments before the interview, I was informed CEO2 would not allow recording of the interview, but I could take notes from the meeting.
[b]Interview conducted in person.

on the amount of time the interviewee volunteered and their role in the Seniors Programme.

I asked interviewees' permission to record the interview, which they all allowed except for CEO2. Though CEO2 did not allow me to record his interview, he allowed me to take notes. His assistant informed me of this only moments before the interview, so I did not have time to plan for someone to take notes on my behalf, which would have allowed me to focus on the interview. Due to the limits of my ability to ask questions, process answers, and type simultaneously, I was unable to record CEO2's answers verbatim but instead paraphrased his responses, though I still managed to capture some quotations. This compromised my ability to identify narratives in his interview. That notwithstanding, I was able to code my summary of his responses, which allowed me to pull out useful data for analysis. The remainder of the interviewees agreed to the recording, and I had these recordings transcribed by Points West Transcription Services. I then analysed these data using the process I describe in the following section.

6.5.   Data Analysis

In this section, I describe how I analysed the texts and interview data. A key element of my analysis was coding my data for relevant structures of values, rationality, and power. I describe this coding process first. Then, I describe my narrative analysis process starting with a rationale justifying the use of narrative analysis followed by the specific method I used. I conclude with a summary of the methodological approach of how I organized and implemented my analysis of the data.

6.5.1.   Coding

I developed my coding, summarized in Table 6.5, based on the theoretical background presented in Chapters 3–5. During my data analysis, I recognized I needed to introduce two modifications to my coding plan. First, I introduced a new value: spread. As described above, the Foundation was an organization devoted to the spread of medical innovations across Canada. The Foundation described its conceptualization of spread as, '[The Foundation] identifies proven innovations and accelerates their spread across Canada by supporting healthcare organizations to adapt, implement and measure improvements in patient care, population health and value-for-money' ('[The Foundation] – What We Do', 2018). From this description, the value spread is a combination of the values of public interest, innovation, dialogue, openness, and effectiveness. Project texts and interviewees referred to spread so frequently, however, that I chose to code it as a separate value. Second, I observed many relationships between different codes within interviewees' responses. These included relations such as conflicts (e.g. between different forms of rationality, like technocratic versus body), priorities (e.g. one value being held in higher esteem than another, like public interest over effectiveness), means-ends (e.g. one value enacted to achieve another, like innovation as a means to achieve public interest), and enabling (e.g. one construct facilitating another, like defining rationality facilitates the production of new power relations). I highlighted these relations and documented them in the summaries of my analysis of each narrative. With this coding process, I began my narrative analysis of interview data, which I describe next.

6.5.2.   Narrative Analysis

In this section, I first present a rationale justifying the use of narrative analysis. I then describe how I specifically performed this analysis on my data. Clegg (2009) stressed how power games frequently involve defining the meaning of discourses. Consequently, any research on power, such as PR, should include methods capable of grasping the underlying meaning of discourses. Narrative research is a means to achieving this understanding (Eriksson & Kovalainen, 2008; Flyvbjerg, 2001, 2004, 2006b). With regard to strategizing, the narrative analysis gives researchers insight into the actions and interactions of actors as they make sense of their roles and the roles of others (Fenton & Langley, 2011). Regarding narratives and understanding power, Landman (2012) explained: 'Narrative analysis can illuminate the ways in which individuals experience, confront and exercise power in ways that are useful if one adopts the phronetic approach' (p. 28).

Table 6.5. Codes Used during Data Analysis.

Coding categories	Codes
Values (per Table 3.1, page 26)	Public interest, altruism, sustainability, regime dignity, majority rule, user democracy, protection of minorities, political loyalty, openness, neutrality, competitiveness, robustness, innovation, effectiveness, self-development of employees, accountability, the rule of law, equity, dialogue, user orientation
	Spread (combines values of public interest, innovation, dialogue, openness, effectiveness)
Rationality (per Townley, 2008b)	Disembedded rationality (economic, bureaucratic, technocratic)
	Embedded rationality (institutional, contextual, situational)
	Embodied rationality (body, emotions, 'irrational' subconscious)
	Collective rationality (collective action, collective reasoning)
	Practical rationality (*phronesis*)
Power	Power and rationality (ignoring rationality, defining rationality, using rationalization as rationality)
Power and rationality/ power relations (per Flyvbjerg, 1998)	Power relations (maintaining stability, conflict, historical power relations, production of power relations, reproduction of power relations)
	Faces of power (episodic [manipulation, coercion], systematic [domination, subjectification])
Faces of power and sites of power (per Fleming & Spicer, 2014)	Sites of power (Power over organizations, power through organizations, power in organizations, power against organizations)
Narrative analysis (per Feldman et al., 2004)	Story, storyline, oppositions and syllogisms

Landman (2012) further identified four advantages of narrative enquires concerning PR. Narrative research provides insights into event details, and the stories told can interact with pervasive impressions and feelings. Furthermore, subjective and inter-subjective understandings are possible using narrative research. Also, this method preserves social, political, and human elements in the interactions between people as well as between people and their environment. Finally, narrative research provides researchers with the opportunity to uncover perceptions, experiences, and feelings of power and organizational constraints. This is reinforced by Pentland (1999), who added that narratives not only describe individuals' social world but are also constitutive of the social world. As a source of data, therefore, narratives are invaluable because they are the same kind of data organizational actors use to enact and evaluate their reality. Townley (2008b) further argued for the role of storytelling and narratives in understanding what is rational.

> In organizations, stories and narratives function as a 'key part of members [*sic*] sense-making' allowing them to 'supplement individual memories with institutional memory.' They function as a means of defining characters and scripting actions (Townley, 2008b, p. 128)

Clegg and Pitsis (2012) added:

> [...] we can only really grasp the nature of interests through deep involvement in practical contexts of everyday life and engagement in the dialogues that constitute these. The basis for grasping social reality is not so much the construction of elegant and internally coherent models of action, but an understanding that the social world has a historical and narrative structure: the one is understood through the other. (p. 73)

Townley (2008b) provided further research guidelines to understand the powerful effects of rationalities. To do this, she claimed the researcher must first identify different rationalities presented by individuals. These rationalities serve as grammars that '[...] structure debate into certain considerations' (p. 211). This understanding allows the researcher to understand the conflicts between different rationalities and contradictions within them. Then, she added, the researcher should observe how power actors use and operate through these rationalities. With the understanding gained from this, the researcher is in a position to provide a meaningful critique (Townley, 2008b). As she explained, meaningful critique involves making transparent what was hidden to initiate self-reflection amongst the actors in the research setting.

Multiple methods of performing narrative analysis exist, depending on the goals of the researcher (Chase, 2005). The purpose of my narrative analysis was to understand the values, rationalities, and power structures behind individuals' actions in the development of the Seniors Programme. Given these objectives, this investigation took the form of an organizational narrative. Specifically, I performed a thematic analysis of acquired narratives (Eriksson & Kovalainen, 2008). I achieved this through application of a rhetorical approach as described by Feldman et al. (2004), which uses tools of rhetoric and semiotics to identify implicit assumptions and values underlying the stories told by respondents. As they described, a narrative analysis occurs on three levels: (1) identifying the storyline; (2) identification of implicit/explicit oppositions in the story to understand elements by learning what the narrator believes the element is not; and (3) identifying arguments and representing the inferential logic behind them, which involves recasting the story in the form of syllogisms.

A brief example will clarify this process. A person may debate whether a pet cat is part of the family. As part of the debate, they may argue that only humans can be part of a human family, and at one point they utter the phrase, 'A cat's got four legs. They're animals!' *Step 1: identify the storyline.* In this example, the individual was telling a story of what constitutes a family. *Step 2: identify implicit/explicit oppositions.* The implicit oppositions in the speaker's quote were human/animal, and two legs/four legs. *Step 3: identify arguments and inferential logic by recasting as syllogisms.* As Feldman et al. (2004) described, a syllogism contains a minimum of three elements: premise 1, premise 2, and a conclusion. Let us recast the speaker's quote as a syllogism.

- Premise 1: Cats have four legs
- Premise 2: ?
- Conclusion: Cats are animals.

A premise is missing. We can, however, infer the missing premise from the context of the statement. We can then revise the syllogism with the inferred premise as follows.

- Premise 1: Cats have four legs
- *Premise 2 (inferred): Only animals have four legs*
- Conclusion: Cats are animals

By applying this process through an entire narrative, the researcher uncovers insights into the speaker's logic and values.

Through my semi-structured, open-ended interviews, I elicited stories from interviewees following the general framework presented by Chase (2005), which proposed three elements. First, the researcher must understand what is story-worthy in the organizational context of interviewees. I accomplished this though preliminary review and analysis of text sources described above, as well as my preliminary meetings with the Mentor and BC Working Group. Next, the researcher develops broad questions that invite stories, which I did with my interview guide. Chase (2005) recommended these questions centre on the processes by which decisions were made, significant events documented within secondary data sources, significant events that remain undocumented but have come to the researcher's attention, interpretation and evaluation of other's actions, and so on. Finally, inviting stories requires the receptiveness of the interviewer to recognize the stories interviewees tell. Feldman et al. (2004) presented guidance on recognizing stories. They suggested the researcher must distinguish between description (a list with no plot) and stories. Stories, as described by

Pentland (1999), contain the following structural elements: sequence, focal actors, voice, moral context, and other indicators. With this understanding of my narrative analysis, I now present the specific methodology that I used to analyse my data.

6.5.3. Methodology

To perform my data analysis, I first uploaded my texts and interview transcripts to QSR NVivo, a software designed to facilitate qualitative data analysis. My analysis then had three stages. Stage 1 involved reading through all the texts and interview transcripts to familiarize myself with their contents and to get a sense of what themes they might contain. In stage 2, I re-read all the texts and interview transcripts and coded them for structures of values, rationality, and power listed in Table 6.5. Stage 3 involved a thorough narrative analysis of my interviews following the process described by Feldman et al. (2004) that I summarized above. This included identifying individual narratives within interviewees' responses, storylines within the narrative, identifying implicit oppositions throughout the storyline, and then recasting each element of the narrative as syllogisms, identifying any inferred premise or conclusion. I then coded the syllogisms using the codes in Table 6.5. After that, I wrote a summary of each narrative, highlighting the major themes I identified through the above process. This yielded a vibrant and detailed understanding of how the structures of values, rationality, and power influenced individuals' actions throughout the life of the Seniors Programme.

In the following chapters, I present my results. In Chapter 7, I present the values inherent in the Seniors Programme. Following this, I explore issues surrounding managerial resistance to the programme in Chapter 8, including why some managers did not support it, how they manifested their lack of support, and actions the BC working group took to build and maintain support for the programme. I then consider in Chapter 9 how CEO1 bound his organization to the Seniors Programme despite the presence of managerial resistance. In Chapter 10, I explore how different rationalities combined and conflicted during the development and implementation of the Seniors Programme. In Chapter 11, I explore how the BC working group reified power within their organization. In Chapters 12 and 13, I investigate spread, evaluating structures that constrain and enable spread in Chapter 12 and then exploring how the Training Fellowship managed to spread the programme as far as they had in Chapter 13. After that, I discuss my results in the remaining chapters of this book.

Chapter 7

The Values Inherent in the Seniors Programme

In Chapters 7–13, I present the results of my study. To facilitate understanding, I had to create an organizing structure with which to present these results. Options for this framework included presenting my results sequentially, thematically, or a combination thereof. I chose to organize the results thematically. When I attempted to organize them sequentially, I found that several themes repeated themselves throughout the life of the programme. Highlighting the learning within the data was difficult when structured sequentially as multiple themes might emerge at one time, and then resurface off and on throughout. I also tried organizing the results according to themes within time categories (e.g. beginning, middle, and end). This structure resulted in chapters that were unwieldy.

Thus, I opted to organize the results along themes that I present in separate chapters. I believe this organizational framework allows the reader the most transparent view of the learning within my data. The cost of this organizational framework, though, is the reader loses the sense of Herculean struggle the individuals creating the Seniors Programme experienced over years of effort that would be evident had I told their story sequentially. What the people creating the programme experienced was Vaill's (1998) permanent white water – that is, a bumpy ride down a wild river with dangers and obstacles they had to navigate around. My role as researcher, however, was to make some sense of this wildness so that we can learn from it. This involved organizing the data in the way that best highlighted the principles within it. I felt a thematic organization accomplished this best. I start first by exploring the values active in the Seniors Programme.

One of the themes I pulled out of my review of organizational wisdom was values guide wise action. By learning what drew people to the Seniors Programme, we can begin to learn their values. As this chapter progresses, I will consider the values the Seniors Programme was created to achieve to assess whether the values drawing people to this programme were consistent with what the programme intended. I will then assess whether the values this programme was intended to achieve were consistent with the values of the Canada Health Act. You will recall from the earlier discussion that I argued that since values are socially constructed, and thus there is no objectively 'right' value, I would, therefore, use the values the organization was created to achieve as the litmus for wise organizational action. That is, the wise organizational action is that which pursues the values the organization was created to pursue. Thus, the chain we want to see is this. The values attracting people to the Seniors Programme were consistent with the values the Seniors Programme intended to achieve, which was itself consistent with the values promulgated by the Canada Health Act. In addition to this chain, you will see that values were inseparable from rationality and power. I will demonstrate that values alone did not motivate participation, but rather it was because the programme pursued these values in the right way. In short, the Seniors Programme applied the appropriate rationality in pursuit of appropriate values. You will also see we cannot separate values from power. Interviewees' responses demonstrated it was only through acts of power creating structures that facilitated their involvement that allowed people to pursue these values.

7.1.   What Attracted People to the Seniors Programme?

I asked each of the seven interviewees what it was about the Seniors Programme that led them to want to participate in its development and coded their responses using the constructs of values, rationality, and power identified in Chapter 6. In Table 7.1 (page 81), I summarize these results. The interviewees became involved at different stages of the project's development, and Table 7.1 presents the order of responses roughly in line with the order in which interviewees became involved. CEO1 initiated the events leading to the development of the Seniors Programme, and he first recruited the Mentor followed by the Site Director, MD Lead, and other members of the working group. At this stage, the team had not developed the details of the Seniors Programme other than they knew that they wanted to do something to improve senior health. Once development of the Senior Programme commenced, the Head Coach became involved. CEO2 became involved near the end of the Training Fellowship, and the Senior Improvement Lead did not get involved until after the fellowship had ended. Thus, by the time the Head Coach, CEO2 and the Senior Improvement Lead became involved, the Senior Programme had been well developed. In the next couple of pages, I present the statements of my interviewees that capture why they chose to participate in the Seniors Programme, along with my assessment of the structures represented in their responses.

With one exception, the value of public interest was a significant driver of individuals' interest in the Seniors Programme, centred exclusively around elderly care.

> We really wanted to find out what intervention might have a significant impact on care of the elderly, and particularly preventing them ending up in hospital, which is an ever-present problem. (CEO1, personal communication, 6 June 2017)

The Site Director echoed this sentiment.

> When I started to read the research and saw that there was real potential to maybe prevent frailty [...] I thought that that was a worthy pursuit of my time. (Site Director, personal communication, 12 May 2017)

Table 7.1. Summary of the Enabling Structures of Values, Rationality, and Power That Led Interviewees to Become Involved in the Seniors Programme.

Name	Prime Value	Instrumental Value	Underlying Rationality	Power Considerations
CEO1	Public Interest	Innovation Dialogue Effectiveness	Technocratic	CEO1 needed to champion programme so that it did not get lost in the bureaucracy
Mentor	Self-development of employees Innovation Effectiveness	Effectiveness Accountability	Technocratic	Initially too busy; CEO1 and her current supervisor had to give her leave from current position Wanted ability to fail; needed agreement and protection of CEO1
Site Director	Public interest Self-development of employees	Effectiveness	Technocratic	
MD Lead	Public interest Self-development of employees	Sustainability Innovation	Technocratic	Defining rationality
Head Coach	Public interest	User orientation Accountability	Body	Required agreement between the BC Coaching Organization & BC Health Authority to collaborate
CEO2	Public interest Innovation		Technocratic	Project Charter required CEO2's presence at Training Fellowship symposium where he learned about the Seniors Programme (discussed later)
Senior Improvement Lead	Public Interest Spread	Effectiveness User orientation Sustainability Innovation	Technocratic Economic	Required agreement between the Foundation & BC Health Authority to collaborate

Underlying this interest in elderly care was a sense the status quo was failing seniors. The Site Director spoke of a '[...] raising awareness that our current approach to managing seniors' care is not working. Even more specific to that is watching the suffering of seniors ageing into frailty' (Site Director, personal communication, 12 May 2017). Similarly, CEO2 stated that no one else was looking at preventing frailty (CEO2, personal communication, 2 June 2017). The above quotes suggested the value of effectiveness also led to several interviewees' interest in the Seniors Programme. They felt current efforts at elderly care were ineffective, and the Seniors Programme was a means to address that. Rather than an end in itself, however, the value of effectiveness seemed to be expressed as a means to achieve public interest. Like effectiveness, innovation also appeared to be a value expressed to achieve public interest through reducing frailty. CEO1, for example, wanted to '[...] look at stimulating innovation and reform in the health sector [...] We really wanted to find out what intervention might have a significant impact on care of the elderly' (CEO1, personal communication 6 June 2017).

Dahl and Lindblom (1953) discussed the differences between prime and instrumental values. *Prime* values were those that were ends in themselves, whereas *instrumental* values were those valued for their perceived ability to achieve other values. From this, I categorize the values expressed by my interviewees as either prime or instrumental in Table 7.1. This table shows several instrumental values in addition to effectiveness and innovation, including dialogue, user orientation, and sustainability.

Whereas most interviewees seemed driven by public interest, the Mentor was an exception. Based on her response, her primary values were self-development of employees and effectiveness. The Training Fellowship interested her because she wanted to know, 'How do we take evidence and then apply it into practice?' (Mentor, personal communication, 19 May 2017). Like other interviewees, she found shortcomings in the status quo. Whereas other respondents found the status quo lacking in its ability to care for seniors, however, the Mentor took issue with current modes of decision-making.

> We talk about words like 'evidence', 'decision-making', 'evidence-based decision-making.' However, I did see on many occasions decisions would be made and then it's like, 'Okay. Well, let's find the evidence to support this decision that we have.' Which is a little bit different than saying: 'What knowledge currently exists based on this particular topic, and how can we synthesize that information and apply it to our situation so that we have I guess the best solution for our environment?' (Mentor, personal communication, 19 May 2017)

For the Mentor, evidence-based decision-making was the gold-standard of which the status quo fell short, and she saw participation in the Training Fellowship as a means to learn how to apply evidence to practice. '[...] [H]ow do we take what researchers have come up with and then implement that? That was the piece that I felt that there was an opportunity inside of the health care system, so that was what drew me to it'. (Mentor, personal communication, 19 May 2017)

The Mentor's focus on evidence-based decision-making segues into the role of rationality in interviewees' interest in the programme. I introduced this section focusing on values, but I do not believe we can separate values from rationality, for it is through rationality we grapple with the question of *how* we will pursue values. From these interviews, technocratic rationality underlaid the reasoning behind interviewees' interest with only few exceptions. A desire to prevent frailty drove most interviewees, and they expressed the assumption that not only was this possible but they could discover the means of prevention through the application of technocratic research methods. For example, the MD Lead stated:

> [...] what I've learned through the literature is so, so compelling, that you can actually take people that are independent and have them really be engaged in lifestyle changes that's going to put them on a different trajectory until they die, that they do not have to become frail. (8 August 2017)

The Site Director (personal communication, 12 May 2017) echoed this sentiment.

> [...] I started to read the research and saw that there was real potential to maybe prevent frailty if we enhanced our assessment techniques in primary care and then connected motivated seniors to coaching [...]'

Moreover, CEO2's (personal communication, 2 June 2017) interest in the Seniors Programme was solidified, in part, because the scientific study conducted by the Seniors Programme demonstrated a decline in frailty as measured by the Rockwood scale, which the interviewees considered the gold standard of measuring frailty. How did this reliance on technocratic rationality motivate interviewees to work on the Seniors Programme? They saw the Training Fellowship as a programme whose purpose was to teach participants how to apply evidence to practice, and they saw the Seniors Programme that developed out of the fellowship as a manifestation of evidence-based decision-making in action. For example, the MD Lead stated:

> [The Training Fellowship] was pitched to me as a way of learning more about research application and how to base interventions on what's in the literature and ensuring that we are evidence-based as we go forward with any interventions (personal communication, 8 August 2017).

I observed two exceptions to the reliance on technocratic rationality: the Head Coach and the Senior Improvement Lead. The Head Coach relied on body rationality. Rather than look to the literature for ways to prevent frailty, she instead relied on her own experience.

> Well, actually physical activity for me is absolutely crucial. I don't want to say it's the panacea to just about everything, but certainly, I find that it's something that everyone can do no matter their health condition. (Head Coach, personal communication, 4 August 2017)

She later added, 'Personally for me, I enjoy physical activity [...] I believe in it, and I find that it's actually quite helpful in terms of my overall balance of life' (Head Coach, personal communication, 4 August 2017). This rationality attracted her to the Senior Programme because this programme sought to study the ability of physical activity to prevent frailty – there was overlap between what her body rationality told her was true and how the Seniors Programme was approaching elderly care. Conversely, economic rationality led the Senior Improvement Lead to the Seniors Programme: '[...] [the Senior Programme's] got some benefits when it comes to reducing costs if we can keep seniors well [...] we can foresee that there would be a reduction in costs [...]' (Senior Improvement Lead, personal communication, 13 June 2017). This economic rationality addressed the Senior Improvement Lead's value of sustainability, which attracted her to the project. In summary, we see in all interviewees their interest in the Seniors Programme was driven not only by their values but because the rationality underlying the programme's approach aligned with the forms of rationality on which they relied. The Seniors Programme was pursuing the right thing in the right way.

In addition to the values and rationality that attracted interviewees to the Seniors Programme, several actors had to exercise power to facilitate individuals' ability to participate. For example, I asked CEO1 why he, the chief executive of a health authority, was personally involved in championing the Seniors Programme. Did he not have subordinates to whom he could delegate this?

> It's simple. Because it's little things like this that actually can have a profound influence, and sometimes it's the little things that get lost in the bureaucracy. And sometimes you need a chief executive or a senior vice president or somebody to nurture a project to ensure that it stays alive and gains momentum and is not relegated to some report that sits on a shelf somewhere and nothing ever happens. Without that kind of leadership, these types of things can drift. And I don't think a CEO's interest is defined by the project cost. It's the impact, potential impact of the outcome, for the elderly in particular. (CEO1, personal communication, 6 June 2017)

Here, we see the CEO1 is drawing a relationship between power and values. It is through an executive's exercise of power in an organization that programmes achieve effectiveness, and through that public interest. In the absence of power, organizations do not implement programmes. CEO1 became directly involved in the creation of the Seniors Programme out of the belief that the programme needed to become a reality, and that only through exercising his power could it achieve that.

This was not the only exercise of power needed to facilitate people's involvement in the Seniors Programme. For example, the Mentor initially rejected the invitation to participate in the Training Fellowship as she was too busy. CEO1 arranged with her direct supervisor a leave from her position that would allow her to participate, which was no minor feat given the Mentor's previous job was demanding, and her supervisor would now have to find a replacement (Mentor, personal communication, 19 May 2017). With the offer of a leave, the Mentor began seriously considering joining the Training Fellowship, but she still had reservations. She felt her position in this fellowship exposed her to political risks.

> But the question I said to him, 'Am I allowed to fail? Because if I'm not allowed to fail, then you're going to end up with something that's not all that innovative or not all that creative. If I'm allowed to fail or be unsuccessful, whatever word you want to call it, then I can deliver you something I think that could be quite good. But we have to enter into it with the mindset that this is a big challenge, there are a lot of barriers, and if something happens and we don't deliver, we have to be okay with that,' because we knew the environment was extremely political. (Mentor, personal communication, 19 May 2017)

She saw this programme as something new, and the risk of failure real. She wanted the assurance and protection of CEO1's position in the organization. Only when he gave her those assurances did she agree to join the Training Fellowship. The source of the political risk the Mentor perceived stemmed from her observation that BC Health Authority's involvement in the Training Fellowship did not have the support of all the Vice Presidents (VPs), which I explore in detail later. One of the power tactics she and CEO1 enacted to protect her from these political risks was an act of defining rationality.

> One of the things that we did is I actually didn't even have a job title. We're like, 'Let's just not even put a job title out there because that'll just make people uncomfortable.' Actually, I was 'the intern.' So 30 years of experience and I had a job title as the intern. (Mentor, personal communication, 19 May 2017)

So already, by merely asking interviewees to tell the story of why they joined the Seniors Programme, we learn of the values that guided them, but we also see links between values, rationality, and power. The Seniors Programme pursued the right values in the right way and required acts of power to create structures that gave the programme life. Recall our initial purpose here to see the chain linking individuals' values with those the programme was intended to achieve and then to the Canada Health Act's values. I have shown what drew people to the Seniors Programme. Let us now turn to whether the project was intended to achieve what people perceived.

7.2.   Values the Seniors Programme Intended to Achieve

The above values are those that the members of the fellowship perceived in the Seniors Programme. Were these the values the Senior Project were initially designed to achieve? To answer this, I looked at the Project Charter. The Project Charter, which I shall later demonstrate was the founding document establishing the Training Fellowship, clearly identified the purposes the fellowship was intended to achieve. It stated its purposes thusly.

> The goals of this joint venture among the Foundation, NS Health Authority, and BC Health Authority are to:
>
> - design, implement, evaluate and potentially spread an improvement initiative related to the senior population, which will not only improve quality and appropriateness of care but will do so in a manner that is sustainable;
> - identify a process of combined collaboration to influence system change and improvement; and
> - demonstrate that an integrated and systematic approach is an effective methodology to spread change, and knowledge exchange across other regional areas (Project Charter: Collaborative Project to Improve Senior Care, 2013, p. 8).

These objectives demonstrated several values. The focus on improving senior care demonstrated the value of public interest, and we see innovation and effectiveness expressed as means to achieve it. Sustainability was a significant value explicitly identified in the first objective. The second and third objectives expressed the value of dialogue to achieve innovation and spread. In addition to values, the second objective expressed bureaucratic rationality with the intention to develop a collaborative process of change and improvement. Table 7.2 lists public sector values (as per Beck Jørgensen & Bozeman, 2007) with the addition of the value of spread and compares the values expressed in the Project Charter with those the members of the Training Fellowship perceived in the Seniors Programme. Values overlap strongly between the programme's intent and the values that led members of the fellowship to join, with the exceptions of self-development of employees, accountability, and user orientation. Though these values were not explicitly mentioned in the Project Charter, they are not

Table 7.2. Comparison of Values in the Project Charter versus Those
Interviewees Perceived in the Seniors Programme.

Public Sector Values	Values Expressed in the Project Charter		Values Perceived in Seniors Programme	
	Prime	Instrumental	Prime	Instrumental
Public interest	✓		✓	
Altruism				
Sustainability	✓			✓
Regime dignity				
Majority rule				
User democracy				
Protection of minorities				
Political loyalty				
Openness				
Neutrality				
Competitiveness				
Robustness				
Innovation		✓	✓	✓
Effectiveness		✓	✓	✓
Self-development of employees			✓	
Accountability				✓
The rule of law				
Equity				
Dialogue		✓		✓
User orientation				✓
Spread	✓		✓	

inconsistent with its aims. Thus, the values that motivated people to join the programme were mostly consistent with the values the programme was intended to achieve.

7.3.   Were the Values of the Seniors Programme Consistent with the Canada Health Act?

One of my research questions was: Does power wielded by stakeholders of the Seniors Programme result in organizational actions in keeping with the values of

Table 7.3 Comparison of Values in the Canada Health Act versus Those Interviewees Perceived in the Seniors Programme.

Public Sector Values	Values in Canada Health Act	Values Expressed in the Project Charter		Values Perceived in Seniors Programme	
		Prime	Instrumental	Prime	Instrumental
Public interest	✓	✓		✓	
Altruism	✓				
Sustainability		✓			✓
Regime dignity					
Majority rule					
User democracy					
Protection of minorities					
Political loyalty					
Openness					
Neutrality	✓				
Competitiveness					
Robustness					
Innovation	✓		✓	✓	✓
Effectiveness			✓	✓	✓
Self-development of employees				✓	
Accountability					✓
The rule of law					
Equity	✓				
Dialogue	✓	✓			✓
User orientation					✓
Spread		✓		✓	

Canada's healthcare system? Table 7.3 compares the values identified in the Canada Health Act (per Table 3.2, page 27) with the values interviewees perceived in the Seniors Programme (per Table 7.1, page 81) and the values identified in the Project Charter (per Table 7.2, page 87) to assess whether the values were in alignment. There was substantial overlap in the values of public interest and innovation. When including instrumental values, there was further overlap in the value of dialogue. Not all values overlapped, though. Neither the Project Charter nor interviewees expressed the values of altruism, neutrality, and equity, which were present in the Canada Health Act. Likewise, interviewees perceived sustainability, accountability, and user orientation in the Seniors Programme, which were not present in the preamble to Canada's Health Act. That notwithstanding, there is no evidence from these interviews suggesting these differences undermined the Canada Health Act. Indeed, in the case of instrumental values, some values in the Seniors Programme that the Canada Health Act does not express are means to achieve values that are. Though there are some values in the Canada Health Act the Seniors Programme does not address, this is not surprising. The programme was developed to employ innovation to address a specific public interest problem, so naturally it focuses on those values relevant to that problem. Nothing in the programme contradicts the other values expressed in the Canada Health Act.

In summary, the values motivating people to participate in the Seniors Programme were consistent with the values the Seniors Programme was created to achieve. These values, in turn, aligned well with the Canada Health Act. As the experience of the Mentor hinted at, however, there were points of power resisting the programme. In the following chapter, I explore why and how some senior managers resisted the Seniors Programme, and then how individuals in the BC Health Authority built and maintained support within the organization.

Chapter 8

Managing Executive Resistance

The stage Assembling the Training Fellowship encompassed the time from when CEO1 first conceived of championing a project devoted to seniors' health to the signing of the Project Charter on 2 December 2013. During this period, CEO1 recruited individuals who would eventually become part of the Training Fellowship. The nascent fellowship had to build support for the programme within the BC Health Authority while CEO1 built relationships with other organizations that would eventually culminate in collaboration with the Foundation and NS Health Authority. In this chapter, I investigate why some senior managers within the BC Health Authority did not support the programme and how they exerted their power to resist it. Following this, I consider the actions the BC working group took to gain support among senior management to launch the programme and then build and maintain that support throughout the programme's life.

8.1. Why Did Some Managers Not Support the Seniors Programme?

In this and the following sections, I first present the views expressed by my interviewees on the topic. I have coded each of their responses using the constructs of values, rationality, and power identified in Chapter 6 and then mapped these constructs onto a critical realist framework. After presenting the interviewees' responses, I analyse the elements of values, rationality, and power embedded in them, and then show how these come together in a critical realist framework to result in the actions and experiences observed. What I drew out of this analysis was that resistance was caused by conflicting values and rationalities between the VPs and the Seniors Programme. As we will see, the value conflict had some surprising and paradoxical elements.

During a meeting of the Training Fellowship held on 1 August 2014, the BC working group cited as a potential barrier to implementing the Seniors Programme their organization's '100% focus on acute care and decongestion'[1] (Training Fellowship, 2014a). As laudable as the Training Fellowship's focus on preventing frailty was, it did not address short-term issues of acute care or

---

[1]Acute care refers to the treatment of medical emergencies, and decongestion refers to addressing the over-crowding of medical facilities under the remit of the BC Health Authority.

decongestion. Several members of the Training Fellowship confirmed this was a source of organizational resistance. The Mentor explained:

> That was certainly not the way that we think from an acute care perspective. If we view that patient's in your emergency department and you've got ambulances lined up outside the door, saying, 'Is this the time you try something different?' and we fail, and patients die while they're sitting in an ambulance, that's not really an option. So it was a little bit different way of thinking, and of course you couldn't run a whole health authority in that innovative space, right? We have to deliver acute care. (personal communication, 19 May 2017)

Consequently, as explained by CEO1 (personal communication, 6 June 2017), senior executives of the BC Health Authority were busy dealing with what he called the 'tyranny of the urgent', and, therefore, possibly viewed the Seniors Programme as a distraction from their day-to-day job. The MD Lead (personal communication, 8 August 2017), Mentor (personal communication, 19 May 2017), and Site Director (personal communication, 12 May 2017) all concurred, adding that dealing with these immediate issues of congestion led to a conservative attitude among senior managers and a hesitancy to devote their limited resources to preventative projects like the Seniors Programme.

Moreover, there were several aspects of the Training Fellowship's approach that were foreign to executives in the BC Health Authority. For example, at the time CEO1 and the Mentor were assembling the Training Fellowship, the details of the intervention that became the Seniors Programme had not yet been developed. As the Mentor identified this was a point of resistance.

> What [senior executives] were used to was somebody coming and saying, 'This is what we're going to do,' and people could see it and they could buy into it or commit to it a little bit easier. I think that that was some of the reluctance that our senior people had. (Mentor, personal communication, 19 May 2017)

That is, the Training Fellowship, at this stage, was a programme that would do *something* to improve senior care, but no one had yet defined what that something was. The nascent fellowship was asking executives to devote resources to a programme that did not align with the daily difficulties VPs were facing and had yet to be developed. Add to this a fear of failure that CEO1 (personal communication, 6 June 2017) suggested was prevalent in many people, and compelling reasons for resisting the Training Fellowship emerge.

In Table 8.1 (page 93), I summarize reasons for VPs lack of support and link them to relevant structures of values, rationality, and power. In Figure 8.1 (page 94), I present a visual representation of this mapped onto a critical realist framework. Through this, the paradoxical aspect of the value conflict between VPs

Table 8.1. Reasons Some VPs Did Not Support the Training Fellowship and Their Relation to Values, Rationality, and Power.

The Reasons Some VPs Did Not Support Seniors Programme	Relevant Structures of Values, Rationality, and Power
Focus on acute care and decongestion	*Values*: Effectiveness, public interest (conflicts with innovation)
	Note: The values effectiveness and public interest also guided the Training Fellowship, but the time scale of when they achieved those values caused it to conflict with acute care management
The tyranny of the urgent	*Values*: Effectiveness
Limited resources	*Values*: Sustainability, robustness, accountability
	Rationality: Economic
	Power: Reproduction of power relations
Unwillingness to fund prevention	*Values*: Accountability
	Power: Reproduction of power relations, power in organizations, coercion
Disagreement with the hypothesis	*Rationality*: Technocratic
	Power: Defining rationality
Managers used to approving specific interventions, but Training Fellowship did not specify an intervention. Instead, it was a process to determine an intervention.	*Rationality*: Bureaucratic (procedures & roles, processes) versus technocratic
	Power: Reproduction of power relations, power in organizations, defining rationality, not adhering to established bureaucratic rationality prevented the production of needed power relations
Fear of failure	*Values*: Effectiveness, accountability, regime dignity
	Rationality: Emotions

and the Training Fellowship becomes evident. The VPs' focus on acute care and decongestion as well as the Training Fellowship's aim to prevent frailty both draw on the prime values of public interest, effectiveness, and sustainability. All sides share the same prime values. Why, then, was there resistance? There were two reasons. First, though they shared prime values, they differed along instrumental values. The instrumental value of robustness guided VPs to focus on

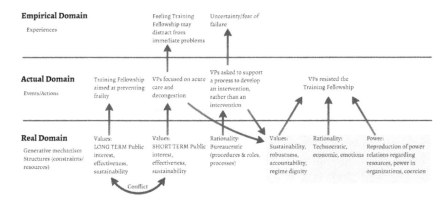

Figure 8.1.   A Critical Realist Perspective of the Reasons Some VPs Did Not Support the Training Fellowship.

acute care and congestion; innovation guided the Training Fellowship. Second, the timing in which these values took effect differed. The Training Fellowship focused on the future while the VPs dealt with the present. Despite shared prime values, the difference in instrumental values and timing brought them into conflict as the 'tyranny of the urgent' sapped the VPs' ability to devote time, energy, and resources to the Training Fellowship's long-term vision. The source of this resistance is an important theme as it also cropped up later in the life of the Seniors Programme when the BC working group attempted to spread it, discussed in Chapter 12.

Moreover, the method used to develop the Training Fellowship violated structures of bureaucratic rationality established in the BC Health Authority. The intention of the fellowship to research the best possible intervention before choosing the intervention was consistent with technocratic rationality. This, however, was not the decision-making process with which VPs were familiar. The Training Fellowship were asking VPs to commit their organization to a course of action that they had not yet developed. This transgression from normal processes resulted in an experience of uncertainty and a fear of failure among some VPs.

Consequently, the members of the BC working group perceived several values triggered in the VPs leading to their lack of support. Not knowing what intervention they were committing the organization to while operating under limited resources may have triggered the value of accountability, sustainability, and robustness among the VPs. That is, they had limited resources, and their role was to deploy those resources productively and responsibly. Not knowing what they were committing to violated those structures. These values were underwritten by economic rationality as VPs chose how to allocate their resources. In those VPs where fear of failure was present, the value of regime dignity and emotional rationality were active too. Technocratic rationality would have further influenced those VPs disagreeing with the Training Fellowship's hypothesis. These structures led some VPs to exercise the power they had within the organization to oppose the Training Fellowship. I next discuss how they resisted it.

8.2. How Did Managers Resist the Seniors Programme?

CEO1 wanted the Seniors Programme developed. Given that, how could VPs resist? Their position was subordinate to the CEO, after all. Despite the organization's hierarchy, VPs exercised power through several mechanisms. At meetings with CEO1, they would challenge the project, asking, 'Is this project worthwhile? [...] Should we be carrying the costs of running it? Was [the Mentor's] position necessary, as a special project leader in [BC Health Authority]?' (CEO1, personal communication, 6 June 2017). At those meetings, however, CEO1 had the authority to push through that resistance. When dealing with the remaining members of the BC working group, though, VPs had more leeway to exercise their resistance. The Mentor provided some examples of this.

> Well, I had to create a team, and I wanted the team to be diverse, and I wasn't hiring this team. This was something that was going to be a part of their job. It's 'How do I engage? How do I get interest from people so that they want to come forward and be a part of this team, but also figure out a way so that the VPs of those particular programs would buy in?' When somebody is going and saying, 'Well, I'd like to be a part of this team,' but then their VP would say, 'Well, how are you going to do it? You don't have enough time to actually take this on. So no, we can't commit to doing it.' (personal communication, 19 May 2017)

Additionally, the Mentor identified that VPs discouraged the Communications department from working with her to socialize the programme to the BC Health Authority. They also prevented her from getting on meeting agendas to present the programme to different departments. In short, unable to dissuade CEO1 from pursuing the Seniors Programme, VPs subsequently prevented the Mentor from recruiting team members and sharing the programme with the broader BC Health Authority.

Table 8.2 (page 96) presents my summary of the means through which VPs resisted the Training Fellowship and links them to relevant structures of values, rationality, and power. Figure 8.2 (page 96) presents my visual representation of this mapped onto a critical realist framework. The power structures of the BC Health Authority gave VPs a position where they had access to CEO1 to discuss their concerns with the Training Fellowship. In these meetings, they would challenge the programme on the value of effectiveness and economic and bureaucratic rationality by questioning whether the programme was worth the resources and personnel associated with it. CEO1, however, exercised his power to override the VPs' concerns and launched the programme. Unable to dissuade CEO1 from his course of action, VPs exercised the authority they had when

Table 8.2. Means of Resistance to the Training Fellowship and Their Relation to Values, Rationality, and Power.

Means of Resistance	Relevant Structures of Values, Rationality, and Power
Questioning CEO1 on whether the project was worth the resources and personnel	*Values*: Effectiveness *Rationality*: Economic, bureaucratic (procedures and roles) *Power*: Reproduction of power relations (to meet with CEO1)
Preventing their staff from working on the project	*Power*: Power in organizations; reproduction of power relations, coercion
Block the Mentor from getting on meeting agendas and accessing communication resources	*Power*: Power in organizations; reproduction of power relations, manipulation

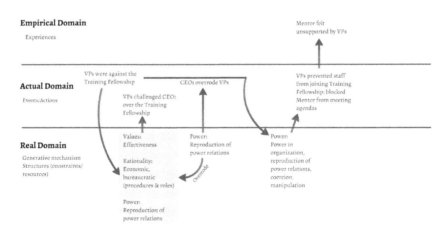

Figure 8.2. A Critical Realist Perspective of the Means of Resistance to the Training Fellowship.

dealing with the Mentor through acts of coercion and manipulation by preventing their staff from working on the project and blocking the Mentor from meeting agendas and communication resources.

Thus far, we understand why and how some VPs resisted the Seniors Programme. Despite these challenges, the BC working group eventually gained support at the VP level. They gained this support through persistent effort and organizational savvy. As I will show in the next section, the BC working group effectively enacted structures of values, rationality, and power to achieve this end.

8.3.   Building Support for the Seniors Programme

Despite resistance from some VPs, the BC working group did manage to build a base of support within senior leadership, which it then maintained and grew throughout the life of the Seniors Programme. In subsequent sections of this chapter, I will demonstrate how the fellowship grew and maintained support for the Seniors Programme. Here, though, I will show how they began to build their coalition. As I will show, they did this through extensive meetings with senior leaders where members of the fellowship appealed to their values and rationality, as well as through exertions of power.

CEO1 (personal communication, 6 June 2017) observed that due to the size and diverse array of communities represented within the BC Health Authority, it had developed a culture of collective decision-making. Thus, rather than a command and control structure where the CEO might drive a project to completion through acts of coercion, the BC working group had to engage with the leadership team to gain their support. This necessitated frequent meetings where the BC working group promoted participation in the Training Fellowship (Mentor, personal communication, 19 May 2017). Additionally, the MD Lead explained that structuring the programme as a Training Fellowship had benefits.

> [W]e were working with just the fellows that went through the [Training Fellowship] and with the Divisions of Family Practice that came on board. We weren't really needing to work internally in [the BC Health Authority] so much. (MD Lead, personal communication, 8 August 2017)

Structuring the programme as a training exercise reduced the fellowship's exposure to the politics of the BC Health Authority during its developmental stages, lowering the bar of support needed to launch the programme.

Earlier, I showed how the Training Fellowship shared with the VPs the prime values of public interest, effectiveness, and sustainability. The difference was in instrumental values (innovation versus robustness) and the time horizon (long term versus short). These differences notwithstanding, during their meetings with senior leaders, the fellowship used these shared values as a bridge to build support. The MD Lead explained it as follows.

> I think [senior management] recognized that they had immediate issues with congestion that they had to deal with today. But they saw that doing this, in the long run, is what's required, that if you keep on going as-is now and just wait for people to deteriorate and then land up in the hospital, it's not sustainable. But if we were to get a population that is healthier and better able to self-management and there's resources in the community to help them, that was what was going to save the day in the end for all of acute care. (personal communication, 8 August 2017)

In short, VPs did not resist supporting the Training Fellowship because they fundamentally disagreed with the ends the fellowship was trying to achieve. Just the opposite – they saw the fellowship's activities as a solution to the problems besetting acute care. They were, however, victims of the 'tyranny of the urgent'. Dealing with the urgent problems of today consumed the energy of the VPs to the point they had few resources left to devote to getting ahead of the problem. We will see this theme arise again when I analyse the challenges the BC working group experienced trying to spread the programme after the fellowship ended.

Given that the VPs resistance stemmed mainly from the 'tyranny of the urgent', I asked the Site Director how the fellowship managed to get the VPs to consider supporting a programme that had its impact on the future.

> I think aligning it to strategic objectives is very important. This was where the support of senior leadership is needed. And publishing. Being considered worthy in your professional group is important. I mean I think that's something that we're even still trying to do. Trying to show people how it aligns with their objectives. Trying to secure time at executive meetings, but not too much time. So it's balancing on how to stay in the discussion but not to be too intrusive. (Site Director, personal communication, 12 May 2017)

In essence, the BC working group emphasized shared prime values (i.e. 'aligning it to strategic objectives') and sought to define rationality in a way that convinced VPs that the programme, though differing in instrumental values and time horizon, still supported the values the VPs pursued.

This mention of defining rationality segues into the role rationality played in securing VP support. Recall from the previous chapter where I explored the values motivating individuals to join the Seniors Programme that rationality was equally important. People were interested in the Seniors Programme because it was doing the right thing (value congruence) in the right way (rationality congruence). This dynamic also played out with gaining support from the VPs. The Site Director explained:

> We think that [senior leadership have] been very supportive because it's evidence-based. We've been able to demonstrate that the researchers in this area, whether it's Dr. Kenneth Rockwood, who developed the Clinical Frailty Scale, the Rockwood Clinical Frailty Scale, as well as the [Comprehensive Geriatric Assessment] [...] People understand that it holds tremendous potential [...] I think that that's why they are supporting it, is it's evidence-based. (personal communication, 12 May 2017)

Thus, VPs did not support the Training Fellowship only because of shared prime values, but rather because it intended to achieve those values using rationality they venerated.

A comment made by the MD Lead suggested that other rationalities beyond technocratic contributed to gaining VP support, also.

> We had to talk about it a lot, and we had to present a lot, especially to leadership groups and senior leadership in particular. They all got it. It's like everybody is so inundated with the demand and congestion, and when you can lift them out of that for just even a few minutes as you talk about prevention, as you talk about the literature and the ability to prevent ageing, and even the audience members are all kind of at that age where they're thinking about themselves, and they could be pre-frail [...] They don't think of themselves as frail, but they realize they got to make some changes to their lives. We've had directors tell us recently, 'It was because of your presentation I've actually started exercising'. (MD Lead, personal communication, 8 August 2017)

That is, VPs personally related to the patient population in question. This is an expression of body rationality. They recognized within themselves the person the Seniors Programme intended to help. They understood this was an important programme not just because it was evidence-based but because they had a visceral experience with ageing.

In addition to technocratic and body rationalities, the Site Director also identified they discussed the programme's '[...] good return-of-investment potential [...]' (Site Director, personal communication, 12 May 2017), or economic rationality. CEO1 and the Mentor further discussed this, explaining it as follows. The Training Fellowship's cost was minimal compared to the BC Health Authority's budget (Mentor, personal communication, 19 May 2017). CEO1 felt this helped justify the programme in the minds of his VPs. 'Keeping the cost down made a huge difference. The neat thing about [the Seniors Programme] is it's not a high-cost model, and that was one of the strengths of it' (CEO1, personal communication, 6 June 2017).

Thus far, we see the BC working group sought to gain VP support by emphasizing shared prime values, demonstrating how the Seniors Programme contributed to achieving those prime values, and expressing multiple rationalities, including technocratic, body, and economic, that the VPs recognized. These are acts of episodic power. Specifically, they are acts of manipulation, for the BC working group was essentially defining rationality that would lead to the production of a supportive power relation with the VPs. Acts of coercion, however, also played a role in securing these power relations. As the Mentor explained:

> [VPs] didn't come along I would say with a lot of enthusiasm. They came along because it is something that the organization had committed to from the most senior level, and I would say actually specifically to the CEO. (personal communication, 19 May 2017)

CEO1 further explained the need for support from the senior leader.

> Unless you have a leader who says, 'I actually believe in this, and I want to see the outcome. I think this could make a difference. I'm nailing my colours to the mast on this,' is an important dimension of keeping something going [...] You got to make sure that everybody knows that the CEO wants this to happen. (personal communication, 6 June 2017)

Table 8.3 (page 101) presents my summary of the means of building support for the Training Fellowship and links them to relevant structures of values, rationality, and power. Figure 8.3 (page 102) presents my visual representation of this mapped onto a critical realist framework. Figure 8.3(a) visualizes the impact of BC Health Authority's culture of collective decision-making on the process of gaining executive support for the Training Fellowship. The collective culture was founded on values of user democracy and dialogue, informed by contextual rationality – that is, the different areas within the BC Health Authority know best what their needs are and how to address them. This collective culture results in the power structures observed within the organization. Rather than coercion, for example, actors within the organization rely on manipulation. Rather than engaging in conflict, individuals opt for strategies that maintain stability. These power structures required the members of the BC working group to meet with VPs to gain their support. Structuring the programme as a Training Fellowship, however, limited the programme's exposure to the power structures within the BC Health Authority by reducing the number of VPs whose approval was needed to launch the fellowship.

Despite this collective decision-making culture, CEO support did have an impact, visualized in Figure 8.3(b). CEO1's unequivocal support for the Training Fellowship led the VPs to (perhaps grudgingly) support the programme. As highlighted in the previous section, VPs had means to erect barriers to the programme, and so it was necessary for the fellowship to obtain VPs' enthusiastic support. If CEO support was insufficient to make VPs enthusiastic, it at least gave the fellowship access to the VPs to seek their favour. The BC working group's presentations to VPs focused on two structures: values and rationality. Figure 8.3(b) shows the BC working group emphasized values of sustainability, robustness, public interest, user orientation, and effectiveness, which it knew were important to the VPs. The fellowship attributed part of the VPs support from their awareness of a conflict between bureaucratic rationality and the value of sustainability – that is, VPs believed the current processes of addressing elderly care were not sustainable. Also, the fellowship highlighted the technocratic and economic rationality of the Seniors Programme. They reproduced power relations and defined rationality to show how the programme aligned with strategic objectives. They engaged in manipulation to obtain access to VPs but maintained stability through not overstaying their welcome. These actions led to the creation of power relations that manifested as VP support and created a sense of excitement surrounding the fellowship.

Table 8.3. Means of Building Support for the Training Fellowship and Their Relation to Values, Rationality, and Power.

Means of Building Support	Relevant Structures of Values, Rationality, and Power
The culture of collective decision making & need to engage	*Values*: User democracy, dialogue *Rationality*: Contextual *Power*: Power in organizations, reproduction of power relations, historical power relations, manipulation, maintaining stability
Meeting with VPs	*Values*: User orientation, effectiveness, sustainability, public interest *Rationality*: Technocratic, economic *Power*: Production of power relations, reproduction of power relations, defining rationality, manipulation, maintaining stability
Reduced the level of executive buy-in needed to launch by structuring programme as Training Fellowship	*Power*: Reproduction of power relations
Using shared values to build support	*Values*: Sustainability, robustness, public interest, effectiveness *Rationality*: Bureaucratic (processes) (current processes conflicted with sustainability) *Power*: Reproduction of power relations
Using different types of rationality	*Values*: Effectiveness, public interest, sustainability *Rationality*: Technocratic, economic, body *Power*: Reproduction of power relations, defining rationality, manipulation, production of power relations
Support from the CEO	*Power*: Power in organizations, reproduction of power relations, coercion

In Figure 8.3(c), I visualize how the BC working group used the power tactic of defining rationality to gain VP support. The rationalities they drew on were technocratic (evidenced through referral to what the literature said about preventing frailty) and economic (this was a low-cost model with a potentially significant impact). Though not purposefully used by the BC working group, the VPs also relied on body rationality – managers recognized they were getting

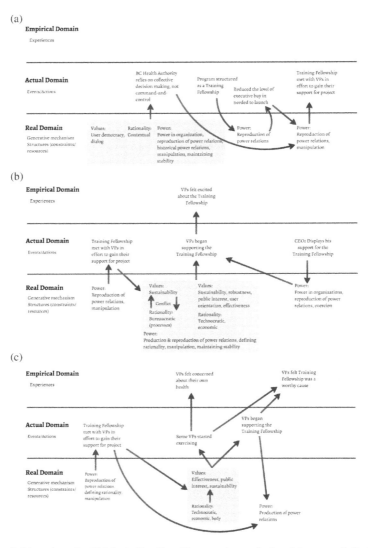

Figure 8.3(a–c). A Critical Realist Perspective of the Means of Building Support for the Training Fellowship. (a) Collective Decision-making. (b) Appeal to Values and CEO Power. (c) Appeal to Rationality.

close to the age where they might be pre-frail. This awareness created an experience of concern for their health. Combined, this led to VP support for the Training Fellowship and a feeling among the VPs that this programme was a worthy cause. As a result, they produced new power relations of support with the Training Fellowship, which I will later show was influential in sustaining the programme during turnover in the CEO office. I will now turn to explore how the BC working group maintained and built on this support for the Seniors Programme.

8.4.   Maintaining Executive Support

As I described earlier, CEO1's departure from the BC Health Authority put the Senior Programme's future at risk. The BC working group, however, took several actions to build support within the organization as they were assembling the Training Fellowship. These efforts continued while the Seniors Programme ran. As surfaced through my interviews, those elements contributing to building this organizational support included the programme's preliminary results. Additionally, the desire to maintain stability along with the alignment between the rationality underpinning the programme and those of the Interim CEO allowed the Seniors Programme to survive as leadership passed from one CEO to another. The BC working group also put considerable effort into managing communications about the programme to communities within the BC Health Authority. Finally, the members of the BC working group had worked hard to gain the support of their VPs. These served as useful allies during periods of CEO turnover. I present my interviewees' discussion of these elements below, following which I present a critical realist perspective of these events.

8.4.1.   *Positive Results − Nothing Wins Like Success*

The Seniors Programme's early results were encouraging. The Mentor discovered that these results, in turn, facilitated support for the programme among senior executives.

> But then when we did the presentation, and we started to show them some of the numbers that we were getting and what that impact, the potential impact would be on the system, then that was really where I started to see the change. That's when the VPs had come to me in follow-up conversations and said like, 'Wow, this is really exciting'. (personal communication, 19 May 2017)

Likewise, with gaining CEO2's support, the Mentor reported:

> Then it was getting a lot of great reviews, it was starting to get nominated for quality awards and things like that, so [CEO2] jumped on board because the evidence was clearly there that this was something that could potentially have significant impact on the system overall. (personal communication, 19 May 2017)

From her experience, the Mentor concluded that people want to associate with winning programmes (Mentor, personal communication, 19 May 2017). Positive results, in sum, showed the programme was working and became a symbol of success that attracted people.

8.4.2. Shared Understanding and Keeping the Peace

Beyond positive results leading to executive support, the Mentor also recognized that shared understanding of the problem led Interim CEO to continue supporting the programme during his tenure. 'I think that having come from another organization, [Interim CEO] was quite aware of the challenges of addressing the ageing population within the health authority, so he could also see where some of those potentials and those opportunities were' (Mentor, personal communication, 19 May 2017). When power transferred from Interim CEO to CEO2, the MD Lead noted CEO2 wanted to avoid conflict within the BC Health Authority before he fully understood the details of all its programmes.

> Well, [CEO2] was really new at the time. It was just maybe six months into his new role, and he was just learning the lay of the land, and we hadn't engaged with him a whole lot. But I think it was one of the remaining things that had to be taken over, and he had to make a decision as to whether he was going to scrap it or whether he was going to continue, and [the BC Health Authority] had invested to a certain extent to that point by sending us. I guess he felt that it was worth having a listen to see whether there was anything there that could be salvaged and carried on. (MD Lead, personal communication, 8 August 2017)

8.4.3. Managing Communications – Don't Rock the Boat

The above elements contributing to support for the Seniors Programme were beyond the fellowship's control – the programme's results were what they were, and the CEOs came with their rationalities and values. The fact they aligned with the needs of the Seniors Programme was fortunate happenstance. When it came to presenting the particulars of the Seniors Programme to the communities within the BC Health Authority, however, the BC working group put considerable effort into controlling their message. For example, during my review of their meeting minutes I noted that a single one-page information sheet of the Seniors Programme underwent at least thirteen revisions between 26 June 2014, and 4 September 2014. I asked members of the Training Fellowship why they paid so much attention on crafting their communication documents. The Mentor answered the following.

> Doing the communication and taking the first stab at it, we were really doing it from the lens and the area that we were coming from, but recognizing that there was a much bigger initiative around seniors and primary care withinside of the health

authority. It was extremely important that we did not do things only from our perspective and say, 'Well, this is the world according to [the Seniors Programme] and the rest of the world really doesn't matter.' We did want to go through that process of engaging with these other stakeholders to ensure that we were not we'll say negatively impacting anything that may have been happening in other strategies and preferably that it would be enhancing things that may be happening in other areas withinside of the health authority with respect to seniors care and communications and things in general. It was I guess out of a strategy of being respectful, but also using it as a way to integrate so that in going forward after we have some of these successes and that, we were now building a greater support network through the health authority to be advocates for the work that was actually happening there. (personal communication, 19 May 2017)

The Mentor further commented on the importance of communication.

[…] even in my job that I have now, communications is always the thing that when you go back and you do reflection and you talk about lessons learned, communications is something that always comes up as a significant piece […] I've had people come back and say, 'There wasn't enough communication. We didn't know what was going on. We felt that we were left out, out of the loop' […] I always go into it thinking I'd rather have somebody say that we communicated too much, or we engaged too much from perspective rather than having people say, 'You know what? I really didn't have an opportunity to have my voice heard'. (personal communication, 19 May 2017)

The MD Lead further commented on the importance of communication in an organization as large and heterogeneous as the BC Health Authority.

Yeah. Well, we had to make sure that when information went out, that it was new and yet it didn't contradict anything that was already happening. There were also a lot of people already working, especially in the field of home health, had already been doing a lot of work with senior care, and residential care also had a lot of work to do with seniors. We wanted to make sure that we were aligning with everything that's out there and using the language that was going to blend rather than be in conflict […] I've had experiences where you write one wrong thing, and you get all kinds of feedback, and then it kind of explodes, and you have to do it all over again. Then it's really difficult to undo something, so better to get it right in the first place. (MD Lead, personal communication, 8 August 2017)

Whereas these comments speak to the importance of communication in avoiding conflict, the Site Director discussed the importance of communication in building support.

> Well, I think communication is central to buy-in. Creating an effective message, that's been a good learning for me. Creating an effective message that is very, you know—what shall we say?—efficient is important [to get] the healthcare providers. So learning to write these messages so that we're representing the project accurately and the intention, and really meeting the intention of the communication strategy. (personal communication, 12 May 2017)

I then asked the MD Lead and Site Director to discuss the impacts of poorly crafted communication. The MD Lead replied:

> Oh yeah, that's a huge thing in the organization. I would expect it's the same everywhere. I'm not sure if it's just [the BC Health Authority]. But if you say something that does not apply to this one community but it applies to another community, and because we're so heterogeneous, it's really difficult to say the same thing and have it apply everywhere [...] When you say things about, say, the hospitals close to the city, it doesn't apply to hospitals like out [in satellite municipalities], and yet they are extremely involved in what goes on out there and really committed to their work. If you say something that applies elsewhere but doesn't apply to them, then there is a shift, is 'They're undoing what we're doing' and it can be seen as undermining. It can get really quite nasty. (personal communication, 8 August 2017)

The Site Director spoke to the risks of losing credibility and disrespecting those who were working on your project.

> Oh, I think there's tons of risk. I think you don't look professional; I think you lose your audience, you lose your credibility. You miscommunicate the intention of the work, so I think you're disrespectful to all those who have done the research ahead of you. I mean there's lots of risk. I mean that's why I think you take the time to do it thirteen times over. You're not only speaking to those people that you're trying to talk to but you're representing the people who've done the research, and I think that's a big responsibility in communication. (personal communication, 12 May 2017)

To emphasize the risks of poor communication, the minutes of the BC working group's meeting on 26 March 2015, reported a complaint about an article they circulated within the BC Health Authority that neglected to mention the work of nurse practitioners in implementing the Seniors Programme (BC Working Group, 2015). Despite all the energy they put into controlling communication, they still managed to upset a group.

8.4.4. *Using the Alliances You Have Created*

The fellowship had put in significant effort gaining the support of VPs within the BC Health Authority. The Mentor explained how this support helped the Seniors Programme as new CEOs came on board.

> Then once the CEO had left the organization, we did have a certain level of engagement and commitment from that senior level. More so than them just saying, 'Yes, I'm going to do it because my boss says I have to do it,' but they could actually see what some of these potentials were. We did have a little bit of I guess voice or support from the VPs for when the new CEOs came on board. (Mentor, personal communication, 19 May 2017)

In Table 8.4 (page 108), I summarize the elements of building and maintaining support for the Seniors Programme and link them to relevant structures of values, rationality, and power. Figure 8.4 (page 109) presents a critical realist perspective of this process. In Figure 8.4(a), I show the critical realist perspective of the impact positive results had on building and maintaining support for the Seniors Programme. In the real domain, the Seniors Programme was an act of technocratic rationality that produced those results. Based on the Senior Programme's design, the Training Fellowship and other audiences perceived these results as positive − an act of defining rationality. When executives in the BC Health Authority learned of these results, it triggered generative mechanisms of the values effectiveness and public interest (the intervention in the Seniors Programme appeared to delay frailty) as well as regime dignity (executives wanted to associate themselves with a successful programme). They then experienced the desire to associate themselves with the Seniors Programme. This desire led to the production of power relations in the real domain, manifesting as support for the Seniors Programme.

Figure 8.4(b) shows my representation of the elements of building and maintaining support at the CEO level during its period of turnover. The Interim CEO shared with the Training Fellowship the value of public interest and contextual rationality about the problems of caring for senior populations. This shared understanding led the Interim CEO to produce power relations with the Senior Programme, allowing it to continue during his tenure. When CEO2 took over, he lacked contextual rationality of the BC Health Authority and chose to engage the power tactic of maintaining stability while he gained contextual and economic rationality about his new operating environment. Finally, previous work the fellowship did to build VP support for the programme resulted in VPs

Table 8.4. Elements of Building and Maintaining Support for the Seniors Programme and Their Relation to Values, Rationality, and Power.

Elements of Building and Maintaining Support for the Seniors Programme	Relevant Structures of Values, Rationality, and Power
The impact of positive results	*Values*: Effectiveness, regime dignity, public interest
	Rationality: Technocratic
	Power: Defining rationality, production of power relations
Shared rationalities	*Values*: Public interest
	Rationality: Contextual
	Power: Production of power relations
Maintaining stability while learning about the organization	*Rationality*: Contextual, economic
	Power: Maintaining stability, production of power relations
Managing communications	*Values*: Dialog, openness, public interest, effectiveness
	Rationality: Contextual
	Power: Power in organizations, reproduction of power relations, production of power relations, maintaining stability, defining rationality, manipulation
Risks of poor communications	*Values*: Effectiveness, regime dignity, competitiveness
	Power: Conflict, defining rationality, reproduction of power relations
Leveraging VP support	*Power*: Production of power relations, power in organizations

using their power in the organization to produce power relations with the new CEOs who were supportive of the Seniors Programme.

Figure 8.4(c) shows my critical realist representation of how the Training Fellowship perceived the role of communication in building and maintaining support for the Seniors Programme. Many generative structures surfaced in my interviews regarding this topic. Values of dialogue and openness created the desire to share information about the programme with communities in the BC Health Authority. Values of public interest created the desire to build a supportive network within the BC Health Authority for the Seniors Programme, and the value effectiveness led to the desire to present relevant programme details

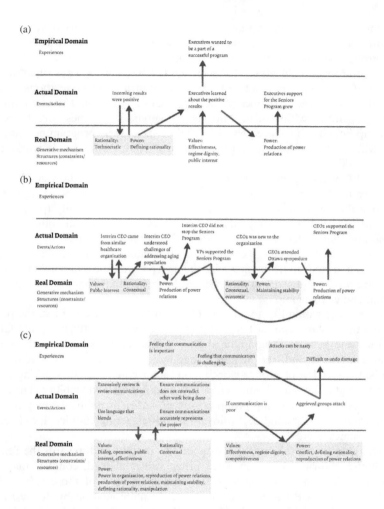

Figure 8.4(a–c). A Critical Realist Perspective of the Elements of Building and Maintaining Support for the Seniors Programme. (a) The Role of Positive Results in Building and Maintaining Support for the Seniors Programme. (b) Maintaining Support during CEO Transitions. (c) The Role of Communications in Maintaining and Building Support for the Seniors Programme.

efficiently and effectively. Contextual rationality informed communication through the BC working group's understanding of the people working on senior health, the work they do to that end, and the political rewards and risks that could result from communications activities. Many power structures also surfaced in my interviews. Communications is an act of defining rationality. The BC working group used communications to exercise power in the organization to position the Seniors Programme in an incumbent community of related programmes. The BC working group also demonstrated their knowledge of how other groups exercised power in their organization, shown in their awareness of how these groups might attack them if they felt threatened. Thus, their careful crafting of communication was an act of reproducing power relations – they understood the power dynamics of the organization and sought to maintain stability by operating within them. Through a combination of these structures, the fellowship hoped to produce new power relations as their programme found its place within this complex community of healthcare professionals working in seniors' health.

If the BC working group crafted communications poorly, they could trigger generative mechanisms such as the values effectiveness (people working hard in their area do not want others to undermine them), regime dignity (people want others to respect their work), and competitiveness (people will want to end a programme that undermines their work). The rationality defined by poor communications is that the new programme is threatening, and so people reproduce power relations to initiate conflict with the new programme. All combined, these generative mechanisms and events created the feeling that communications were essential and challenging.

The themes I would like to pull out of this are the following. First, the power relations they established earlier with the VPs as well as with incoming CEOs supported the Seniors Programme during a time of turbulence at the senior executive level. Second, the Seniors Programme was integrating itself into an incumbent collection of groups working on senior care. The BC working group put significant effort into doing so in a way that maintained stability. Third, the members of the BC working group possessed sufficient political savvy in their organization to understand and (mostly) avoid triggering conflict. I will return to these themes later.

In this chapter, I explored the resistance VPs initially had towards the Seniors Programme, showing that even when prime values aligned, conflicts may still occur along instrumental values or temporal realization of those values. VPs resisted the Seniors Programme through acts of manipulation by, for example, discouraging their staff from working on the programme and keeping the BC working group off meeting agendas. The BC working group overcame this resistance, however, by focusing on shared prime values and defining rationality to show that, despite different instrumental values and timelines, the Seniors Programme aligned with VPs' strategic objectives. They built on this support during the life of the Seniors Programme though focusing on its positive results, relying on shared understanding of the problem with Interim CEO, carefully managing communications within the organization, and then using the alliances they built with VPs to protect the programme during periods of CEO turnover. In the next chapter, I focus on the actions of CEO1 because he performed several acts that created structures binding the BC Health Authority to the Seniors Programme that persisted after he left the organization.

Chapter 9

Binding the Organization to the Seniors Programme

As described in the previous chapter, several points of resistance existed within the BC Health Authority towards the Training Fellowship and subsequent Seniors Programme. A key pillar of support sustaining the programme through this time was the support of CEO1. In June 2014, however, CEO1 left the organization. Though CEO1 was hopeful the programme would continue in his absence, he did worry the project might falter (CEO1, personal communication, 6 June 2017). The Mentor was acutely aware of the dangers to the Seniors Programme.

> Whereas in a lot of other projects, what happens is we start to do things and even if it is evidence-informed, but soon as the landscape starts to shift a little bit, then the priorities change and then really good projects are vulnerable to being put to the side [...] (Mentor, personal communication, 19 May 2017)

CEO2 reinforced how close the Seniors Programme came to ending. '[The Seniors Programme] got lucky. If I hadn't gone to Ottawa, it would have died' (CEO2, personal communication, 2 June 2017). I will turn to the importance of CEO2's trip to Ottawa shortly. For now, not only did the Seniors Programme survive the transition from CEO1 to Interim CEO, and then to CEO2, in the end, CEO2 chose to become the programme's new executive champion. None of these events happened by accident. CEO1 purposefully put in place several structures that led to its survival. I will now explore these structures.

CEO1 said the programme's survival was a testament to its resiliency (CEO1, personal communication, 6 June 2017). When I asked him what created this resiliency, he said:

> Where a project that is sensible, got a good engine room of committed people, and is asking really legitimate questions and is starting to come up with some really good answers, it's hard to shut something down that's so good. (CEO1, personal communication, 6 June 2017)

He further elaborated:

> There's a good structure in place. There are people that are committed. There's good evidence. And the pan-Canadian thing

absolutely helped a lot. Hard to pull yourself out of something
that's so unique. Also, with the connection and help from [the
Foundation] in Ottawa, that also helped put up some protection,
a force field if you wish of commitment. Maybe that's the language, 'the force field of commitment' from many stakeholders
that were involved and believed in what this project could do.
(CEO1, personal communication, 6 June 2017)

From these replies, combined with similar responses from other interviewees,
I have identified the following elements that built the Seniors Programme's resiliency: (1) people (building the engine room), (2) structure (protecting and arming
your people), (3) collaboration (creating a force field of commitment), (4) a sensible programme (the confluence of values and rationality), and (5) results (nothing
wins like success). Two of these five elements I have discussed in the previous
chapter. I have explored the narratives covering the development of a 'sensible'
programme through the confluence of values and rationality in Chapter 7. Suffice
it to say the Training Fellowship pursued a goal that leaders perceived as necessary (i.e. value congruence) using means these leaders accepted as legitimate
(i.e. rationality congruence). I also analysed the impact of positive results in the
previous chapter. Recall that positive results demonstrated the effectiveness of the
intervention and attracted individuals who wanted to associate with a successful
programme. In this chapter, I focus on the remaining three elements: people, structure, and collaboration, highlighting the role of values, rationality, and power.
Following this, I will show how these elements conspired to keep the programme
alive as the organization transitioned from CEO1 to Interim CEO to CEO2.

9.1.   People – Building the Engine Room

Regarding people, from my interviews with CEO1, CEO2, and the Senior
Improvement Lead, the critical characteristics of the people needed on a project to
drive it to success are those who are willing and capable of doing what is needed
to overcome barriers, as well as an ability to forge relations with relevant stakeholders. CEO2 stated these people need endless enthusiasm, optimism, and resilience (CEO2, personal communication, 2 June 2017). CEO1 further explained,

I think you're looking for people who really want to make a difference, that are passionate about the project itself, and I would
dare add really try to make a difference to pre-frail elderly.
You've got to have disciples that are committed to that endeavour. (CEO1, personal communication, 6 June 2017)

Both CEO1 and CEO2 felt the Mentor, Site Director, and MD Lead possessed
these qualities.
The Senior Improvement Lead (personal communication, 13 June 2017) further
identified qualities the Site Director and MD Lead possessed that contributed to

project success. These qualities included possessing a realistic appreciation of what individuals in the organization could and could not do, combined with a willingness to change and adapt as the project progressed. In the case of the Site Director:

> [...] she's built a solid infrastructure to support [the Seniors Programme]. I think she recognized how important it was to do the stakeholder engagement and ensure that the right people were involved. (Senior Improvement Lead, personal communication, 13 June 2017)

The Senior Improvement Lead also believed that the Site Director was willing to make changes to the Senior Programme as the project progressed and she learned more about the needs and limitations of critical stakeholders. For example:

> I think initially when there was a lot of a feedback from physicians around spreading [the Seniors Programme] and using the comprehensive geriatric assessment tool, the feedback was loud and clear 'Great, but if it's not embedded in my [electronic medical records], I'm not going to use it.' So [the Site Director] realized how important that was, and while that wasn't part of the original [Seniors Programme], she saw that that was a critical success factor, and she moved forward with that and put forward the necessary proposals within [the BC Health Authority] to make that happen [...] (Senior Improvement Lead, personal communication, 13 June 2017)

The Senior Improvement Lead (personal communication, 13 June 2017) added that projects need people who are willing to do hands-on work and have the technical competence to do it. She related the story of how shortages of nursing support in physician offices participating in the Seniors Programme threatened to delay the Seniors Programme. The Site Director was a nurse, and so she went to these physician offices and filled the gap left by the nursing shortfall. Similarly, the Senior Improvement Lead spoke of the MD Lead's importance in providing the physician's perspective in programme design as well as being the programme's champion among primary care doctors. Finally, the Senior Improvement Lead identified passion as an essential element. Speaking of the Site Director, she said:

> She doesn't need a script. [The Site Director] speaks from the heart and passionately about the issue [...] With any kind of spread initiative, having that spokesperson-like lead is an important ingredient. (Senior Improvement Lead, personal communication, 13 June 2017)

From these stories, Table 9.1 (page 114) presents my summary of the critical attributes members of the Seniors Programme perceived as contributing to project resiliency and links them to relevant structures of values, rationality, and power. Figure 9.1 (page 115) presents my visual representation of these attributes mapped

Table 9.1. Attributes of People That Kept the Seniors Programme Alive and Their Relation to Values, Rationality, and Power.

Attributes	Relevant Structures of Values, Rationality, and Power
Enthusiasm	*Values*: Public interest, effectiveness, innovation, user orientation, dialogue
	Rationality: Contextual/institutional
Optimism	*Values*: Public interest, effectiveness, innovation, user orientation, dialogue
	Rationality: Contextual/institutional
Committed, resilient	*Values*: Effectiveness
Want to make a difference to pre-frail elderly	*Values*: Effectiveness/innovation to achieve public interest
	Rationality: Contextual/institutional (that status quo ineffective)
A realistic appreciation of what people can and cannot in the organization	*Rationality*: Contextual, institutional
Willingness to change and adapt	*Values*: Effectiveness
	Power: Power in organizations (to implement changes)
Ability to build a supportive infrastructure; having the right people involved	*Rationality*: Bureaucratic (procedures and roles; processes)
	Power: Production of power relations
Competency in stakeholder engagement	*Values*: User orientation, dialogue
	Rationality: Contextual
Has the technical competence to do the actual work required by the project and willingness to do the work when needed	*Values*: Effectiveness
	Rationality: Contextual, institutional, bureaucracy (procedures and roles, processes)
A peer of project stakeholders	*Values*: User orientation
	Rationality: Contextual
	Power: Reproduction of power relations (doctors listen to doctors); production of power relations (physician champion builds physician support)
Passion. Doesn't need a script; speaks from the heart	*Experience*: Feels project is a worthy cause
	Rationality: Body, emotional

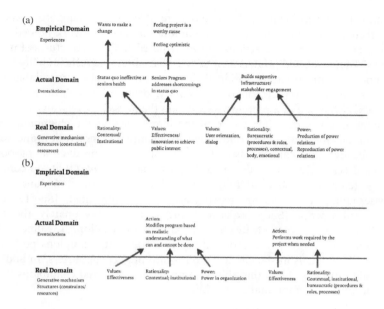

Figure 9.1(a–b). A Critical Realist Perspective of the Attributes of People That Kept the Seniors Programme Alive. (a) Sources of Optimism and Enthusiasm; Ability to Build Supportive Infrastructure and Stakeholder Relations. (b) Willingness to Adapt and Do the Work Required for the Project.

onto a critical realist framework. Project champions exhibited several values: public interest achieved through effectiveness and innovation, user orientation, and dialogue. Note the alignment between these values and those that interviewees perceived in the Senior Programme summarized in Table 7.1 (page 81). That is, the values possessed by project champions closely matched the values the Seniors Programme embodied. These values, when combined with an understanding of the shortcomings of our current treatment of senior health gained through contextual and institutional rationality, gave champions the understanding that the status quo was insufficient, creating within them the desire to make a change. This insight, when combined with the Seniors Programme's potential to improve care, created feelings of optimism and a belief that the Seniors Programme was a worthy cause. I believe these dynamics created within champions the motivation and resilience to do whatever it took to succeed.

Motivation and resiliency alone, however, were not enough to create success. Champions also exhibited contextual and institutional rationality that informed two types of actions. First, they needed the understanding these rationalities provided of their health authority to modify the Seniors Programme to make it work in their organization. Second, they needed an understanding of the contexts of critical stakeholders that allowed champions to recruit their support for the programme. Further, by combining contextual and institutional rationality with bureaucratic rationality, champions were able to build supportive systems within their organization, as well as step in and do hands-on work needed to fill resource gaps. Making these actions happen required enabling structures of power. We see champions could produce new power relations through their ability to create supportive infrastructures within their organization. They also exhibited the ability to reproduce power relations effectively, demonstrated through the MD Lead's ability to serve as a peer-advocate within the physician community.

Finally, interviewees often spoke of the importance of the champions' passion. This passion may have contributed to champions' motivation and resiliency. I believe this passion also played a role in the production of power relations. Recall CEO1's words: 'You've got to have *disciples* that are committed [...]' (emphasis added) (CEO1, personal communication, 6 June 2017). Likewise, remember the Senior Improvement Lead commented, '[Site Director] doesn't need a script. [She] speaks from the heart and passionately about the issue' (Senior Improvement Lead, personal communication, 13 June 2017). These comments suggested a proselytizing function that champions performed to convert individuals in stakeholder groups into project supporters. In addition to the values driving them, this ability to proselytize required champions to tap into their body and emotional rationalities.

9.2.   Structure – Protecting and Arming Your People

The developers of the Seniors Programme did more than ensure project champions existed within the team. Despite the passion of members of the Training Fellowship, the Seniors Programme nearly died during the wrap-up stage. It was only at a symposium attended by CEO2 held in Ottawa where the Training Fellowship presented their project that the programme found its new executive champion and, subsequently, life after the fellowship. The MD Lead corroborated this: '[...] it was after that presentation, and we were all coming home, and we were at the airport and had a beverage together, [CEO2] sort of said, 'Yeah, I sort of get it now. And I was skeptical at first, but I think it makes sense [...]'' (MD Lead, personal communication, 8 August 2017). What structures led CEO2 to attend the Ottawa symposium?

This is not a trivial question, because he had the authority to choose not to go. The Project Charter identified the cost to the BC Health Authority for its participation in the Training Fellowship was just over $44,000, a nearly insignificant fraction of the budget of which CEO2 was responsible (*Project Charter: Collaborative Project to Improve Senior Care*, 2013, p. 20). CEO2 had been in his position less than a year and had no history with the programme. Why did he take time out of his busy schedule to travel across the country to hear the presentation of what, budget-wise, was an insignificant study? It turns out the members of the Training Fellowship built structures, most of them created during the nascent stages of the project's life, that not only kept the project alive as the Interim CEO came and left but led CEO2 to that Ottawa symposium. These structures include documentation, collaboration, building support within the organization, and the project's positive results. In the following pages, I will focus on the role of documentation. In later sections, I explore the remaining structures.

Considering documentation, the seminal document binding the organization to the Training Fellowship was the Project Charter. This document served three purposes. First, it documented a common understanding of the objectives, scope, expectations, and requirements of the Training Fellowship between the Foundation and the BC and NS Health Authorities. Second, it supported the submission of the Training Fellowship's work to the Training Programme run by the Foundation. Third, it established a common understanding of the project's purpose, expected results, and delineated how and who would deliver those results. Senior executives from the Foundation and the BC and NS Health Authorities signed the document. Upon signing, the Project Charter defined the contract between the three organizations (*Project Charter: Collaborative Project to Improve Senior Care*, 2013, p. 7).

The Mentor explained the rationale for joining the Training Fellowship and committing the BC Health Authority to the Project Charter.

> [...] we went back and said, 'Well, you know what? Why don't we develop a team that would go through the [Training Fellowship]?' So once again there would be these signatures on the paper, the commitment from the most senior level. Then if the senior people moved, at least we had the documentation – when we would engage with whatever the next leadership would be, that we could then say, 'Well, you know what? This was the commitment.' Of course, any new leadership has the prerogative I guess to slash and get rid of whatever they want, but at least we would be well positioned to get on the agenda because we would have had these meetings set up all the time. So the [Training Fellowship] was one of the strategies to help to give us that strength. (Mentor, personal communication, 19 May 2017)

One of these commitments was for the CEO of the BC Health Authority to attend the Ottawa symposium.

Beyond committing the organization to this multi-partner project, documentation also served to protect and assist the members of the Training Fellowship within their organizations. For example, the Mentor explained how the Project Charter facilitated the advancement of the Seniors Programme within the BC Health Authority.

> [...] one of the things that I observed when I actually did the programme was that by having the commitment of the organization from the most senior level and signatures on the paper[...] they had their sweat in the game, which then really enabled the focus for the project to go to completion. (Mentor, personal communication, 19 May 2017)

Additionally, CEO1 described how documentation developed by the Foundation protected members of the Training Fellowship, allowing them to focus their efforts on the project. As described in Chapter 7, the Mentor felt exposed to political risks due to her involvement in the fellowship. According to CEO1, '[…] we had the syllabus and the curriculum of the [Training Fellowship] that was very nurturing and protective of its students' (CEO1, personal communication, 6 June 2017). He related that the protective effects of these documents enabled members of the Training Fellowship to focus on developing the programme while minimizing their worries about political risks to their career if the programme failed.

Table 9.2 (page 119) presents my summary of the role documentation had in keeping the Seniors Programme alive during turnover at the CEO level and links them to relevant structures of values, rationality, and power. Figure 9.2 (page 120) presents my visual representation of this mapped onto a critical realist framework. From the narratives summarized above, part of the reason to join the Training Fellowship was to overcome resistance at the VP level to the Senior Programme. As the document establishing this fellowship, the Project Charter defined rationality, and it relied on bureaucratic rationality to do so. Through this document, the charter defined the boundaries of the programme as well as the procedures, roles, processes, and rules of the fellowship. Once executed, this document created the structure of the Training Fellowship. It was the means through which people reified power. We will see bureaucratic rationality reifying power throughout the life of the Seniors Programme. For now, it was through CEO1's power in the organization that once he signed the charter, the organization was committed through several power and value structures. The signing of this document defined rationality by communicating to stakeholders the organization's commitment to the project. It established power relations through a commitment to collaboration between the Foundation and the BC and NS Health Authorities. CEO1 reproduced power relations as this commitment overrode resistance to the programme at the VP level.

Moreover, it gave members of the BC working group the ability to engage in manipulation through getting on the agenda to highlight the programme to any future CEO. It engaged the value of regime dignity as once the organization had entered a signed commitment to other stakeholders, exiting that commitment may have adversely impacted the organization's reputation. During the implementation of the Training Fellowship, the Foundation's syllabus and curriculum exercised power over organizations by producing power relations that protected the fellowship from political repercussions should the project fail. Combined, this act of documentation contributed to the programme's survival and created a sense of obligation for CEO2 to attend the Ottawa symposium. I will now consider how collaboration (the force field of commitment) served to bind the organization to the Seniors Programme.

9.3.   Collaboration − Creating a Force Field of Commitment

MD Lead (personal communication, 8 August 2017) explained that one of the last responsibilities of the chief executive for the Training Programme was to

Table 9.2. Role of Documentation in Keeping the Seniors Programme Alive and Its Relation to Values, Rationality, and Power.

Documentation	Relevant Structures of Values, Rationality, and Power
Project Charter: documented objectives, scope, expectations, and requirements	*Rationality*: Bureaucratic (boundaries, documentation, rules) *Power*: Defining rationality
Project Charter: supporting submission of Training Fellowship to the Foundation	*Rationality*: Bureaucratic (documentation) Power: Defining rationality
Project Charter: established project's purpose, expected results, and how/who delivered results	*Rationality*: Bureaucratic (boundaries, documentation, procedures and roles, processes, rules) *Power*: Defining rationality
Project Charter: sign off	*Values*: Regime dignity (breaking a signed agreement impacts reputation) *Rationality*: Bureaucratic (documentation) *Power*: Defining rationality (leaders are committed to this project), power in organizations (authority to commit organization to action), production of power relations (committing to collaboration), manipulation (ability to get on agenda with new leaders), power in organizations/reproduction of power relations (senior managers committed to the project),
Training Fellowship syllabus and curriculum was nurturing and protective	*Rationality*: Bureaucratic (boundaries, documentation, procedures and roles, processes, rules) *Power*: Power over organizations (the Foundation could protect participants in BC Health Authority), production of power relations (protecting Training Fellowship)

attend the final symposium in Ottawa. Despite the structures of power tied to the Project Charter, the charter specified any party could terminate its agreement with three months' notice without penalty (*Project Charter: Collaborative Project to Improve Senior Care*, 2013, p. 19). Thus, CEO2 could have ended the

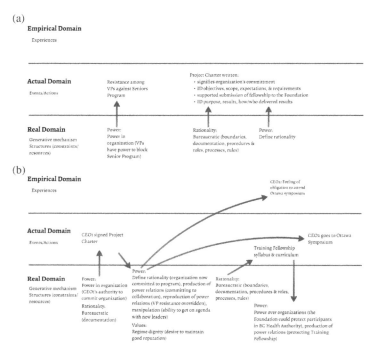

Figure 9.2(a–b).   A Critical Realist Perspective of the Role of Documentation in Keeping the Seniors Programme Alive. (a) The Project Charter. (b) The Project Charter's Role in Bringing CEO2 to Ottawa.

project rather than go to Ottawa at no cost. Instead, CEO2 chose to go to Ottawa. I now consider the role the BC Health Authority's collaboration with other partners had in binding the organization to the Senior Programme.

The Project Charter did not commit the BC Health Authority to the Seniors Programme. Instead, it committed the BC Health Authority to a multi-institution collaboration to participate in a Training Fellowship that then developed the Seniors Programme (*Project Charter: Collaborative Project to Improve Senior Care*, 2013). Relative to the size of studies often performed by health authorities, the Seniors Programme was small (CEO1, personal communication, 6 June 2017). It was unlikely the BC Health Authority needed help from other organizations to perform the study. Moreover, one of its collaborators was a health authority on the opposite side of the country in Nova Scotia. What could a Nova Scotian health authority possibly contribute that the BC Health Authority could not supply on its own, or at least source closer to home? What was the rationale for incurring the extra logistical challenges of collaborating with organizations flung across the country for such a small study?

Different members of the Training Fellowship perceived varied reasons for the collaboration. Both the Mentor (personal communication, 19 May 2017) and MD Lead (personal communication, 8 August 2017) identified that both the BC and NS Health Authorities faced similar issues with their senior population's health and subsequent utilization of resources, and so both wanted to find a way to improve the situation. Despite this common cause, however, there were differences between the two senior populations across these regions. According to CEO1 (personal communication, 6 June 2017), these differences gave them the ability to test the programme's robustness in more than one region. That said, these differences did cause resistance at the VP level within the BC Health Authority as some members of the executive team questioned whether the organization should be spending time and resources working on problems outside their region (Mentor, personal communication, 19 May 2017). The Mentor added, however, that CEO1 was a visionary leader who wanted to be innovative and learn from what other organizations were doing. In CEO1's own words:

> I think any health authority who becomes insular and inward-looking is going to have problems. You need to have an inclusive mind that allows you to consider what's happening not only in your province in other health authorities but in your neighbouring provinces like Alberta and others internationally. Bringing these differences just adds strength. It adds strength to the form and structure of potential innovation. (personal communication, 6 June 2017)

Regardless of the reasons for the collaboration, once established, it contributed to keeping the Seniors Programme alive as CEOs turned over. As mentioned earlier, the pan-Canadian collaboration between health authorities and federal agencies created what CEO1 called a 'force field of commitment' (CEO1, personal communication, 6 June 2017). Moreover, at the Ottawa symposium where CEO2 decided on the Seniors Programme's fate, the support of the Foundation played an important role in gaining his support. The MD Lead explained.

> [...] we had a really great reception at [the Foundation]. We had a lot of positive feedback from the [Foundation] board, and they were very encouraging in us to continue with this work. They wanted to support the ongoing work towards getting it to be able to spread [...] They felt that [the Seniors Programme] actually had the potential to become another project that could go Canada-wide, so I think that was also very helpful. (MD Lead, personal communication, 8 August 2017)

In Table 9.3 (page 122), I summarize the reasons for collaboration and the role it had in keeping the Seniors Programme alive during turnover at the CEO level and link them to relevant structures of values, rationality, and power. Figure 9.3 (page 123) presents my visual representation of this mapped onto a critical realist framework. From the narratives summarized above, the value of

Table 9.3. Role of Collaboration in Keeping the Seniors Programme Alive and Its Relation to Values, Rationality, and Power.

Elements of Collaboration	Relevant Structures of Values, Rationality, and Power
Shared issues regarding senior care	*Values*: Dialogue, public interest, sustainability
	Rationality: Collective reasoning, contextual
	Power: Power in the organization, reproduction of power relations
Differences between the senior population	*Values*: Dialogue
	Rationality: Technocratic (test robustness of model across regions)
Differences between regions led VPs to question collaboration	*Values*: Accountability
	Rationality: Bureaucratic (boundaries)
	Power: Power in organizations, reproduction of power relations
Learning from others	*Values*: Dialogue strengthens innovation and effectiveness
	Rationality: Collective reasoning, contextual
Force field of commitment	*Values*: Dialogue
	Power: Production of power relations
Support from Foundation	*Values*: Spread
	Power: Power over organization through manipulation via defining rationality (external validation of programme contributed to CEO2's support), reproduction of power relations (CEO2 respected the Foundation's previous work)

dialogue strongly drove CEO1. He saw dialogue as a way to enhance the values of effectiveness, innovation, and sustainability, all with the aim of achieving public interest. Several forms of rationality supported these values. The commonality of the problem shared between BC and NS spoke to a shared contextual rationality that led to the belief each region had something of relevance to teach the other. One of the reasons for the collaboration was to engage with collective reasoning under the belief that this form of rationality led to superior solutions. My interviewees perceived the differences that existed between the two

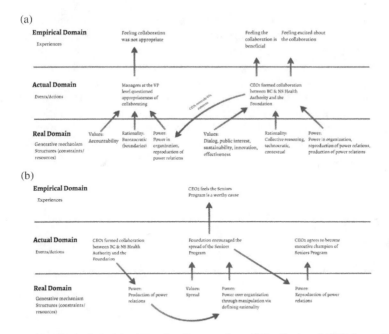

Figure 9.3(a–b). A Critical Realist Perspective of the Role of Collaboration in Keeping the Seniors Programme Alive. (a) Perceptions of the Collaboration at Senior Management Levels. (b) The Role of Collaboration in Gaining CEO2's Support for the Senior Programme.

health authorities as an opportunity to test the robustness of the Seniors Programme in different settings, which strengthened the programme's technocratic rationality. These differences between the regions, however, raised concerns at the VP level in the BC Health Authority. Here, dissenting VPs seem driven by the value of accountability as informed through bureaucratic rationality, specifically boundaries. That is, the VPs questioned whether collaborating with NS Health Authority was beyond their organization's remit. Nonetheless, CEO1 exercised his power in the organization to override the VPs and commit the organization to the collaboration by signing the Project Charter.

Once executed, the Project Charter produced power relations between the BC Health Authority and its partners. In the case of the Foundation, these power relations allowed it to host the Ottawa symposium CEO2 attended. The Foundation then had the opportunity to exert power over the BC Health Authority through defining rationality by expressing its strong support for the Seniors Programme, which contributed to CEO2 experiencing the feeling that this programme was worthy. These actions, consequently, contributed to CEO2 becoming the new executive champion of the Seniors Programme in the BC Health Authority once the Training Fellowship ended.

This chapter highlighted several means through which CEO1 bound his organization to the Seniors Programme despite initial resistance from his VPs. This included recruiting project champions who possessed passion, drive, and political savvy to move the project along. We see bureaucratic rationality in the form of documentation, specifically the Project Charter and Training Programme documents, that committed the organization to collaboration on this project and nurtured those project champions working on it. Plus, the collaboration, beyond contributing to the rationalities of the programme, also created a 'force field of commitment' that assisted in recruiting a new executive champion. I now turn in the next chapter to explore how different forms of rationality combined and conflicted throughout the life of the Seniors Programme.

Chapter 10

Multiple Rationalities at Play

Once senior executives of the BC Health Authority, NS Health Authority, and the Foundation signed the Project Charter in December 2013, the Training Programme commenced. Activities included the official formation of the Training Fellowship, who then set to the task of developing the Seniors Programme. This period was a very active phase of the programme's life. During this time, the geographically diverse team started developing the details of the Seniors Programme, including how to create an intervention that delays frailty and then applying that intervention across different regions. Additionally, the study the Training Fellowship designed required the use of community coaches, so the BC working group had to devise a method to identify and select a partner organization to administer this coaching. Notably, throughout this period the Training Fellowship engaged in three important processes of defining rationality described later.

In this chapter, I will explore the preliminary research the Training Fellowship performed followed by an analysis of the troubles they had designing a standardized approach to apply across two healthcare regions. Through that analysis, I will surface some of the benefits and difficulties of blending rationalities. Then, I will consider how the Training Fellowship selected the BC Coaching Organization, as this, again, highlights the importance of different rationalities in this project. Finally, I will evaluate several processes of defining rationality the Training Fellowship undertook which highlighted important connections between values, rationality, and power. I turn first to an exploration of the preliminary research they did to learn how to prevent frailty.

10.1. Learning How to Prevent Frailty

The goal of the Training Fellowship was to improve senior health by preventing frailty (*Project Charter: Collaborative Project to Improve Senior Care*, 2013, p. 8). One of the first actions the fellowship took was to educate themselves on what researchers already knew about this. Meeting minutes for the BC Health Authority working group record that from January 2014 to July 2014, the fellowship performed a literature review and attended conferences where experts spoke on the topic. The MD Lead related it was at a conference held in April 2014 where they learned something that would impact the path of their further research into the area.

So we went to one of their conferences in Chicago [...] and learned a lot about the importance of asking the question of 'What matters to you?' to the senior. Rather than coming down with what is good for you, we are going to ask, 'What matters to you most?' That was one of the first sort of changes in thinking that we had to come to in that it was really important that we're not dealing with children that have nothing, no thoughts of their own really. They're seniors that have had a wealth of experience and usually if they're pre-frail, they're still very high-functioning and independent and they have ideas of what is important to them. (MD Lead, personal communication, 8 August 2017)

The fellowship adopted this advice and in early May 2014 developed a plan to engage with seniors' groups (BC Working Group, 2014a). By the end of May 2014, the BC working group had met with four different seniors' organizations ('Minutes: CARES Project – FH Working Group Planning Meeting 2014-05-22', 2014). The MD Lead described what information they asked of seniors at these meetings, and how that impacted the Seniors Programme's development.

[...] [W]e asked questions of seniors as to what it would take for them to take the advice of healthier lifestyles. What kind of information? In what way would it compel them to move forward to take that up? We heard quite strongly in several settings that if it came from their doctor, whom they trusted, that would go a lot further than if they saw a poster at the swimming pool [...] But hearing that if it came through their primary care provider it would be adhered to a bit better, that's where we decided that with the [Seniors Programme] the model would be in the primary care office. (MD Lead, personal communication, 8 August 2017)

Table 10.1 summarizes the means of preliminary research the Training Fellowship undertook and links them to relevant constructs of values, rationality, and power. Figure 10.1 presents a visual representation of this mapped onto a critical realist framework. Initially, the fellowship relied on technocratic rationality to learn what researchers had discovered about preventing frailty. They did this through a literature review and attending conferences. An epiphany occurred at a conference they attended in April 2014. They gained an appreciation for the knowledge contained within the senior population. That is, they saw the value of contextual rationality in the development of the Seniors Programme. They immediately modified their research plan and met with four seniors groups. According to the MD Lead, the decision to base the Seniors Programme out of primary care offices came out of this contextual rationality. The use of primary care offices spoke to power structures within the senior community. Seniors said they listened to what their doctor told them – a reproduction of power relations. The above use of multiple rationalities demonstrated the

Table 10.1. Means of Preliminary Research and Their Relation to Values, Rationality, and Power.

Means of Preliminary Research	Relevant Constructs
Literature review and conferences	*Experiences*: Unknowledgeable; epiphany
	Action: Literature review and attending conferences
	Rationality: Technocratic
Meeting with seniors' groups	*Actions*: Met with seniors' groups
	Values: User orientation, dialogue
	Rationality: Contextual
Seniors Programme developed, including learnings from literature review and meetings with seniors' groups (e.g. designed around primary care)	*Action*: Designed Seniors Programme around primary care
	Rationality: Technocratic, contextual
	Power: Reproduction of power relations, defining rationality

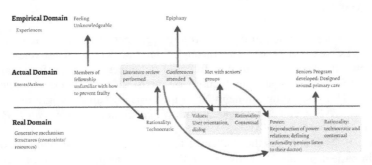

Figure 10.1.   A Critical Realist Perspective of the Means of Preliminary Research.

Seniors Programme was the result of blending technocratic and contextual rationalities, a theme that will arise again.

10.2.   Reconciling Differences between Regions

You will recall from the previous chapter that my interviewees had several rationales for why the BC Health Authority collaborated with NS. Some of these reasons included similar problems with an ageing population, as well as testing their intervention in different regions to establish their model's robustness. Despite that reasoning, the Mentor acknowledged that the differences between the patient populations served by the BC and NS Health Authorities posed challenges.

> [...] [I]n [the BC Health Authority], we have a large subpopulation, which is the South Asian community, and in Nova Scotia they have a similar subpopulation. I could be wrong, but I think it's maybe Middle Eastern. I can't remember now, but I think it's Middle Eastern subpopulation [...] Both provinces have an ageing population, but in Nova Scotia they actually have a declining overall population, whereas BC has a growing number.' (Mentor, personal communication, 19 May 2017)

The fellowship struggled with reconciling these differences and ended up taking what the Mentor called a 'staged' approach.

> [...] [W]e ended up developing I would call it a staged type of implementation – that there was that higher-level strategy, 'What are the key elements from a strategic perspective that we want to put into this model?' and then how does that then translate down into something from a more local level, so 'What might work inside of Nova Scotia?' or 'What might work inside of [the BC Health Authority]?' (Mentor, personal communication, 19 May 2017)

These differences resulted in different trial designs between the two regions. For example, BC selected participants through family physician offices versus a privately owned care provider in NS. BC used volunteer versus professional coaches in NS. In BC, coaching focused on physical activity/social connection versus the Harmony Programme in NS, which was a wellness programme exclusive to the NS Coaching Organization (*[The Seniors Programme] Project Intervention Summary*, 2014).

Table 10.2 summarizes the challenges the fellowship had managing the differences in patient population between the BC and NS health authorities and links them to relevant constructs from the critical realist framework I am applying.

Table 10.2. Challenges the Fellowship Had Managing the Differences in Patient Population between the BC and NS Health Authorities and Their Relation to Values, Rationality, and Power.

Challenge	Relevant Structures of Values, Rationality, and Power
Differences in patient population between BC and NS	*Values*: Spread *Rationality*: Technocratic conflicting with contextual

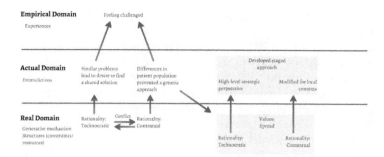

Figure 10.2.   A Critical Realist Perspective of Managing the Differences in Patient Population between the BC and NS Health Authorities.

Figure 10.2 presents a visual representation of this mapped onto a critical realist framework. As I have shown previously, members of the fellowship valued technocratic rationality. Given the similarities in problems between BC and NS, the veneration of technocratic rationality led to a desire to develop a standard solution. The differences in patient population, however, revealed contextual rationality that the Training Fellowship was unable to ignore. These differences were significant enough to preclude a standardized approach to the problem both regions shared. The conflict between technocratic and contextual rationality posed a challenge. Unwilling to forego technocratic rationality, and unable to ignore contextual rationality, the fellowship developed an approach that incorporated both. This approach had a high-level strategic perspective that encompassed shared aims between the regions embodying technocratic rationality that each healthcare authority then modified for their local area by applying contextual rationality. This was not the only example of the tension between technocratic and other forms of rationality, and I will explore these tensions in more depth later. For now, I will turn to the BC working group's decision to work with the BC Coaching Organization.

10.3.   Selecting the BC Coaching Organization

The BC Coaching Organization was one of the last collaborators brought into the Seniors Programme, and it was the only organization identified and selected exclusively by the BC working group – all other collaborators had either been selected by CEO1 or the NS working group. For nine months between January and September 2014, the BC working group met with several community groups they could potentially use to administer the coaching to participants in the Seniors Programme. Suddenly, during the 4th September 2014 meeting, the minutes mentioned the BC Coaching Organization for the first time ('Minutes: CARES Project – FH Working Group Planning Meeting 2014-09-04', 2014). A week later, the Head Coach presented an overview of the BC Coaching Organization to the fellows ('Minutes: CARES Project – FH Working Group Planning Meeting 2014-09-11', 2014). A week after that, the working relationship with the BC Coaching Organizations appeared finalized (Training Fellowship, 2014b).

What was it about the BC Coaching Organization that led the BC working group to quickly adopt them as their partner after months of meeting with other groups? The Site Director explained, 'Well, again it was back to what was evidence-based [...] we were looking for an evidence-based coaching initiative and self-management programs' (Site Director, personal communication, 12 May 2017). The MD Lead concurred, citing that the BC Coaching Organization relied on the Stanford model (MD Lead, personal communication, 8 August 2017). The Stanford model she referred to is the Chronic Disease Self-management Programme developed at Stanford University and licenced through the Self-management Resource Center. It was a widely used and researched model of how to develop the capacity of patients with chronic diseases to manage their health (Self-management Resource Center, 2018). Rather than applying the Stanford model in a standardized way, however, the BC Coaching Organization customized the fitness goals and programme to the individual senior (Head Coach, personal communication, 4 August 2017).

Table 10.3 summarizes the process of selecting the BC Coaching Organization and links it to relevant constructs from the critical realist framework I am applying. Figure 10.3 (page 131) presents a visual representation of this mapped onto a critical realist framework. The BC working group perceived that technocratic rationality informed the operations of the BC Coaching Organization, which was an important form of rationality to the BC working group. The coaching organization's reliance on technocratic rationality reassured

Table 10.3. Selecting the BC Coaching Organization and Its Relation to Values, Rationality, and Power.

Elements of the Selection Process	Relevant Structures of Values, Rationality, and Power
Complimentary needs (one needed participants, the other coaches)	*Values*: Dialogue, effectiveness *Rationality*: Collective action
Allowed the team to choose a coaching organization	*Values*: Dialogue, user democracy *Rationality*: Collective reasoning *Power*: Reproduction of power relations
Choosing BC Coaching Organization	*Values*: Effectiveness, user orientation *Rationality*: Technocratic, body *Power*: Production of power relations

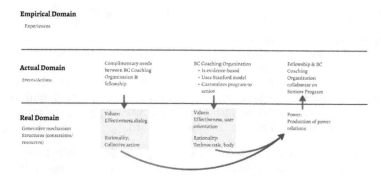

Figure 10.3. A Critical Realist Perspective of the Selection of the BC Coaching Organization.

the BC working group that the programme satisfied their value of effectiveness. Recall that technocratic rationality presumes a single best solution to a problem discoverable through the scientific process (Townley, 2008b, pp. 66–88). The Head Coach, however, stated that their coaches customized fitness programmes to seniors' needs, which reflected body rationality as well as the value of user orientation. Thus, the BC Coaching Organization blended two forms of rationality in the delivery of coaching. I will return to this tension between rationalities later. For now, these attributes satisfied the BC working group, which led to the production of new power relations manifested through their agreement to collaborate on the Seniors Programme.

10.4. Defining Rationality

During the development of the Seniors Programme, the Training Fellowship undertook three significant processes of defining rationality. These processes included determining what name to give their programme, what to call the population that was the focus of the Seniors Programme, and developing a vision statement. These may seem trivial, and indeed some members of the fellowship did trivialize these endeavours, but they demonstrate a thoughtful and deliberate blending of values and rationality by some individuals. In this section, I look at two of the three processes of defining rationality. The one act I am omitting is the process through which they developed the project's name. There are two reasons for excluding this process. One, I cannot discuss the process of developing the programme's real name without mentioning the name, thereby compromising the confidentiality of my interviewees. Two, the remaining two acts of defining rationality (identifying what to call the patient and developing a vision statement) sufficiently represent the themes apparent in the process of naming the programme. Given that, I first explore the Training Fellowship's process of determining what to call their target patient population.

10.4.1.   *Defining Rationality I: What Do We Call Our Target Population?*

During my review of project documentation, I noticed an array of terms the Training Fellowship used when referring to the population they wanted to target with the Seniors Programme. These terms included healthy, not frail, non-frail, not-yet-frail, pre-frail, and frail. The team seemed to settle on pre-frail in some documents, non-frail in others, before finally choosing 'pre-frail seniors with chronic conditions'. I asked members of the BC working group to explain this diversity of terminology. The Site Director explained:

> I think it was just those were early days [...] we didn't really know how to define our population [...] So I think those were just sort of our earlier attempts to know what direction we were heading in. We knew that we weren't going to work with the advanced frail senior and we didn't [...] It really just had to speak to our inexperience and our lack of exposure to the literature and the experts. (personal communication, 12 May 2017)

The Mentor suggested part of their confusion came from a lack of consistent terminology within the healthcare community.

> [...] there's very little understanding of what these terms were amongst any community that we spoke with. Truly there was no consistency. When we say 'child,' we create a mental picture of to some degree what that might like look like. It's 18 and under, 15 and under − something along those lines, but it's a little bit clearer. (Mentor, personal communication, 19 May 2017)

The first step the Training Fellowship took to define their target population was to see what language the literature and experts used (Site Director, personal communication, 12 May 2017). The differences between some of the terms under consideration may seem trivial. Is the difference between non-frail, pre-frail, or not-yet-frail meaningful? The Site Director suggested these differences were significant in the literature, specifically with regards to the Clinical Frailty Scale.[1]

> Well, I think they're important in that 'pre-frail' and 'non-frail' speak a little bit more to the literature. There's more definition emerging around what the 'pre-frail senior' is. And the 'non-frail senior' is someone who we're looking at [...] if you're looking at the Clinical Frailty Scale, you're looking at 1 to 3 for the 'non-frail.' They don't really have the chronic disease component. But the 'pre-frail' are those that are still well enough but have chronic health conditions, and without the intervention to support

---

[1]Rockwood et al. (2005) developed the Clinical Frailty Scale. It describes seven levels of frailty, ranging from 'very fit' at level one to 'severely frail' at level seven.

health-protective factors, those people will descend quickly into frailty. So I believe that we have achieved some clarity in the definitions, but we defer to what the literature and the experts say. (personal communication, 12 May 2017)

The Training Fellowship eventually settled on the term pre-frail. The MD Lead, however, suggested this term was not without problems, and may yet change.

[...] Ken Rockwood was saying that 'pre-frail' in the literature actually means something different from what we're working on, so we may evolve to something else [...] because I mean yeah, it depends on what's in the literature too because they started using terminology in different ways. (MD Lead, personal communication, 8 August 2017)

Despite their initial reliance on the literature and expert opinion, the Training Fellowship also spoke directly with the population they wanted to target to gain their input on what to call that population. Through these meetings, the Training Fellowship used the process of defining rationality as a means of engaging stakeholders. The Mentor explained,

[...] [I]t was a strategy that we used to have stakeholder engagement. The literature might tell us what these terms might mean, and we might see them multiple different ways. But 'Hey, why don't we just ask people what they want to be referred to?' And what we learned through that process is they don't want to be called 'a silver tsunami,' because they think that 'Tsunamis are horrible, so why are you going to tell us that we're going to be horrible on our environment?' So that was the other strategy then as well, is like, 'Okay, let's use this as an engagement tool to go out and to engage with this population, who we don't only learn what they want to be referred to, but we learn lots of other things as a part of that engagement as well.' In designing strategically some of the strategies of us being able to have this team work as a team and be able to get a solution that was not health authority—driven, it included the needs of the health authority, the needs of the practitioners, as well as the needs of the target population. So the seniors, pre-frail, whatever, whatever we want to call them, but we wanted them to be a part of this process. (personal communication, 19 May 2017)

Bringing in the opinion of the target population, though, posed a problem. Finding a term that was consistent with the literature yet palatable to the target population challenged the fellowship. As the Mentor reported, the target population wanted a label they perceived as positive.

It was 'We want to be using something that's more positive,' because this is the feedback that we were getting from the senior population that we engaged with and we wanted the initiative to be in a positive light, not to be something that was negative. (personal communication, 19 May 2017)

The MD Lead explained how challenging this was.

[…] [L]ately we're finding that 'pre-frail' is even really not appropriate because the patients that are pre-frail don't really think that they're frail. The ones that we're trying to address are still quite active, so they're not focused on being on the negative side of things. So, we've got to try and figure out how we're going to address them […] There's this negative kind of connotation to the word 'seniors' and 'pre-frail,' but we haven't come up with anything positive about it, either. It's 'How do you prevent frail?' That's what we also talk about, is preventing frailty. But what do you call the patient that you want to prevent frailty on? When we say 'pre-frail,' we're saying they're not yet frail, but then they don't even want to consider the word 'frail' because they don't feel that they're anywhere near it. That's the dilemma, and I don't think we've come up with anything quite right yet'. (personal communication, 8 August 2017)

Thus, there was no ideal term the Training Fellowship could use. Pre-frail, the term they settled on, does not quite align with the literature's use of that word, and the target population did not perceive the term favourably. Given such imperfections, why did the fellowship use it? The Site Director explained it had utility in the clinic.

We settled on 'pre-frail seniors with chronic conditions' because that described the population we were most accurately trying to achieve and where we further gave clinicians additional criteria, saying that 'What you're really looking for are seniors 65 to 85 with chronic health conditions who you suspect from your assessment land between 3 and 5 on the Clinical Frailty Scale […] (personal communication, 12 May 2017)

That is, the term pre-frail was close enough to the literature that it guided physicians to identify candidates for the Seniors Programme successfully, yet flexible enough to allow them to exercise their discretion within guidelines provided by the Training Fellowship when enrolling patients.

In Table 10.4, I summarize the elements of defining the target patient population and link them to relevant structures of values, rationality, and power. Figure 10.4 presents my visual representation of a critical realist perspective of this process. Figure 10.4(a) shows the process whereby the Training Fellowship

Table 10.4. Elements of Defining the Target Patient Population and Their Relation to Values, Rationality, and Power.

Elements of the Developing Terminology	Relevant Structures of Values, Rationality, and Power
Initially considered many different terms	*Power*: Defining rationality
Inconsistent use of the term in healthcare communities	*Power*: Reproduction of power relations; defining rationality (had not been done across communities)
The Training Fellowship assumed responsibility for choosing terminology	*Values*: User democracy *Power*: Power in the organization, reproduction of power relations, defining rationality
Identified candidate terms through researching literature and expert opinion	*Values*: Effectiveness (learning what's achievable with different populations) *Rationality*: Technocratic *Power*: Defining rationality
Spoke with target population to learn what terminology they preferred	*Values*: User orientation, dialogue *Rationality*: Contextual *Power*: Defining rationality, produce power relations
Chose the term 'pre-frail seniors with chronic conditions'	*Values*: Public interest, user orientation (clinician > patient), effectiveness *Rationality*: Technocratic, contextual, emotions, body *Power*: Defining rationality, production of power relations, reproduction of power relations (terminology chosen for clinician use)

established the need and assigned responsibility for the act of defining rationality by naming the population the Seniors Programme targeted. Naming the target population was important, for without an appropriate identifier, clinicians would be unable to recruit appropriate seniors to the programme. The inconsistent use of terms among healthcare communities suggested current power structures within those communities lacked enough strength or will that enabled them to formalize the naming of different senior categories. Consequently, the Training Fellowship experienced discomfort with the array of names for their target population. Over time, it became clear that no ideal name existed for their target population, and so, someone would have to create it for the Seniors

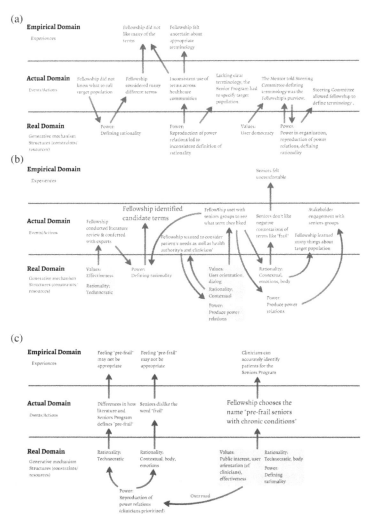

Figure 10.4(a–c). A Critical Realist Perspective of the Elements of Defining the Target Patient Population. (a) Establishing the Need and Responsibility for Defining the Target Patient Population. (b) Identifying Candidate Terms to Define the Target Patient Population. (c) Selecting the Term Used to Define the Target Patient Population.

Programme. The Mentor, driven by the value of user democracy, exercised her power within the organization to establish with the Steering Committee the right and responsibility of the Training Fellowship to define the target population.

Figure 10.4(b) visualizes the fellowship's process of defining the target population. Driven by values of effectiveness, underwritten by technocratic rationality, the fellowship first reviewed the literature and expert opinion to gain an understanding of ways to categorize seniors. The fellowship, however, did not feel this was adequate. Values of user orientation and dialogue, fuelled by a desire to gain contextual rationality of the seniors' community, led the fellowship to meet with seniors' groups to learn what terms they preferred. This act also produced new power relations with this important stakeholder group. The fellowship wanted to develop a programme that would honour the needs of the patient at an equal level as those of the health authority and clinicians, and meeting with seniors' groups was a means to establishing this. Moreover, the fellowship used these meetings as a means of stakeholder engagement where they not only informed seniors about the development of this programme but learned about the wishes of these seniors, too. Through these meetings, seniors expressed contextual, body, and emotional rationalities – they disliked terms such as 'frail' or 'seniors', for they did not feel they were frail, and they disliked the negative connotations associated with those words. Seniors' preferences set up a conflict with technocratic rationality, for the terms defined in the literature relied on the words 'frail' and 'seniors'.

Figure 10.4(c) visualizes how the fellowship resolved this conflict. The name of the target population the fellowship selected was 'pre-frail seniors with chronic conditions'. Members of the fellowship acknowledged this name was not ideal. It violated technocratic rationality, for the way the literature defines 'pre-frail' differed slightly from how the Seniors Programme used it. It violated the contextual, body, and emotional rationality of the seniors' groups, as the name included both the words 'frail' and 'seniors'. It provided clinical utility, however, which satisfied values of public interest, effectiveness, and user orientation (with clinicians defined as the users). It possessed technocratic rationality, as the fellowship derived 'pre-frail' from the literature, but it gave physicians leeway to exercise their body rationality – that is, it allowed clinicians to exercise their judgement when evaluating candidates for the Seniors Programme.

When selecting the official name, the fellowship chose to preference the needs of clinicians over the literature and seniors. Between the literature and seniors, the fellowship seemed to prefer the literature, for the elements within the chosen name were derived from the literature, even if they do not align perfectly. The name, however, possessed terms seniors explicitly disliked. Members of the fellowship acknowledged this was not ideal, but that discomfort did not translate into action. Though the fellowship may have wanted a solution that met the needs of the patient, health authority, and clinicians, when it came to choosing a name for the target population, the fellowship subordinated patient's desires.

Was this a bad thing? The fellowship selected a name that would guide clinicians to select appropriate seniors into the programme. The fellowship believed that the intervention they were developing would, if applied to appropriate patients, improve health. They chose to preference the clinicians due to their values of public interest and effectiveness. Though seniors may dislike words like 'frail' or 'seniors', there were no other terms that had meaning to the clinicians tasked with recruiting patients for the programme. Thus, the fellowship made seniors' desires subordinate to the needs of clinicians. I now turn to an exploration of the Training Fellowship's development of their vision statement.

10.4.2.   *Defining Rationality II: The Vision Statement − Defining Rationality to Drive Action*

Age well, die fit. This is the vision statement the Training Fellowship developed. Several interviewees found it contentious and jarring and, thus, deeply disliked it. The purpose of a vision statement is to summarize a programme's intention. The Seniors Programme intended to demonstrate that seniors could slow, if not reverse, the progression of frailty through lifestyle choices. This idea is contrary to our view of ageing and frailty. Our society and medical establishment view frailty and senescence as inevitable components of the body's decline towards death. The MD Lead explained.

> I, up to that point, hadn't really thought about assessing anybody for frailty. When we talked about frailty, we just thought of people when they came frail already. I would think, 'Oh, this person's going to land up in the hospital one day soon,' and didn't think about 'What can we do to prevent this person from getting more frail?' or 'Could we have done anything about this person earlier on?' (personal communication, 8 August 2017)

Despite its provocative nature, I will show that several members of the fellowship believed the vision statement did capture the intent of the Seniors Programme. The jarring nature of the vision statement made it a powerful tool that the Training Fellowship used to redefine rationality in seniors' minds. This new rationality then led seniors to adopt lifestyle changes that the fellowship's earlier literature review suggested could slow or reverse frailty's advance. Quoting from my interviewees, I will show why the Training Fellowship developed this vision statement, their source of discomfort with it, and why, despite this discomfort, the fellowship ultimately accepted it. I will then show how the Training Fellowship used this vision in conjunction with an anecdotal story of a uniquely healthy senior to change attitudes towards frailty and ageing.

The Mentor played a role in focusing the fellowship's attention on the development of its vision statement. She explained her rationale for this as follows.

> [...] [W]hen we started to talk about vision, the team was really like, 'Well, we just want to jump in and get the work done.' But it was 'We need to know where we're going and we need to understand what it is that we're working towards or what is it that we're trying to accomplish.' By going through that process and landing on 'Age well, die fit,' it really solidified what it is that we're trying to accomplish − not necessarily trying to help people to live longer, we're trying to help the seniors to live the life that they want to live. That came from what we heard from people. (Mentor, personal communication, 19 May 2017)

The vision statement was controversial due to its reference to dying. The Mentor explained.

> [...] It was not a vision that everybody was necessarily really comfortable with. I think everybody on the team bought into the vision, but there was a little bit of concern of 'Age well, die fit'? So we're talking about dying, and in healthcare, we're not comfortable in talking about people dying. Which seems kind of odd, but the individuals, the seniors, said that they were okay. (personal communication, 19 May 2017)

In addition to discomfort among members of the Training Fellowship, executive leadership within the BC Health Authority expressed reservation.

> [...] [E]ven with [CEO1], he was like, 'Oh, you're going to say 'Age well, die fit'?' and it was like, 'Yeah, that's what we were going to use,' and he was like, 'Oh, okay.' But the VPs were like, 'Are you really sure you want to use that term? Because that actually might be a turnoff'. (Mentor, personal communication, 19 May 2017)

Whereas the Mentor implied patients accepted the vision, the MD Lead and Site Director presented alternate views. The MD Lead said, '[...] nobody wants to talk about dying either. You know? 'Dying fit' is a bit of a jolt, and so people don't like that [...]' (MD Lead, personal communication, 8 August 2017). The Site Director further explained.

> Moving forward, I would actually like to move away, because they may find it jarring for the professional and for [...] We're trying to raise awareness in academic communities and in physicians, and they may respond to it. But I'll tell you who does find it offensive, is when I'm working with patients, they don't like that [...] I don't think you and I would want to be sitting with someone who said, 'Let's age well and die fit.' I mean it's not particularity sensitive or culturally sensitive. I mean many cultures do not find that [...] Having said that, what I'd like to do moving forward is maybe change that to 'Age well and avoid frailty.' Something that is more sensitive and is more culturally appropriate across multiple cultures. So 'Age well, die fit,' yeah, that had its place and time. But moving forward and being more patient-centred and now spending more time with seniors, they respond generally more favourably to something that's a little bit more sensitive, culturally appropriate, and is positive. Many people don't like to reflect on death. (personal communication, 12 May 2017)

Given these reservations, what was the rationale for choosing the vision? To explain this, I first need to introduce Olga Kotelko. Her story was emblematic of what the Seniors Programme was developed to accomplish, and the Training Fellowship used the vision statement in conjunction with Olga's story to define rationality. The book *What Makes Olga Run?* (Grierson, 2014) summarizes Olga's story. Briefly, Olga started competing in track and field at the age of 77. By the time she entered her 90s, she had competed globally and broken numerous world records. Her physical and mental capabilities were far beyond what our society attributed to those of advanced old age. The Mentor explained the relation between Olga and the vision statement.

> Through this process, I went to a lot of seniors' things on the weekends and even during the weekdays too, but there was one lady that was a [...] Senior Olympic athlete. She had won, I don't know, like hundreds of medals in track and field. I went to a book signing that she had. She had wrote a book that was [*What Makes Olga Run*] [...] We went to that book signing, and she was a very vibrant person and she talked about she had still lots of things that she wanted to do. But what she really wanted in life was that she wanted to be active and doing the things that she was currently doing until she died. She did not want to be in a residential care bed, she did not want to be housebound, and that's what we heard from all of the seniors. And a week after that book signing – she was very active and everything that day – a week afterwards she actually took a stroke and she died two days later. So she actually did age well and she died fit. She was actually fit when she died. She could walk, she could run, she could jump, she could do all of the things that she wanted to do. She kept herself fit until her body said, 'You know what? You're done. You're wore out.' And we actually learned from the research as well that that's actually quite possible. We think that as we get older, we think that our body breaks down and our muscles and things break down, but there's a lot of things that we can do to keep ourself active and well while our body ages [...] (personal communication, 19 May 2017)

The Head Coach further explained how she used Olga's story to counter patients' discomfort with the vision statement.

> Then I've had a couple of smarties say to me, 'Well, if I'm going to die, why do I have to die fit?' And I say, 'Well [...]' and I would use the example of Olga from West Vancouver [...] Two Decembers ago, she died at age ninety-four, and she literally I would say died with her boots on. She was just back from Budapest competing in the track and field. She has won more gold medals in her age group than anybody else. Because she was so fit and did such good stuff, she was studied at McGill University to see if she had some super cell or some super

something, and she was studied at UBC. I think she was also studied at Stanford. She was just an ordinary woman with nothing else. Nothing. So she came back from Budapest from her track and field. Two days after that, she had a stroke, and a day after that she died. She literally died fit. So when I use the [Seniors Programme] mission, people, they get [...] as I said, it's very provocative, then I would go into sort of all that [...] (personal communication, 4 August 2017)

So, despite its provocative nature, the vision statement accurately reflected what the Seniors Programme was designed to achieve, and Olga's story became a striking exemplar that you could age well and die fit. The MD Lead justified the selection of the vision statement by linking the anecdotal story of Olga with the research in the field.

Yeah. We liked [the vision statement] in the beginning because we were actually looking at senior Olga somebody-or-other who was an athlete and she was ninety-some years old. She died and she was obviously fit. [...] So dying fit is possible. You don't have to live your life into frailty and then die. We know with data recently that people are living longer, but now a good number of years of that longer lifespan is spent in frailty, and so people assume that they get frail as they get older. 'Dying fit' reminds you that you don't have to get frail before you die. (personal communication, 8 August 2017)

Despite reservations, the Site Director noted that the Foundation liked the vision statement. '[...] [T]hey thought it was jarring, it really sent a very strong message' (Site Director, personal communication, 12 May 2017). I asked her to explain why they liked it.

[...] They just felt that there's so much happening out there for research or innovation, they just felt that you needed something that was a little bit grabbing if you really wanted to get people's attention. (Site Director, personal communication, 12 May 2017)

Though this was only a brief comment, it suggested that during this stage of the Seniors Programme's life, the Foundation felt getting the attention of those with interest in ongoing research in the field was important enough to risk offending seniors.

Turning back to the target patient population, the MD Lead further explained that during the implementation of the Seniors Programme, the vision's provocative nature would get seniors' attention and make them curious to learn more.

> [...] I think it's a strong statement and it's okay in certain audiences, and it's okay as something to sort of draw your eyes to. But then it kind of compels you to go on and read about what we mean by that. (MD Lead, personal communication, 8 August 2017)

The Head Coach provided details on how this worked in practice.

> I think [the vision statement is] a very provocative one. I think it gets people's attention because I know when I used to repeat it, it would 'Ooh. Yes. Well, ooh.' [...] Yeah, they were shocked. But then after I related this with Olga, then they thought, 'Oh yeah, that makes sense,' because then they started thinking, 'Well, there's nothing worse than being put in a corner in some care facility waiting for someone to come and give you a cup of tea.' So they started looking at the contrast of how that could be beneficial to actually die fit, if at all possible. Some would say, 'Well, I have so many joint pains, I don't see that can happen,' and then we'd go into concept where they talk about how physical activity, the research shows that it reduces inflammation. (personal communication, 4 August 2017)

Table 10.5 presents my summary of the elements of the vision statement and links them to relevant structures of values, rationality, and power. Figure 10.5 presents a critical realist perspective of this process. In Figure 10.5(a), I show the process whereby the Training Fellowship began developing the vision statement. The Mentor, driven by the generative mechanism of defining rationality, felt the need to have the vision to guide the Training Fellowship's activities. For their part, the generative mechanism of effectiveness motivated the Training Fellowship to focus on the developing the Senior Programme rather than pay attention to the vision. That notwithstanding, the Mentor was able to effectively exercise her power within the fellowship to focus the team on creating a vision. The Mentor did not (or could not?) impose a vision. Instead, drawing from generative structures of the values dialogue, public interest, and user orientation, along with the rationality of collective reasoning, the fellowship began developing their vision as a team and met with seniors' groups for their input. The fellowship learned seniors experienced a desire to die fit during these meetings. Through this process, the vision 'Age well, die fit' formed.

In Figure 10.5(b), I present the perceptions of this vision statement among the Training Fellowship. The vision statement referenced death, which triggered several generative mechanisms for the Training Fellowship that led some members to dislike it. These generative mechanisms included values of user orientation – the fellowship believed seniors felt uncomfortable speaking of death. The vision also violated several forms of rationality: institutional rationality (healthcare systems do not help people to die), contextual (speaking of death offended cultural sensitivities of patient groups), and emotions (people felt fear

Table 10.5. Elements of the Vision Statement and Their Relation to Values, Rationality, and Power.

Elements of the Vision Statement	Relevant Structures of Values, Rationality, and Power
Current attitudes towards frailty	*Rationality*: Body
	Power: Domination, defining rationality (historical power relations, reproduction of power relations)
Choosing a vision statement that solidified what the Seniors Programme was trying to accomplish	*Values*: Dialog, effectiveness, public interest, user orientation
	Rationality: Collective reasoning
	Power: Defining rationality, reproduction of power relations
Discomfort including dying in the vision statement	*Values*: User orientation
	Rationality: Institutional, contextual (cultural), emotions
	Power: Maintaining stability, reproduction of power relations, ignoring rationality (no one wants to talk about death), conflict (statement may turn people off)
The Foundation liked the vision statement's ability to grab researchers' attention	*Values*: Competitiveness
	Power: Production of power relations
Olga's story	*Values*: Public interest, user orientation
	Rationality: Body, situational (her ability linked to exercise), technocratic (Olga was studied)
	Power: Defining rationality
The vision statement plus Olga story draw patients in to learn more about the Senior Programme	*Values*: User orientation, effectiveness
	Rationality: Contextual, emotional, body (I cannot do this), technocratic (yes you can)
	Power: Defining rationality, conflict

and discomfort talking about dying). The current power structures in healthcare ignore rationality — that is, they do not talk about patients dying, even though that is the eventual fate of all people the healthcare system serves. With the phrase 'die fit', the Training Fellowship engaged in a tactic of conflict. They directly confronted patients and healthcare workers with the idea that seniors will

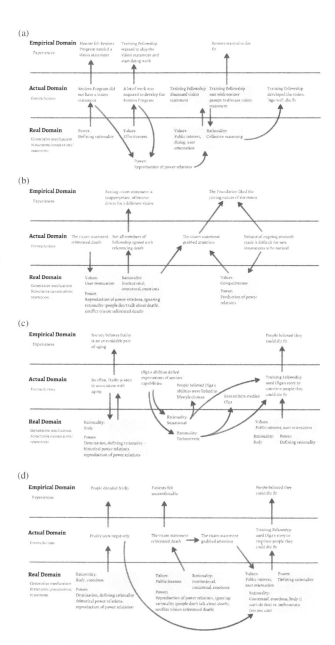

Figure 10.5(a–d). A Critical Realist Perspective of the Elements of the Vision Statement. (a) Developing the Vision Statement. (b) Mixed Reviews of the Vision Statement. (c) How Olga's Story Defied People's Perception of Ageing and Frailty. (d) Using the Vision Statement and Olga's Story to Redefine Rationality.

die, and that the fellowship's goal was not to prevent that, but rather to allow them to 'die fit'.

In Figure 10.5(b), I also show the Foundation had a different reaction to the vision statement. They liked it. Because of the taboos it violated, the vision statement grabbed the attention of listeners. Rather than concern over what seniors felt about the vision, the Foundation focused instead on other researchers. A large volume of ongoing studies bombarded researchers. The Foundation, driven by the values of competitiveness and the desire to produce power relations with these researchers, wanted the research community to notice the Seniors Programme. The jarring nature of the vision statement made it a useful tool for this aim.

Despite reservations of some fellowship members, the team adopted the vision statement. Part of the reason may have been to get the attention of other researchers. I, however, also believe the team accepted it because the jarring nature of the vision made it a powerful tool in redefining well-entrenched rationality surrounding ageing and frailty. For the Seniors Programme to have an effect, it needed to redefine how we age in the minds of healthcare workers and patients. In Figure 10.5(c) and (d), I show how the fellowship achieved this redefinition using the vision statement in conjunction with Olga's story.

Figure 10.5(c) shows my representation of society's current views on ageing and frailty and how Olga's story challenged those views. In the actual domain, we see frailty associated with old age. This creates structures that constrained our understanding of ageing. It fed body rationality — we see frailty advance in others (and ourselves) in lockstep with age — leading to the conclusion that the two are linked. It also generated several power structures. This body rationality defined rationality that, over time, became dominating. People saw frailty as inevitable. Members of society, including the healthcare community, continually reproduced this understanding. Consequently, healthcare systems made little effort to prevent frailty, which resulted in seniors continued descent into frailty. Thus, society experienced frailty as an unavoidable component of ageing.

Olga's story, however, contradicted this. The Training Fellowship, perhaps influenced by their research of the literature, exhibited situational rationality in the real domain whereby they attributed Olga's exceptional capabilities to her lifestyle choices. Enabled through structures of technocratic rationality, researchers in the field studied Olga to assess the source of her abilities. These two forms of rationality enabled the fellowship to tell Olga's story to seniors to convince them that they might delay, if not prevent frailty. Body rationality and the values of public interest and user orientation enabled this process as coaches worked with seniors to uncover their physical capacities. Through this effort, the fellowship defined rationality where seniors came to believe that frailty was not inevitable and that they could, indeed, die fit.

In Figure 10.5(d), I bring all these ideas together. Through the structures I have described previously, people saw frailty as inevitable and negative — people dreaded it. Due to the underlying structures of values, rationality, and power, the vision statement was jarring. Even though its reference to death made patients uncomfortable, it grabbed the attention. Once the fellowship had that attention, it related the Olga story, which, as described above, redefined rationality so that patients believed they could avoid frailty and die fit. With seniors' new understanding, coaches then worked with them to implement frailty-preventing lifestyle changes.

In this chapter, I discussed the fellowship's approach to preliminary research where they blended technocratic and contextual rationalities. I discussed the challenge they had in reconciling the differences between the two healthcare regions when designing the programme. That is, technocratic and contextual rationalities conflicted and needed resolution. I also discussed how the BC working group chose the BC Coaching Organization to implement coaching of seniors. Technocratic rationality was an important factor here, but we see again other rationalities conflicting with it. I then concluded with a description of two acts of defining rationality: naming the target population and developing a vision statement. In both of those examples, we again see different rationalities conflict.

This blending and tension between rationalities is the dominant theme I want to draw out of this chapter. In some instances, this blending gave insights into how to drive action, such as learning from seniors that running the Seniors Programme through physician offices would increase participation rates. In other instances, tensions led to compromises, such as modifying the Seniors Programme to allow for differences in implementation between BC and NS. These are essential considerations in the development of organizational wisdom, and I will return to discuss them in more detail later. For now, I will focus on how individuals reified power during the life of the Seniors Programme in the next chapter.

Chapter 11

Reifying Power

My discussion with the Head Coach surfaced several means through which the BC working group turned the idea of the Seniors Programme into reality, highlighting how actors reified power structures. These structures included shared values that led to production of power relations. Additionally, several individuals enacted forms of bureaucratic rationality that guided the actions of coaches, including goal setting, establishing clear processes, and coordination. These structures also permitted coaches to exercise contextual and body rationalities, demonstrated through the empowerment of coaches to modify the programme to the needs of the senior. Other structures centred around acts of communication between stakeholders. Finally, the BC working group enacted structures of power to shield coaches from the politics within the BC Health Authority, allowing coaches to focus on the work at hand. I will start this analysis with an exploration of the impact of shared values. Following my presentation of these results, I will present a critical realist summary of how individuals reified power.

11.1.   Shared Values as a Basis for Producing Power Relations

One thing that came across in my interviews with the Head Coach was her respect for members of the Training Fellowship with whom she interacted. This respect derived from shared values. For example, this is her assessment of the MD Lead.

> [...] I think [the MD Lead's] head is in the right direction. I really do. I really respect her. Her role and her goal was to keep people out of hospitals, which for a doctor that's pretty weird. Fortunately I understand it because my own personal doctor just around the corner is pretty well the same thing – 'If you don't have to go there, don't go there.' But [the MD Lead's] idea was really connecting, working with community programs to keep people healthy [...] (Head Coach, personal communication, 4 August 2017).

In addition to this personal connection, the Seniors Programme also aligned with the Head Coach's values. '[...] That for me was the exciting thing about this programme because I believe in prevention. You know, I was about to say, "An ounce of prevention is worth a pound of cure" or something along those lines' (Head Coach, personal communication, 4 August 2017). This value-alignment motivated the Head Coach to go beyond the mere requirements of the job to ensure the success of the programme. For example,

> [...] one of the things that I did with the [BC Coaching Organization] [...] I would do the odd education session for the participants as well. We'd bring them all together and we would talk about maybe the same thing, motivation, how physical activity affects the brain, those kind of things. Those were the kinds of extras that they got so that they can see 'Yeah, this is important, and I'm doing it because I need to do it, not because the doctor tells me to do it.' (Head Coach, personal communication, 4 August 2017)

The Head Coach also described the motivation of the coaches they recruited. '[...] [O]ver the province there were about 500 coaches all in total. I think because the people that came forward were invested in physical activity themselves, they understand it, they believed in it [...]' (Head Coach, personal communication, 4 August 2017). Across the board, from the BC working group to Seniors Programme to Head Coach to other coaches, values aligned, motivating action and producing supportive relations.

In Table 11.1, I summarize the elements of implementing the Seniors Programme and link them to relevant structures of values, rationality, and power. In Figure 11.1, I show that in the real domain the Head Coach and MD Lead shared values of dialogue and public interest, which manifested as a desire to connect with communities to keep people healthy and out of the hospital. The Training Fellowship founded the Seniors Programme to implement these same values. These shared values served as the basis to produce power relations – they facilitated the Head Coach's engagement with the Senior Programme and attracted coaches who possessed unique body rationality through their

Table 11.1. Elements of the Motivational Capacity of Shared Values and Their Relation to Values, Rationality, and Power.

Elements of Implementing the Seniors Programme	Relevant Structures of Values, Rationality, and Power
Shared values	*Values*: Public interest, dialogue
	Power: Production of power relations
Motivated workers	*Values*: Public interest, dialogue
	Rationality: Body (coaches had a relationship with physical activity), bureaucratic (processes, procedures and roles)
	Power: Defining rationality, reproduction of power relations

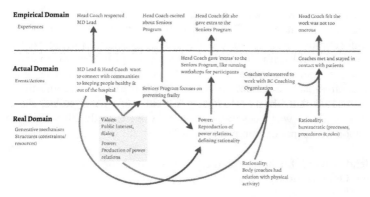

Figure 11.1.   A Critical Realist Perspective of the Motivational Capacity of Shared Values.

relationship with physical activity to the BC Coaching Organization. The Head Coach reproduced power relations to exercise her ability to define rationality by running workshops for seniors participating in the programme. These activities were outside the scope of the Seniors Programme, and thus the Head Coach considered them 'extras'. Through combinations of these structures and events, the Head Coach respected the MD Lead, was excited about working on the Senior Programme, and felt she gave extra to the programme. Combined, I believe this created a community of coaches within the BC Coaching Organization that were motivated to do the work of the Seniors Programme.

11.2.   Reifying Power through Bureaucratic Rationality

Beyond shared values building a relationship of respect and attracting motivated coaches, the BC Coaching Organization had specific goals that gave the Head Coach direction.

> Well [...] Because of course the funding also came from the Ministry of Health, and I think my numbers were supposed to be about forty per month, forty coaches/participants combined a month in around. (Head Coach, personal communication, 4 August 2017)

The Head Coach seemed to enjoy working with the BC working group. As the following quotes demonstrate, she derived part of this pleasure from the clarity in processes and coordination with the Training Fellowship.

> Actually, working with [the Site Director] and [the MD Lead] and all the parties involved from the [BC Health Authority] side was absolutely wonderful. It was great. It's something I would do

again. They were clear where they wanted to go, they were clear on the measurements [...]They were available. The transfer of information was very smooth. As I said, I work from home, so all of the referrals came to my email at home [...] My role was to contact new patients within 24 hours of receiving that email. They got the email, so the patient knew exactly when I called, because they were told that [the Head Coach] will call. So when I called, they knew who I was, they were clear, they were ready, they understood. (personal communication, 4 August 2017)

The Head Coach further explained the internal processes within the BC Coaching Organization.

[...] The program was a two-pronged system. I would train coaches [...] After I've matched a coach with a participant, they told them would meet in person and the coach will help that person to design their physical activity goals one week at a time. Then the coach would call the person once a week, they would arrange at what time and place, and the coach would say, 'How did you make out with your goals? Were you able to obtain your goals?' If they'd had, then, of course, they will just set the goals for the next week. If they hadn't, then they would do problem-solving. (personal communication, 4 August 2017)

The above quotes highlighted the importance of clarity in procedure and communication creating a pleasurable work environment.

In Table 11.2 (page 151), I summarize the elements of implementing the Seniors Programme and link them to relevant structures of values, rationality, and power. In Figure 11.2(a) (page 152), I show the critical role of bureaucratic rationality in implementing the Seniors Programme. For example, the Ministry of Health, driven by values of effectiveness, reproduced power relations through its funding of the BC Coaching Organization and used that to exercise power over the organization. It used that power to establish a structure of bureaucratic rationality – it created a target of forty coaches trained per month. This target was specific and measurable, and, according to the Head Coach, achievable, and it gave the BC Coaching Organization a clear understanding of what it must do to maintain its funding. Similarly, the Head Coach found working with the BC working group 'wonderful,' and this experience traced back to structures of bureaucratic rationality. In the real domain, driven by values of dialogue and effectiveness, the Training Fellowship reproduced its power relations and defined rationality with the BC Coaching Organization to establish structures of bureaucratic rationality, including clear lines of communication, smooth transfer of information, and ensuring participating seniors knew what to expect from the Head Coach.

In Figure 11.2(b), I continue my representation of bureaucratic rationality's role in implementing the Seniors Programme. Motivated by values of

Table 11.2. Elements of Reifying Power through Bureaucratic Rationality and
Their Relation to Values, Rationality, and Power.

Elements of Implementing the Seniors Programme	Relevant Structures of Values, Rationality, and Power
Goal setting	*Values*: Effectiveness
	Rationality: Bureaucratic (procedures and roles)
	Power: Reproduction of power relations, power over organizations
Clear processes and communication (between BC Coaching Organization and BC Health Authority)	*Values*: Dialog, effectiveness
	Rationality: Bureaucratic (processes, procedures and roles)
	Power: Reproduction of power relations, defining rationality
Clear processes and communication (within BC Coaching Organization)	*Values*: Dialog, user orientation, accountability, effectiveness, sustainability
	Rationality: Bureaucratic (procedures and roles), body
	Power: Defining rationality, reproduction of power relations, production of power relations

dialogue and effectiveness, the Head Coach reproduced power relations to
define bureaucratic rationality for patients as she oriented them to the programme. Through this process, the Head Coach produced power relations
between the patient and the Seniors Programme. Likewise, the Head Coach
also trained new coaches in the BC Coaching Organization. Bureaucratic
rationality guided the interaction between coaches and patients. The values
of dialogue and user orientation led coaches to produce and reproduce power
relations with their patients as they applied body rationality to develop individualized physical activity programmes. Motivated by values of accountability and effectiveness, coaches applied bureaucratic rationality to establish
goals with their patients and would then check in with them regularly to
monitor and adapt those goals. The value of sustainability combined with
bureaucratic rationality to establish the frequency with which coaches
checked in with their patients, and this frequency decreased over time to
avoid the patient's dependency on their coach. In sum, the BC working group
and BC Coaching Organization applied bureaucratic rationality effectively,
resulting in a pleasurable work environment where processes flowed
smoothly. It was through bureaucratic rationality that individuals channelled
power to create desired action.

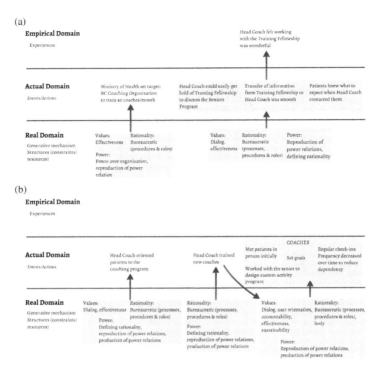

Figure 11.2(a–b). A Critical Realist Perspective of Reifying Power through Bureaucratic Rationality. (a) Clarity of Goals, Procedures, and Flow of Information. (b) Processes within the BC Coaching Organization.

11.3. Empowerment – Letting Contextual and Body Rationalities Rise

Though the Head Coach identified the clarity of processes as a reason she enjoyed working with the BC working group, these processes did not stifle personal discretion. For example, the Seniors Programme empowered the Head Coach, allowing her to use her discretion in achieving the aims of the programme. As she explained,

> [...] For one thing, as you know, the training manual came from Stanford [...] I adapted it because Stanford is in the United States. We're talking a program for British Columbians where it snows, nine months of the year or rains or some such thing, so we had to adapt some of the exercises that they were recommending and how they were recommending it. I think one of the things was, and I always remember this, 'If you have the flu, you can still go out and exercise.' Well, if it's 40 below, no way in God's green earth anybody's going to go, and I wouldn't be so stupid as

to recommend that to people. Those are the kind of things, and I would go, and I would say, 'Okay, fine. If you have the flu today, don't beat yourself up. Work with it. I mean have your tea, do whatever you need to do to make you feel good, knowing that you are going to get back to exercise at some point.' You put that future build into, not 'Go out and get pneumonia and fall over in the snow, don't find you till spring.' [laughs] So those were some of the things. Also, the ads, I created the ads myself where I put it in the paper to get people. Any flyers that I had to do. The additional education pieces, all of the education pieces like physical activity in the brain and how it works, motivation, all of that was my creation. (Head Coach, personal communication, 4 August 2017)

I asked if the BC working group required the Head Coach to submit the ads and educational materials she developed for their review and approval

No. I was fortunate. I think they knew [...] I've been a facilitator for over years and I've run groups and I've prepared workshops, and I was very blessed they actually didn't have to [...]. (personal communication, 4 August 2017)

In addition to the Head Coach's empowerment, the Head Coach, in turn, empowered the coaches she paired with patients.

[...] [W]hat I told the participants, the coaches, 'I leave it up to. I'll let you have your personal understanding of your participant, because I'm [no] longer there. If it looks like the person needs you to call them every week coming up to the second month, do so. (personal communication, 4 August 2017)

Moreover, the Head Coach empowered the coaches to work with participating seniors to develop customized physical activity programmes for the patient.

The other one was yes, the coach and the participant sat down and designed a program that the participant wants. The coach did not walk in and say, 'Well, you know, I think you should be swimming' or 'I think you should be walking 30 minutes a day.' Because this is what the recommendation is, but if you haven't walked or moved in months and you have a joint pain here and a joint pain there, walking 30 minutes a day is not going to get you where you're going. It's going to get you in the hospital.' So we encourage people to say, 'Look. Walk five minutes. And think about it. When you leave home and walk for five minutes, you still have to get back, so you've already got 10 minutes down. So monitor yourself, self-manage, and build yourself up'. (Head Coach, personal communication, 4 August 2017)

Notice in the above quotes that through empowering the coaches, the BC working group allowed coaches to apply their own contextual and body rationalities to the situation. They modified the Stanford model to account for climate differences (contextual rationality). They also allowed coaches to design individualized physical activity plans in conjunction with their participants (body rationality). This blending of rationalities is a theme we have encountered before during the development of the Seniors Programme. Later, I will discuss this in more depth.

In Table 11.3, I summarize the elements of implementing the Seniors Programme and link them to relevant structures of values, rationality, and power. Figure 11.3 shows my representation of how coaches exercised their empowerment. In the actual domain, I show the Head Coach had 30 years of experience, which led the BC working group to trust her judgement. Consequently, they allowed the Head Coach to exercise her power to define bureaucratic rationality through the creation of ads and educational materials. Likewise, the BC working group allowed the Head Coach to similarly exercise

Table 11.3. Elements of Empowerment and Their Relation to Values, Rationality, and Power.

Elements of Implementing the Seniors Programme	Relevant Structures of Values, Rationality, and Power
Empowerment	*Values*: Effectiveness, public interest, user orientation
	Rationality: Bureaucratic (documentation, processes, procedures and roles), contextual, body technocratic
	Power: Reproduction of power relations, defining rationality

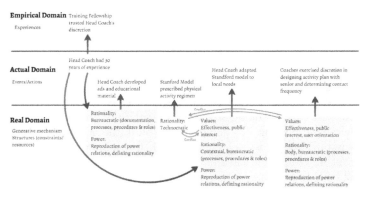

Figure 11.3.   A Critical Realist Perspective of Empowerment.

her power to define rationality by applying her contextual rationality to the Stanford Model that prescribed physical activities for seniors. The Head Coach felt that for the model to achieve the values of effectiveness and public interest, she had to modify it for the BC context. This act was also an exercise of bureaucratic rationality in that she was defining the processes, procedures, and roles of coaches in the Seniors Programme. Modifying the Stanford Model conflicted with the technocratic rationality that served as the model's foundation. Whereas technocratic rationality maintained there is a knowable best way to achieve an end, the Head Coach instead exercised contextual rationality to modify it to the environment. Likewise conflicting with technocratic rationality, the Head Coach empowered her coaches to individualize the physical activity plans for each of their patients. This empowerment gave coaches the power to define bureaucratic rationality with their patients. Values of effectiveness, public interest, and user orientation led the Head Coach to empower her coaches. Whereas the Head Coach's modification of the Stanford Model was a result of contextual rationality, here the coaches worked with patients to employ body rationality as they developed their activity programme. Once again, this was incongruent with technocratic rationality.

11.4. Building and Maintaining Power Structures through Communication

Once the coaches were actively working with patients, the Head Coach stayed in regular contact with them and expressed the sentiment that this was key to maintaining motivation. 'Then once a month I hosted teleconferencing conversations with coaches around the province. I think those were the kinds of activities that actually kept the coaches engaged' (Head Coach, personal communication, 4 August 2017). Additionally, the Head Coach further said:

> What I also did too, once a year I hosted [a BC Coaching Organization] conversation. What that meant was we brought coaches and participants together in a dialogue [...] What that dialogue served was an opportunity to say, 'Well, what's it like for you being part of this project? How is it working? What would you change? How is the training for you? How is the connection?' We had both coaches and participants giving feedback, and that was really, really good. That was very helpful [...] (personal communication, 4 August 2017)

In short, this open, consistent communication reinforced power structures that kept coaches motivated, as well as gathered contextual rationality from those coaches to strengthen the programme.

In Table 11.4, I summarize the elements of implementing the Seniors Programme and link them to relevant structures of values, rationality, and power. In Figure 11.4, I present how the Head Coach kept her coaches engaged.

Table 11.4. Elements of Communication and Their Relation to Values, Rationality, and Power.

Elements of Implementing the Seniors Programme	Relevant Structures of Values, Rationality, and Power
Communication	*Values*: Dialog, sustainability
	Rationality: Bureaucratic (procedures and roles), contextual
	Power: Reproduction of power relation, defining rationality

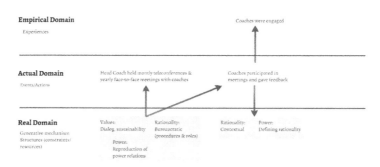

Figure 11.4. A Critical Realist Perspective of Communication.

The Head Coach acted on the generative mechanism of the values dialogue and sustainability to implement bureaucratic rationality manifesting as monthly teleconferences and annual face-to-face meetings. In these meetings, coaches gave feedback on how they perceived the programme was progressing, which was an act of defining contextual rationality for the Head Coach. These conversations also created the coaches' experience of engagement with the programme.

11.5. Shielding Workers from Political Turmoil

As the BC Health Authority underwent turnover at the CEO level, I asked whether the Head Coach felt any of this turmoil during the life of the Seniors Programme. Her replies suggested that the BC working group effectively shielded her from the politics of their organization, allowing her to focus on the work at hand (Head Coach, personal communication, 4 August 2017). Similarly, I asked the Head Coach if she perceived any of the resistance from the VPs within the BC Health Authority towards the Seniors Programme. She replied, 'So constantly working with [the MD Lead] and not with the whole administrative machinery, I was spared that' (Head Coach, personal communication, 4 August 2017).

The above responses suggested a clear separation between the politics of the BC Health Authority and the coaches implementing the Seniors Programme. In a similar vein, when I spoke with CEO1 about the creation of the Seniors Programme he discussed actions he took very early on to create an organizational structure separate from that of the BC Health Authority that focused on innovations.

> Well, the origins of the [Seniors Programme] came from the work of the institute, which if you go way back, the institute was created by myself and the chairman of the board at the time [...] We created an institute to look at stimulating innovation and reform in the health sector, and that was separate from our organization, separate from government, and had some independence. Over a period of months, we held some workshops and seminars. We really wanted to find out what intervention might have a significant impact on care of the elderly, and particularly preventing them ending up in hospital, which is an ever-present problem. (CEO1, personal communication, 6 June 2017)

In Table 11.5, I summarize the elements of implementing the Seniors Programme and link them to relevant structures of values, rationality, and power. In Figure 11.5, I present how managers protected aspects of the Seniors Programme from political turmoil. The BC working group exercised their power to enact bureaucratic rationality. They did this by creating procedures where the Head Coach only worked with the MD Lead. The MD Lead exercised her power to maintain stability for the Head Coach by keeping the political turmoil within the BC Health Authority as CEOs turned over separate from the Head Coach's sphere of activity. Likewise, before the Training Fellowship even existed, CEO1, driven by generative structures of the value innovation, exercised his power to create an institute separate from the BC Health Authority that could focus on healthcare innovation. Though he does not explicitly state why he created a separate institute for this, doing so would have insulated it from the

Table 11.5. Elements of Shielding Workers from Political Turmoil and Their Relation to Values, Rationality, and Power.

Elements of Implementing the Seniors Programme	Relevant Structures of Values, Rationality, and Power
Shielding from politics	*Values*: Innovation
	Rationality: Bureaucratic (procedures and roles)
	Power: Reproduction of power relations, maintain stability, production of power relations

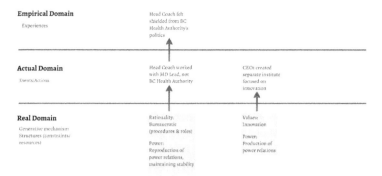

Figure 11.5.   A Critical Realist Perspective of Shielding Workers from Political Turmoil.

power structures active within the BC Health Authority. I believe this process shielded people from political turmoil, which allowed them to focus on the work at hand.

I want to pull out the following themes from the above analysis. First, we see here that alignment between the values of individuals with the programme attracted people to work with the Seniors Programme, thereby producing supportive power relations. It also motivated front-line workers to go above and beyond the requirements of their job. Second, it was through bureaucratic rationality that the BC working group reified power. That is, clarity in processes and communications led to the smooth implementation of the Seniors Programme. Third, we see the blending of rationalities again as bureaucratic structures allowed for the empowerment of coaches. Finally, several actors reified a power structure through the bureaucratic rationality of boundaries that shielded workers from the political turmoil the BC Health Authority experienced. These boundaries allowed individuals to focus on their jobs without distraction. This concludes my analysis of how individuals reified power during the life of the Seniors Programme. I now turn to assess the goal to spread the Seniors Programme nationally.

Chapter 12

Structures Constraining Spread

There is a significant value underpinning the Seniors Programme that I have thus far not addressed in detail: spread. Indeed, the Foundation's mission was to promote the spread of medical innovations across Canada ('[The Foundation] — What We Do', 2018). In this chapter, I explore whether other members of the Training Fellowship were as focused on spread as the Foundation, or if the Foundation was only a means for the BC Health Authority to collaborate with other organizations in an aim to create CEO1's 'forcefield of commitment' that I described in Chapter 9. I uncovered that spread was a fundamental value of many members of the Training Fellowship. I then analysed whether my interviewees felt the collaboration between the BC and NS health authorities was a success. Their response was nuanced. They thought it was of great benefit to seniors, but it was only spreading regionally within the BC Health Authority, rather than across Canada as hoped.

12.1. Was the Initial Goal to Spread the Seniors Programme?

Whereas the Foundation had a mandate to promote the pan-Canadian spread of healthcare innovations, members of the BC Health Authority were accountable to the region in which they worked in Metro Vancouver. Earlier, I explored the reasons the fellowship had for collaborating with the NS Health Authority. Here, I want to explore the importance of spread to members of the BC Health Authority involved in the Seniors Programme. Was the collaboration undertaken primarily to gain access to knowledge and resources that the fellowship could apply in their region, or was it the goal from the start to spread this innovation across Canada? I asked CEO1 as the original mover of this programme whether spread was an essential goal of his for the Seniors Programme.

> Oh, totally, totally. That's why we took this pan-Canadian approach, is that we wanted potentially other provinces to join in the analysis and the momentum of this research project. And choosing a coast-to-coast connection really gave that signal that we did want spread, and that's why we wanted to work with the [Foundation], to tap into their resources at the federal level. (CEO1, personal communication, 6 June 2017)

The Site Director concurred:

> They were always hopeful that we would maximize the return of investment in both the studying of it, the learning from it, but also the intention in creating it was to spread it in a pan-Canadian effort. (personal communication, 12 May 2017)

The above quotes demonstrated that CEO1 and the Site Director saw the intention for the programme to spread nationally. Others, however, were more focused on regional rather than national spread. For example, the Mentor explained:

> Oh, [spread] was always a focus. That was the conversation from day one. The idea with spread is we want to have something that's going to span across [the BC Health Authority]. And potentially something that could go provincially, but our focus being that I worked inside of [the BC Health Authority] was specific to [the BC Health Authority]. But if you were to look at something and to say, 'We're going to do this right across [the BC Health Authority],' the planning and the time that it would take to get to that level, just nothing would have ever happened. So the idea was, is that 'Okay, we're going to give ourselves a 14-month time period. We're going to do this level of work in 14 months. Then we're going to have these successes, because that'll help us to bring people along. And then we will look at rolling it out to a broader geographic region'. (personal communication, 19 May 2017)

The MD Lead also suggested CEO2 was more interested in spread within the region rather than nationally.

> [...] I think [CEO2] is interested in ensuring that we have this project spread through the region. He's more interested in having a [BC Health Authority] kind of base to this, but he's aware that there is great potential to spread this work and he's supportive of that. (personal communication, 8 August 2017)

The BC Health Authority was responsible for administering healthcare within its geographic region. Though we saw some individuals focused their attention within their territory, others were interested in national spread. Why would employees of the BC Health Authority care whether a programme they developed spread beyond its borders? Earlier, when discussing ways to bind an organization to the Seniors Programme, I presented a quote from CEO1 explaining his rationale for looking beyond his health authority. As a reminder, he said,

> I think any health authority who becomes insular and inward-looking is going to have problems. You need to have an inclusive

mind that allows you to consider what's happening not only in your province in other health authorities but in your neighbouring provinces like Alberta and others internationally. Bringing these differences just adds strength. It adds strength to the form and structure of potential innovation. (CEO1, personal communication, 6 June 2017)

Recall that the Senior Improvement Lead worked for the Foundation. Given its mandate to promote spread, the Senior Improvement Lead works with many health authorities. I asked her why any health authority, tasked by the province to administer healthcare in a specific region, would care enough about spreading innovations beyond their border to commit time and resources to the endeavour.

I'm not sure I could speak generally about health authorities, but when I reflect on our experience certainly working with [the BC Health Authority], I think they've been very open and quite excited to be considered leaders in certain areas and to be able to spread innovative practices to other areas across Canada. Not only with [the Seniors Programme] for example, but we have another initiative we're working with them [...] [The BC Health Authority] really has been seen a leader and is keen to spread those initiatives [...] I would say our experience has been quite often people are very keen to spread something that they know that's working, and that quite often it comes down to knowing that it is benefitting patients and residents and that the outcomes are so much better. People just get really excited about that. (Senior Improvement Lead, personal communication, 13 June 2017)

In Table 12.1 (page 162), I summarize the elements of the intention to spread the Seniors Programme and link them to relevant structures of values, rationality, and power. Figure 12.1 (page 163) presents a critical realist perspective of this process. Figure 12.1(a) shows my conceptualization of my interviewee's reason to spread the Seniors Programme. With CEO1, structures such as the value dialogue underpinned by the rationality of collective reasoning created a desire to learn from others that would occur through a spread initiative. These learnings activated other structures, such as the values of effectiveness and innovation, bureaucratic rationality, and the production of power relations to create what CEO1 called stronger structures of innovation. In the Site Director's response, I saw structures such as the value sustainability underpinned by economic rationality leading to the observation that spread was a means to increase an innovation's return on investment. In her response, she stated that not spreading was 'wasteful' (Site Director, personal communication, 12 May 2017). The response of the Senior Improvement Lead suggested structures of the value of public interest justified spread. Spreading innovations helped more patients as opposed to maintaining a regional base for an intervention. She also identified

Table 12.1. Elements of the Intention to Spread the Seniors Programme and
Their Relation to Values, Rationality, and Power.

Elements of the Intention to Spread	Relevant Structures of Values, Rationality, and Power
Reasons to spread	*Values*: Dialog, sustainability, public interest, effectiveness, innovation, regime dignity
	Rationality: Collective reasoning, economic, bureaucratic (processes)
	Power: Defining rationality
Different ways to approach spread: Pan-Canadian versus regional, all at once versus staged	*Values*: Spread, dialogue, accountability, openness, effectiveness, regime dignity
	Rationality: Economic, contextual, bureaucratic (processes, boundaries)
	Power: Reproduction of power relations, production of power relations, defining rationality, power through organizations

structures, including the value of regime dignity and the act of power to define
rationality created the desire in health authorities for others to see them as leaders
in the field. They see spread initiatives as a means to enhance their reputation.

In Figure 12.1(b), I compare the desire to spread nationally versus focusing
on spread within a localized health authority. Driven by values of dialogue and
spread, in addition to other structures described earlier, CEO1 envisioned pan-
Canadian spread of the Seniors Programme. Likewise, acts of power resulted in
the Foundation's mandate to spread healthcare innovations nationally, underpinned by values of spread, dialogue, and openness. This commonality of purpose led CEO1 and the Foundation to produce power relations creating the
collaboration between the BC Health Authority and the Foundation. Through
this collaboration, each organization could exercise power through the other to
fulfil its ambition of spread. For CEO1, this collaboration was also an act of
defining rationality because it communicated his intention to see the Seniors
Programme spread nationally.

CEO2 focused on different structures. The value of accountability, underwritten by the bureaucratic rationality of boundaries and empowered by historical
power relations, led CEO2 to focus on spread limited to the region to which he
was responsible. According to the MD Lead, CEO2 saw the potential for
national spread and provided some support for it. His focus, however, was in
the local boundary defined by the BC Health Authority. It was likely that these
same structures also acted on CEO1. He was, after all, CEO of the BC Health
Authority, and would have been responsible for administering healthcare within
that region. It would seem, however, that other values promoting national

(a)

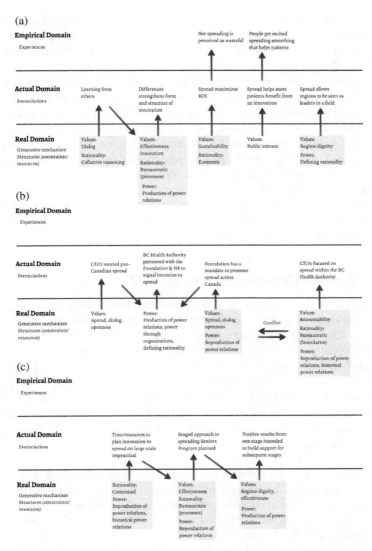

Figure 12.1(a−c). A Critical Realist Perspective of the Elements of the Intention to Spread the Seniors Programme. (a) Reasons to Spread Seniors Programme. (b) Pan-Canadian versus Regional Spread. (c) A Staged Approach to Spread.

spread were more strongly activated in him than in CEO2, leading to the difference in focus.

Figure 12.1(c) shows my representation of the Mentor's comments regarding taking a staged approach to spread. She exhibited contextual rationality of the power structures within the BC Health Authority when she stated that launching a new programme even region-wide would be a massive undertaking, let alone nationally. Driven by the value of effectiveness, she and the initial founders of the Seniors Programme exercised bureaucratic rationality to construct a staged process to implementing the Seniors Programme and then exercised their power to make that happen. The thinking behind this plan was the following. Positive results from initial stages would activate values of regime dignity and effectiveness in other stakeholders, allowing for the production of new power relations that would manifest as support for expanding the programme in subsequent stages. Overall, a theme I would like to draw out of this is many of the individuals involved in the Seniors Programme were genuinely interested in spreading it. There was a tension, however, between the desire to spread nationally and regionally. I will explore this further in the next section where I analyse whether my interviewees felt the collaboration between the Foundation and the BC and NS health authorities was successful.

12.2.   Was the Collaboration Successful?

As described above, the intervention the Seniors Programme tested appeared to have a positive impact on senior health. Recall that the BC Health Authority developed this programme in collaboration with the NS Health Authority. Earlier, I questioned the rationale for collaboration between two health authorities on opposite sides of the country, and my interviewees provided their perceptions of the reasons. I then asked several members of the fellowship who were present from the start to the conclusion of the Training Programme whether they believed the collaboration had been successful. Were the anticipated benefits of collaborating realized? Generally, the answer was not really. The Mentor said:

> I would say probably not. I mean I'm not within the organization anymore, but from what I understand, that partnership and that collaboration has not necessarily continued on, or certainly not in the way that it was. There's probably some relationship back and forth, but not to be working and to say that 'We are a team and we're going to do this together.' I would also say that the larger vision is not [...] Like the project is moving on, but it's moving on with the element that was designed in the first phase for the rollout [...] Like it's just rolling out to a larger stakeholder group and not necessarily reaching that broader context or opportunity that I believe would be existing – something that could be rolled out provincially, maybe even nationally fairly quickly, which is not necessarily what's happening as I understand it. (personal communication, 19 May 2017)

The Site Director had similar sentiments.

> Well, I think you sensed the potential, but I'm not sure if we achieved it. Because in the end, the regions are undergoing such rapid change and they have a new [...] they went through all sorts of reorganization, and in the end they couldn't sustain their commitment to it. So I think for sure it's important to share this information across Canada. But at the same time, I think you have to be aware that different cultures are in different health care systems, and how they roll it out will be up to them. (personal communication, 12 May 2017)

The MD Lead had a more positive response.

> [...] we learned a lot from being with the groups in Halifax, and we continue to collaborate with [two physicians] from Halifax. That is out of our relationships that were built through the [Foundation] connection. Their mandate to spread good work across the country, I think [the Foundation] wanted to support that and they continue to help us with development of educational material and things. So, we stay in touch with them, and they're also helping us with the evaluation components of our project. (personal communication, 8 August 2017)

In Table 12.2, I summarize the elements of the fellowship's assessment of the collaboration and link them to relevant structures of values, rationality, and power.

Table 12.2. Elements of the BC Working Group's Assessment of the Collaboration and Their Relation to Values, Rationality, and Power.

Elements of the Fellowship's Assessment of the Collaboration	Relevant Structures of Values, Rationality, and Power
The collaboration's objective was to foster spread	*Values*: Spread, dialogue
	Rationality: Body, collective reasoning
	Power: Reproduction of power relations
Falling short of the goal	*Values*: Spread, effectiveness
	Rationality: Contextual, collective reasoning
	Power: Collapse of power relations, production of power relations, historical power relations
The current state of collaboration	*Values*: Spread, dialogue, accountability
	Rationality: Technocratic
	Power: Reproduction of power relations, defining rationality

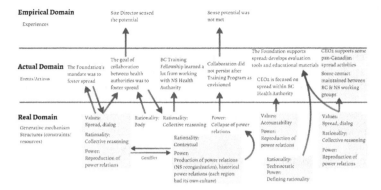

Figure 12.2.   A Critical Realist Perspective of the Elements of the Fellowship's Assessment of the Collaboration.

Figure 12.2 presents a critical realist perspective of this process. As I have discussed earlier, several stakeholders, including the Foundation, exercised power to form the collaboration between NS and BC health authorities to facilitate the spread of the Seniors Programme. Structures such as the values of spread and dialogue, combined with the rationality of collective reasoning, motivated this action. These actions, in turn, led some members of the fellowship to experience a sense of potential. The MD Lead perceived that the BC working group learned a lot from engaging in collective reasoning with the NS working group. Despite this, the collaboration did not persist after the Training Programme, creating the feeling that the collaboration did not meet its potential. Several constraining structures caused this. For example, the NS Health Authority underwent a restructuring, creating new power relations within the organization. The will to maintain collaboration did not survive this restructuring. Moreover, the Site Director referred to differing cultures, which speaks to structures of contextual rationality and historical power relations that constrained organizations' ability to collaborate. She consequently maintained that each region should be left to roll out programmes in their own way.

In the previous sections, I established that national spread was a goal of the Seniors Programme. Actual spread, however, was slow and geographically limited. Why was this? Why was spreading healthcare innovations across Canada so difficult it justified the creation of the Foundation, an organization devoted to fostering spread? My interviews surfaced several structures that constrained spread, as well as actions the BC working group took to overcome those structures. I present these findings in the following pages, starting first with constraining structures.

12.3.   Structures Constraining Spread

The results of the Seniors Programme as perceived by the Training Fellowship was that it meaningfully delayed, and in some cases reversed, frailty. Who would not want to delay, if not reverse, frailty? Assuming these results were real, why does the Seniors Programme not spread like wildfire across Canada? I asked my interviewees what forces obstruct the spread of useful healthcare innovations. They identified several such forces, including risk aversion, structural constraints, and limited resources of time, energy, and money. I explore these in turn.

12.3.1. Risk Aversion

CEO2 raised an issue that I touched on earlier when discussing why executives within the BC Health Authority might resist the Seniors Programme. 'It is hard to spread these types of new programmes. We are parochial' (CEO2, personal communication, 2 June 2017). When I asked him to expand on the resistance points, he explained, 'The resistance points are we are a conservative business. We are risk averse. We are driven by risk profiles. We don't do risk. Therefore we shut down new ideas' (CEO2, personal communication, 2 June 2017). I explored this risk aversion earlier — recall the Mentor's comments that the health authority must deliver acute care where lives are on the line, and so the entire authority cannot be operated in an innovative space (see Chapter 8). I do not belabour that point here other than to say this risk aversion was not limited to stopping programmes locally, but also in spreading innovations from one authority to another. I turn, instead, to analyse structural constraints limiting the spread of the Seniors Programme.

12.3.2. Structural Constraints

Beyond risk aversion, there are often structural issues that constrain the adoption of innovations. For example, as the MD Lead explained, fee codes may not facilitate physician adoption of innovations. Regarding the Seniors Programme, she said:

> Yeah, it is a challenge, and it's really too bad because family physicians are having to work at the pace that they do. The fee code seems to reward short, limited kind of assessments and doesn't allow time and doesn't reward people for taking a more fulsome assessment of somebody who's got multiple problems. We know with seniors and especially with frailty, that there's a whole host of different [...] it's multifaceted, so it takes time. That's been something that we've heard repeatedly from physicians, that they cannot take the time really to do a comprehensive assessment. (MD Lead, personal communication, 8 August 2017)

The above comment is a general one regarding assessing frailty. The following statement from the MD Lead spoke to the specific activities physicians performed when implementing the Seniors Programme.

> I just remember the [general practitioners] GPs saying, 'This takes too long.' That was the pilot phase. When they went to the paper [frailty assessment] format and they said, 'Can't we just send patients somewhere and have somebody else fill it out?' I remember

that feedback because that really embodied a big concern that we felt was a risk of having to take up so much of the physician's time. (MD Lead, personal communication, 8 August 2017)

The Site Director also saw this barrier.

[…] [T]he challenge is really physician and senior executive adoption. You see […] I get the great opportunity to work in physicians' offices and you see just how very busy they are. They haven't got time to adopt some of the newer innovation. You see that if it's not located in a billing framework, they can see that it's well-intentioned, but if they can't bill for it, they can't adopt the practice. (personal communication, 12 May 2017)

The Senior Improvement Lead suggested another structural issue constraining the spread of the Seniors Programme was how the Province delivered primary care. At the time of this book, family physicians were solely responsible for administering primary care. The Senior Improvement Lead suggested an alternate system where a network of healthcare professionals shared care for seniors might facilitate the adoption of the Seniors Programme. The Site Director echoed this concern.

The other thing I really see is the challenge, that needs to be located. I think the care of seniors going forward is best located in primary care health teams. Not just the physician but in a multidisciplinary team. I mean best of all is if you can have a physician, a nurse, a social worker, and an [occupational therapist/physiotherapist] OT/PT, and a pharmacist. Those are the kind of teams that I think we have the best opportunity in launching something like the [Seniors Programme] that really identifies those seniors early, assesses them, prevents them from sliding into frailty by developing health care plans with them and getting the coaching they need to stay well. Then following and using the [electronic Comprehensive Geriatric Assessment] eCGA either every six months or yearly or having a billing code that allows those primary care providers to do that so that they can trend over time the progression toward or away from frailty, so they can affirm the senior's self-capacity to manage their health or help support them towards more effective means of managing their chronic health conditions. (personal communication, 12 May 2017)

The Senior Improvement Lead also identified that bureaucratic processes within a physician's office could pose a barrier to spread.

[…] I mean [the Seniors Programme] right now the way that [the BC Health Authority] is implementing it with the use of the electronic comprehensive geriatric assessment, some of the barriers around that are automatically wrapped up in the electronic version of that tool. So there's some development stuff that would need to happen. Of course embedding it into an [electronic medical record] EMR, you'd be aware that there are all [...] there's not just one EMR per province or anything like that [...] So you've automatically got a number of platforms and that means development costs for each one. I mean that automatically creates something that is [...] I'm also loath to call it a 'barrier' as much as it's a challenge [...] (personal communication, 13 June 2017)

Regarding national spread, differences in the administration of healthcare between provinces created another challenge. The Senior Improvement Lead explained:

I think working with all of the different primary care models across Canada. Again, we've got a number of ways that this is organized. That again could represent another level of challenge. If you were looking to spread nationally, you'd have to take that into consideration. [The Seniors Programme] relies currently on wellness coaches. Right now they're with the [local university] self-management program, and I believe it's a volunteer model. Now in Ontario, there's a very similar self-management model that also relies on volunteers [...] But again, if you're looking at volunteers, that could raise challenges in terms of capacity and so forth. If you use paid staff, then that could become a problem in terms of having the resources and the funding to do that. (personal communication, 13 June 2017)

The main message from the above quotes is even though people may want to adopt an innovation, existing bureaucratic rationalities — i.e., the billing framework, processes, documentation, roles, and procedures — may prevent adoption. These constraining structures, however, could be overcome with enough energy and resources. As the next section explores, though, these resources are often limited.

12.3.3. *Limited Time, Energy, and Money*

The MD Lead suggested that directors of health authorities work in an environment where many issues pull on their attention that constrain spread.

But then as we're doing the work to spread, we've had to go to executive directors, and we've had to go to other directors in the health authority and different regions as we wanted to bring the project to their communities. There we've had to sort of I think compete a bit for their attention, because they've got so much activity going on already and this is something new, and it's beyond what they immediately are familiar with. They've had to sort of rearrange things to try and provide some staff time as we try and do some integrated work with Divisions of Family Practice. (personal communication, 8 August 2017)

Consequently, if a region was not in a stage of its activities where it could take on a change initiative, spread faltered. The Senior Improvement Lead explained:

[...] I think when it comes to spreading innovation generally and sort of general barriers around that, I think often it's people are not resistant to the great ideas. It's often around 'Is it the right time?' and it's often about their readiness to receive the innovation. If something is deemed spreadable − it has all of the right ingredients and it's ready to go − it's often about that site's ability to take on something new. Do they have the capacity? Is it the right timing? Are there competing priorities? Those kinds of things I think can create barriers to spread. (personal communication, 13 June 2017)

The Site Director identified that even if you can get the attention of executives, locating the funds needed to finance the adoption of innovations can pose a challenge.

[...] I mean some of the challenges are [...] things like funds, in you have to create the funding to develop the eCGA frailty index and the EMRs. And that's a substantial cost. That's about fifty-to sixty-thousand for each EMR. So of course you need to secure those funds. That's one. The other challenge of course is it just takes money too, whether it's to develop the hardware, to test the hardware, to have the resources to keep someone like myself employed so that I can work with academics to write the CIHR grant. (personal communication, 12 May 2017)

Finally, as the Senior Improvement Lead explained, sometimes the pressure the health care regions are under can lead to tiredness that limits people's capacity to adopt innovations.

[...] I think that kind of comes with what I call those competing demands [...] if we have patients lining hallways, and certainly the flow is forever an issue [...] I think then people [...] there's the fatigue that follows that when forever people are trying to find ways to change that, and so they're just feeling like, 'Well, it doesn't seem to be working. Nothing seems to be working.' There can be a bit of that fatigue, that change fatigue that would compound your crisis management, and so you've got these two factors kind of coming together, (personal communication, 13 June 2017)

12.3.4. A Critical Realist Summary of Structures Constraining Spread

In Table 12.3, I summarize the elements that are posing barriers to spread and link them to relevant structures of values, rationality, and power. Figure 12.3 (page 172) presents a critical realist perspective of this process. Figure 12.3(a) shows my representation of the impact risk tolerance and fee structures had on spread. CEO2 said health authorities were 'parochial' and they avoid risk. Risk aversion spoke to the value of public interest. As discussed earlier in this book, healthcare systems manage human lives and, therefore, cannot afford to take risks. This risk aversion indicated the presence of underlying power structures that assigned responsibility for managing human lives and assigned blame for mismanagement of those lives. Combined, these created structures that constrain those attempting to spread new programmes.

Figure 12.3(a) also shows my depiction of how fee structures posed barriers to the spread of the Seniors Programme. Premised on structures of bureaucratic rationality, specifically regarding procedures and roles, physicians were responsible for assessing frailty. This task was time-consuming. Driven by structures of economic rationality, the Province exercised its power to assign fee codes, and

Table 12.3. Elements Posing Barriers to Spread and Their Relation to Values, Rationality, and Power.

Elements Posing a Barrier to Spread	Relevant Structures of Values, Rationality, and Power
Risk aversion	*Values*: Public interest; opposed to dialogue and innovation
	Power: Reproduction of power relations
Structural restraints	*Values*: Spread
	Rationality: Bureaucratic (processes, procedures and roles, documentation), economic
	Power: Reproduction of power relations, ignoring rationality, historical power relations
Limited resources of time, energy, and money	*Values*: Spread, sustainability, effectiveness
	Rationality: Bureaucratic (procedures and roles), economic
	Power: Production of power relations, reproduction of power relations, defining rationality, manipulation, coercion

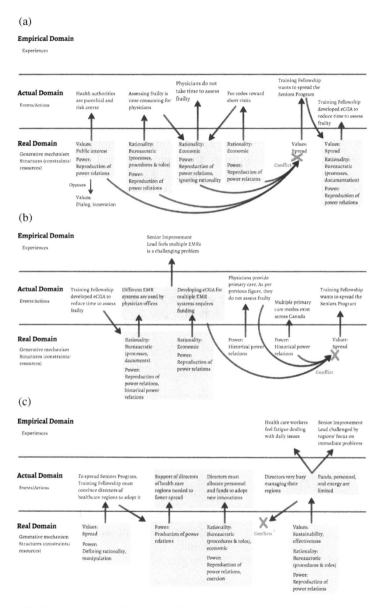

Figure 12.3(a–c). A Critical Realist Perspective of the Elements Posing Barriers to Spread. (a) How Risk Tolerance and Payment Structures Posed Barriers to Spread. (b) How Diverse Systems Posed Barriers to Spread. (c) How Managing Daily Pressures in Healthcare Regions Posed Barriers to Spread.

these codes rewarded short visits. The organization of primary care gave physi-cians the power to decide what assessments to perform during patient visits. Guided by economic rationality, physicians exercised their power to choose not to assess frailty. Since assessing frailty is an essential component of the Seniors Programme, this posed a barrier to the programme's spread. In response to this barrier, the BC working group exercised the power they had to develop an elec-tronic comprehensive geriatric assessment (eCGA) that reduced the time required to assess frailty. Developing the eCGA was an act of bureaucratic rationality, specifically processes and documentation, to overcome a barrier posed by economic rationality.

In Figure 12.3(b), I show that though the creation of the eCGA may have overcome one barrier, it created others. Historical power structures, informed by bureaucratic rationality, led to a situation where different physician offices use different electronic medical record (EMR) systems. Therefore, the fellowship had to design an eCGA for each EMR system. This development effort cost money. Exercising sufficient power and economic rationality to secure needed funds posed a barrier to spread. I also show in Figure 12.3(b) that because of historical power structures, physicians were solely responsible for assessing frailty, which, as described above, posed economic barriers. There was not yet a mechanism whereby different healthcare professionals could assess frailty and coordinate their findings with the physician. Thus, physicians remained exclu-sively responsible for assessing frailty, which was time-consuming and which fee structures did not reward. Attempts to reduce the time through the creation of eCGA ran into further structural barriers of electronic compatibility and devel-opment costs.

In Figure 12.3(b), I also look at barriers beyond the physician's office. Due to historical power structures, Canada has multiple modes of administering pri-mary care. Different regions have different challenges would-be spreaders needed to overcome, which added to the difficulty of diffusing innovations nationwide. For example, the Senior Improvement Lead spoke of some regions using volunteer coaches to administer the Seniors Programme, leading to cap-acity concerns, versus other regions that might hire paid coaches, leading to funding issues.

In Figure 12.3(c), I look at the experiences of healthcare administrators, and how those caused barriers to spread. In order to spread the Seniors Programme, the fellowship had to exercise their ability to manipulate and define rationality in the minds of healthcare administrators, convincing them to adopt the pro-gramme. Adoption of innovations required administrators to exercise bureau-cratic rationality and power to allocate personnel and resources to the adoption process. These administrators, however, driven by values of sustainability and effectiveness, and perhaps trapped by bureaucratic rationality and prevailing power structures, found their funds, personnel, and energy were limited. These resources were already devoted to managing daily issues of their region. With their energy and resources exhausted, administrators experienced fatigue. Not only might they lack the physical resources to adopt an innovation, but they may also lack the mental energy needed to try adopting something new.

I would like to pull out the following theme from this chapter. The responses of my interviewees highlighted that even though different groups and individuals may share values with the BC working group, even if they saw the benefit of the programme and wanted to adopt it, there existed constraints undermining their ability to do so. These constraints were deeply embedded in systems of power and did not yield themselves easily to change. People, however, were not powerless in the face of these structures. Spread still happened. How? I explore the answer to that question in the following chapter.

Chapter 13

Structures Enabling Spread

Given the structures that constrain the spread of innovations, what can be done to facilitate it? The Site Director, MD Lead, and Senior Improvement Lead were most actively involved with efforts to spread the Seniors Programme within the BC Health Authority after the close of the Training Programme. I asked them what they had done to make the progress they have made. Their responses surfaced several elements that facilitated spread. These included strong leadership, project champions, the characteristics of the programme, developing the eCGA, activities that support general practitioners [GPs], changes currently occurring in how physicians practice primary care, and the approach they took to convince regions to adopt the Seniors Programme. I will present their discussions of each of these elements, and then summarize them using a critical realist framework. I first explore the role of leadership in facilitating spread.

13.1. Leadership

The Senior Improvement Lead spoke at length about the importance of strong leadership in driving a spread initiative. For example, she attributed much of the spread the Seniors Programme achieved within the BC Health Authority to CEO2.

> They have strong leadership, and that's [CEO2] recognizes a good thing when he sees it and he doesn't need seven years of research and paper that will kind of tell him what he already knew in the first year sort of thing. He's willing to go forward with it based on what he's seeing and he has that sort of quality improvement mentality. He is a strong leader, so I think that's another contributing factor. (Senior Improvement Lead, personal communication, 13 June 2017)

The MD Lead concurred and elaborated on the role CEO2 played in spreading the Seniors Programme within the BC Health Authority.

> Then the other thing is we've had the CEO support, which has been really tremendous. I think he really bought in [...] [CEO2 has] actually been nudging the communities to be ready as well. Particularly with the prototype communities that are being given

extra funds to proceed with senior care, they're being encouraged directly from the CEO to take on the [Seniors Programme]. (MD Lead, personal communication, 8 August 2017)

The above quote suggested that under CEO2, the BC Health Authority provided funding to facilitate the spread of the Seniors Programme within its region. The Senior Improvement Lead commented further on how the BC Health Authority has supported the spread of this programme.

I would say that one of the things that [the BC Health Authority] has done that has enabled I think the success of [the Seniors Programme] to date in that health authority is that they've resourced well. They have kind of put their money where their mouth is. They created the position to bring [the Site Director] in so that she's there as the lead. They fund [the MD Lead's] position so she is able to dedicate those critical hours and be that primary care provider voice, both to guide the project but also then to be the peer among other physicians to talk about it. I think those are two really important critical success factors with [the Seniors Programme] [...] (Senior Improvement Lead, personal communication, 13 June 2017)

In short, the BC working group and Senior Improvement Lead spoke highly of CEO2's leadership. What they liked about it was he took action, and he provided necessary resources to spread the programme.

In Table 13.1, I summarize elements of how leadership facilitated spread and link them to relevant structures of values, rationality, and power. Figure 13.1 presents a critical realist perspective of this process. The Senior Improvement Lead's comments that CEO2 did not require years of data, that he knew a good thing 'when he sees it' spoke to values of effectiveness and a body rationality. These structures conflicted with technocratic rationality, which would emphasize making a data-driven decision. The Senior Improvement Lead respected this propensity to act rather than analyse and felt it was an important driver of the Senior Programme's spread. The Senior Improvement Lead, however, did not

Table 13.1. Elements of How Leadership Facilitated Spread and Their Relation to Values, Rationality, and Power.

Elements Facilitating Spread	Relevant Structures of Values, Rationality, and Power
Leadership	*Values*: Effectiveness, user orientation
	Rationality: Body; technocratic, contextual
	Power: Reproduction of power relations, power in organizations, coercion, production of power relations

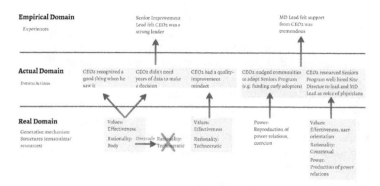

Figure 13.1. A Critical Realist Perspective of How Leadership Can Facilitate Spread.

abandon technocratic rationality. She also referenced CEO2's quality improvement mindset, which implied structures such as the value effectiveness and technocratic rationality. From this reply, the Senior Improvement Lead seemed to suggest that leaders who act decisively despite incomplete data, but then follow up by monitoring and improving the results of those decisions, were important drivers of spread. These attributes led the Senior Improvement Lead to experience feelings of respect for CEO2. The MD Lead also experienced positive feelings of support from CEO2. She identified CEO2 'nudged' communities to adopt the Seniors Programme through funding early adopters. The ability to do this rested on structures of coercion and reproduction of power relations that gave CEO2 the authority to direct funds within the BC Health Authority. Additionally, founded on structures of the values effectiveness and user orientation, underwritten by contextual rationality, CEO2 exercised his power to produce power relations, manifested as adequately staffing the initiative to spread the Seniors Programme.

13.2. Programme Champions

In addition to leadership, the Senior Improvement Lead stressed the importance of the champions promoting the spread of the programme. Thus, in her mind, the funding to pay for the Site Director and MD Lead was of critical importance. Here, she explained some of the work they do.

> The work that [the Site Director] and all of the folks in [the BC Health Authority] have been doing to connect with the primary care teams, the work that she's been doing to connect with Intrahealth[1] and get that eCGA up and off the ground, that's [the

---

[1]Intrahealth is an EMR provider.

Site Director] and the work that they've been doing there. It's just been a phenomenal amount that she has undertaken and I think she's the queen of building connections. (Senior Improvement Lead, personal communication, 13 June 2017)

Later, the Senior Improvement Lead elaborated:

I think [the Site Director] has [...] the team rather has [...] she's built a solid infrastructure to support [the Seniors Programme]. I think she recognized how important it was to do the stakeholder engagement and ensure that the right people were involved. She does have the steering committee and evaluation committee, so that it's not just a couple of individuals moving it forward, so when you've got those stakeholders involved, then they can kind of pave the way at different times. She's also been realistic and willing to course-correct or adjust I should say. (personal communication, 13 June 2017)

In sum, effective project champions were skilled at building needed power relations with key stakeholders, creating appropriate bureaucratic infrastructure for the project, were adaptable, and were realistic about what they could accomplish.

In Table 13.2, I summarize the elements of how programme champions facilitated spread and link them to relevant structures of values, rationality, and power. Figure 13.2 presents a critical realist perspective of this process. I developed this figure from the Senior Improvement Lead's description of the Site Director. She referred to the Site Director as the 'queen of building connections', under which she described several activities. These activities included stakeholder engagement, ensuring the right people were involved with the spread initiative, and connecting with primary care teams and Intrahealth, all of which implied structures such as the values of dialogue and the ability to produce power relations. The Senior Improvement Lead commented that the Site Director had built a supportive infrastructure, such as the Steering Committee and Evaluation Committee, which ensured she was not a lone voice seeking

Table 13.2. Elements of How Programme Champions Facilitated Spread and Their Relation to Values, Rationality, and Power.

Elements Facilitating Spread	Relevant Structures of Values, Rationality, and Power
Project champions	*Values*: Dialog, effectiveness, user orientation
	Rationality: Bureaucratic (documentation, processes, procedures and roles), contextual
	Power: Production of power relations

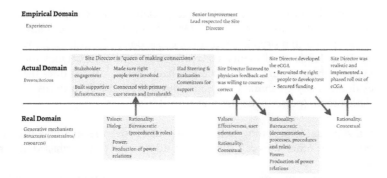

Figure 13.2. A Critical Realist Perspective of the Attributes of People that Facilitate Spread.

the spread of the Seniors Programme. These activities spoke to bureaucratic rationality, specifically the ability to define procedures and roles that supported spread.

Additionally, several other structures influenced the Site Director. These included the values of effectiveness and user orientation, supported by contextual rationality that enabled her to listen to physician feedback and modify the Seniors Programme based on that feedback, specifically regarding the development of the eCGA. From the Senior Improvement Lead's comments, developing the eCGA was a significant effort. The Site Director had to exercise power structures within the healthcare institution to secure funding to develop the eCGA. She also had to exercise bureaucratic rationality, focused on documentation, processes, procedures, and roles, to bring in the right people to develop and test the eCGA. Once developed, the Site Director displayed contextual rationality, enabling her with an awareness of what she could realistically achieve. The consequence of this was a phased rollout of the eCGA. Taken together, the Senior Improvement Lead appeared to experience a feeling of respect for the Site Director.

13.3. Programme Characteristics

Beyond having the right people in place, the Senior Improvement Lead spoke at length about the characteristics of a programme that could spread.

> A lot [of] things could be successful, and then we might say, 'But it might not be ready for spread.' Sometimes it might be a readiness for something to spread. I think in terms of its success, is it demonstrating that it's meeting the outcomes that were established? [...] Then in addition to that though, there are a lot of other elements that need to align in terms of whether or not something is ready to be spread. That's things like 'Can you

replicate it? Is there a clear change package, for example, that could be taken to another site? Or is it such a unique circumstance within the original that no one else could do it? [...] Some of those kinds of elements are really important. And 'Does the evidence bear it out?' certainly come back to that. 'What does the evaluation say?' I think all of those pieces fit together in terms of that spread. (personal communication, 13 June 2017)

In short, a spreadable programme is one that has proven results, has generalizable elements that other sites can successfully adopt, and can be phased in across a region.

In Table 13.3, I summarize the elements of spreadable programmes and link them to relevant structures of values, rationality, and power. Figure 13.3 presents a critical realist perspective of this process. A spreadable programme reflected the structure of the value effectiveness, in that it met expected outcomes. It embodied technocratic rationality in that it had a testable hypothesis, and there existed a causal connection between the programme and the observed outcome. A spreadable programme also had a change package, that is it exhibited bureaucratic

Table 13.3. Elements of How Programme Characteristics Facilitated Spread and Their Relation to Values, Rationality, and Power.

Elements Facilitating Spread	Relevant Structures of Values, Rationality, and Power
Programme characteristics	*Values*: Effectiveness
	Rationality: Technocratic, bureaucratic (processes, procedures and roles)
	Power: Production of power relations

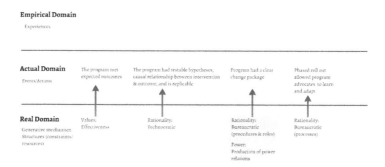

Figure 13.3.   A Critical Realist Perspective of Programme Characteristics that Facilitate Spread.

rationality regarding procedures and roles that facilitated the production of power relations in the new community. Such a programme also exhibited bureaucratic rationality resulting in a phased rollout of the programme that allowed programme champions the ability to learn and adapt as the programme spread.

13.4.   Developing the eCGA

When discussing the barriers to spread, I identified several structural barriers. One of them was the time it took physicians to assess frailty combined with the lack of fee code for that work effort. When discussing that constraint, I mentioned that the fellowship created an eCGA to reduce assessment time. The Site Director elaborated on the importance of this development:

> The real magic ingredients in [the Seniors Programme] has been the electronic comprehensive geriatric assessment that generates the frailty index at point of service. So finally primary care providers [...] They used to look at seniors and, sort of from a gestalt place, they would estimate their frailty. Now they really have an evidence-based tool, yeah, to generate a frailty index, which is a highly sensitive measure of people's frailty. (personal communication, 12 May 2017).

The MD Lead concurred. '[...] [W]e've taken the comprehensive assessment from the paper form, which takes a long time, to an electronic form, so it's embedded in the doctor's EMR [...] it's way faster than having to read through on the paper' (MD Lead, personal communication, 8 August 2017). Note that this was an application of bureaucratic rationality to address the constraints of more powerful bureaucratic rationalities. That is, when they could not change the prevailing bureaucratic rationality, the BC working group created new bureaucratic rationalities to work around the constraints.

In Table 13.4, I summarize the elements of how developing the eCGA facilitated spread and link them to relevant structures of values, rationality, and power. Figure 13.4 presents a critical realist perspective of this process. From earlier in this book, interviewees identified several structures restraining

Table 13.4. Elements of How Developing the eCGA Facilitated Spread and Their Relation to Values, Rationality, and Power.

Elements Facilitating Spread	Relevant Structures of Values, Rationality, and Power
Developing eCGA	*Values*: Effectiveness, user orientation
	Rationality: Technocratic, body, bureaucratic (processes, documentation)
	Power: Reproduction of power relations, manipulation

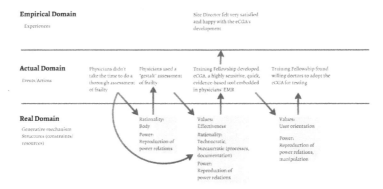

Figure 13.4.   A Critical Realist Perspective of How the Development of eCGA
Facilitated Spread.

physicians from doing a thorough frailty assessment. Instead, they performed what the Site Director called a 'gestalt' assessment, where they merely estimated frailty (Site Director, personal communication, 12 May 2017). This process of frailty assessment implied the physician exercised their power as providers of medical care to use body rationality to assess frailty (i.e. they estimated it) rather than technocratic rationality. Enabled by structures such as the value effectiveness and technocratic rationality, the BC working group exercised a form of bureaucratic rationality to develop an electronic version of the CGA. The eCGA was a form of technocratic rationality reified through the tools of bureaucratic rationality. Members of the fellowship could not force physicians to adopt the eCGA. Thus, they resorted to manipulation, enabled further by the values of user orientation, to find doctors willing to adopt and test the eCGA. Overall, the Site Director's comments suggested she experienced a sense of satisfaction with the development of the eCGA.

13.5.   Supporting GPs

In addition to the time and fee structure, earlier sections described other barriers such as the inability of physicians to offload assessment onto other healthcare professionals. The MD Lead's following quote described how they addressed these barriers.

> [...] [W]e're using a team-based model, so having a nurse or an OT from [the BC Health Authority] to be able to help the GP to complete the assessment takes away from the time that's required by the GP. We've actually whittled down the assessment that by paper was taking 30 minutes, we can get it down to about 15 minutes now because it's electronic and a good part of it actually is done by a nurse. So in the last launch in [neighbouring municipality], we had a [BC Health Authority] clinical nurse specialist

in geriatrics go in and help with some of the components of the assessment. That's really cut down on the time required for the GP. (personal communication, 8 August 2017)

Moreover, the MD Lead also specified how they helped physicians bill for this time in the absence of a fee code for frailty assessment.

[...] [T]here is a fee code that addresses the longer-than-average office visit and also another fee code that talks about some preventative advice for preventing diseases, in particular people with chronic diseases. So there is some sort of ability to bill beyond just the straight office visit. We make mention of that when we go and do the education for the GPs. (personal communication, 8 August 2017)

Note again; the BC working group were developing new bureaucratic rationalities to work around entrenched bureaucratic constraints.

In Table 13.5, I summarize how supporting GPs facilitated spread and link them to relevant structures of values, rationality, and power. Figure 13.5

Table 13.5. Elements of How Supporting GPs Facilitated Spread and Their Relation to Values, Rationality, and Power.

Elements Facilitating Spread	Relevant Structures of Values, Rationality, and Power
Supporting GPs	*Rationality*: Bureaucratic (procedures and roles), economic
	Power: Reproduction of power relations, production of power relations, define rationality

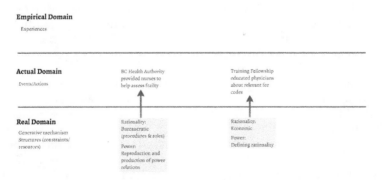

Figure 13.5.   A Critical Realist Perspective of Providing Support to Physicians to Facilitate Spread.

presents a critical realist perspective of this process. In the previous section discussing barriers to spread, I identified the current structure of primary care where physicians were solely responsible for performing frailty assessments as a challenge, especially considering how time-consuming the process was. The lack of a fee code to perform these assessments exacerbated this challenge. The BC Health Authority under CEO2's leadership enacted the enabling structure of bureaucratic rationality to provide nurses to assist those physician offices adopting the Seniors Programme to assess frailty. Also, the fellowship educated physicians on those fee codes that were available to help receive remuneration for the time taken to assess frailty.

13.6.   Changes in How the Province Delivered Primary Care

The above section highlighted that the BC Health Authority provided nurses to help physicians perform the frailty assessment. One might ask whether that is sustainable (can a nurse be provided to every physician's office?) and spreadable (are other regions willing to provide nurses to physicians?). I believe the MD Lead shared these concerns, and she spoke to how permanent and wide-spread changes in how the province delivered primary care was needed to facilitate the spread of the Seniors Programme – and the good news is, these changes were happening.

> The sustainability will come if we get full integration. If we have primary care homes, that means we will have allied health professionals attached to GP offices, so we will have team-based care in the GP clinic. If you have an OT that works with your patient population and you have seniors and they're coming in for yearly exams, you can actually have the OT do portions of their CGA, save it, and then when you see them next, you complete it, and so that it can become a periodic geriatric assessment in a comprehensive way. That would build in sustainability, but we do need to have the primary care homes. The good thing is the BC government is requiring primary care homes to become a reality. (MD Lead, personal communication, 8 August 2017)

In the previous section, I highlighted how the BC working group developed new bureaucratic rationalities to work around entrenched bureaucratic constraints. What the MD Lead was saying here is that by fortuitous happenstance, the Province is acting to alter those entrenched bureaucratic constraints.

In Table 13.6, I summarize the elements that are facilitating spread and link them to relevant structures of values, rationality, and power. Figure 13.6 presents a critical realist perspective of this process. The province of BC was leading primary care providers to adopt a new model of delivering healthcare, the primary care home. Under this model, primary care moved from a model where

Table 13.6. Elements of How Changes to the Delivery of Primary Care Facilitated Spread and Their Relation to Values, Rationality, and Power.

Elements Facilitating Spread	Relevant Structures of Values, Rationality, and Power
Changes to the delivery of primary care	*Values*: Dialog, effectiveness
	Rationality: Bureaucratic (procedures and roles, processes)
	Power: Production of power relations, reproduction of power relations, power over organizations, power through organizations, defining rationality

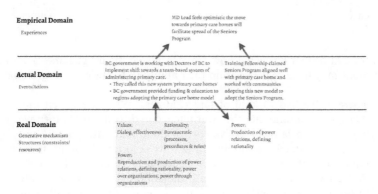

Figure 13.6.   A Critical Realist Perspective of How Changes to Primary Care Facilitate Spread.

the family physician was primarily responsible for administering healthcare to one where an integrated body of professionals share patient care (The College of Family Physicians of Canada, 2018). Restructuring how physicians across the province administered primary care was a significant act of power that empowered structures of bureaucratic rationality to develop new processes, procedures, and roles within the healthcare system. This new model implied the values of dialogue and effectiveness motivated the BC government to undertake these changes. Making such a structural change province-wide was a significant undertaking, and this restructuring was still ongoing as I was writing this book. Regardless, the distribution of care across healthcare professionals provided a means to share the responsibility of frailty assessment. The fellowship recognized this opportunity and took action to define rationality such that stakeholders recognized the Seniors Programme aligned with the move to primary care homes and had subsequently focused their efforts to spread in communities adopting the primary care home model.

13.7.   Convincing Regions to Adopt Seniors Programme

In the previous chapter, I described how fatigue and the daily pressures of managing a healthcare region created structural constraints by sapping the time and energy of the people needed to drive spread. The MD Lead described how they have been selecting communities to spread by identifying those areas that were early adopters of the primary care home model:

> Then I think [communities are] gradually working toward a different mandate that's come through the ministry and now in all of the health authorities in BC [...] to develop primary care homes [...] That lines up really well with the [Seniors Programme] project. So we've been sort of aligning ourselves with communities that are sort of forging ahead with the primary care home development. (personal communication, 8 August 2017)

The MD Lead further discussed how they addressed the fatigue and lack of capacity regions may have that constrain their ability to adopt new programmes:

> There we've had to kind of find readiness. When we've felt that there was a community that was aligned and ready to go, then we would do the launch. We've sort of done that with [city 1] and we're now launching in [city 2], and we're probably going to be going to [city 3] and to [city 4] in the near future, and [city 5]. We're trying to sort of wait until the community becomes ready to do some of the internal work that's required that will allow us to do the spread. It's not so much resistance, but it's just waiting until they have room for us and staff availability to do some of the changes that are required. (personal communication, 8 August 2017)

She further explained that while the fellowship waited for regions to become ready to take on the Seniors Programme, they would lay the groundwork in the minds of administrators and use success in other regions to facilitate adoption.

> Well, a lot of the groundwork has been in speaking with the managers or all of the home health offices [...] When we have meetings, and we have ongoing regular meetings with the managers, I've been able to speak about the [Seniors Programme], so a little bit of seed planting here and there, then continue to talk about it as there is one community that is willing to take it up. As we do the work in that one community, we get to speak about the successes and all of the barriers that need to get removed. So the other communities are listening as we go. (MD Lead, personal communication, 8 August 2017)

Another barrier I identified earlier was how differences between healthcare regions prevented spread. Regarding this, the Mentor discussed the importance of being able to adapt to different regions:

> To me, one of the exciting things about this initiative overall, we now have a really good understanding of how you have to do things from we'll say a high-level generic perspective to map out what an intervention might be, but then you have to allow it to be adaptable to a local context. (personal communication, 19 May 2017)

In sum, the BC working group recognized how shifts towards the primary care home model reduced barriers to the Seniors Programme, and so they approached regions undergoing this change. In response to the lack of capacity of many regions to take on new programmes, the BC working group provided information to candidate regions about the Seniors Programme and waited for that region's readiness to tackle adoption before pushing ahead. They further maintained a willingness to adapt the programme to the specific needs of each region.

In Table 13.7, I summarize the elements that facilitated spread and link them to relevant structures of values, rationality, and power. Figure 13.7 presents a

Table 13.7. Elements of How the Methods Used to Approach Regions Facilitated Spread and Their Relation to Values, Rationality, and Power.

Elements Facilitating Spread	Relevant Structures of Values, Rationality, and Power
Convincing regions to adopt Seniors Programme	*Rationality*: Technocratic, contextual *Power*: Reproduction of power relations, manipulation, defining rationality, production of power relations

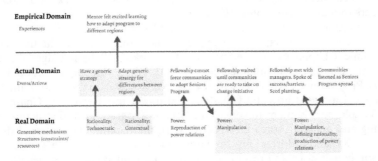

Figure 13.7.   A Critical Realist Perspective of How to Approach Regions to Facilitate Spread.

critical realist perspective of this process. The BC working group lacked the power to force communities to adopt the Seniors Programme. Rather than hoping managers choose to add adoption of the Seniors Programme to their to-do list, the BC working group approached communities adopting the primary care home model and demonstrated through an act of defining rationality how the Seniors Programme aligned with that shift. As described in the previous chapter discussing barriers to spread, managers of communities may not be ready to take on a new programme since managing the daily issues of their region consumed their energy. The BC working group, thus, enacted tactics of manipulation to facilitate spread. They waited until communities were ready to take on a change initiative before attempting to spread the Seniors Programme. Meanwhile, they defined rationality though meeting with managers to discuss the programme, its success, and barriers to overcome. Each community that adopted the Seniors Programme became another case study for the BC working group to share. They believed this created interest in the Seniors Programme that they could later translate into spread once the community had the energy to change.

Moreover, the Mentor's comments identified a tension between technocratic and contextual forms of rationality. Her comment suggested that developing and spreading a single best intervention − the goal of technocratic rationality − was not possible. Instead, the fellowship had to contextualize a generic strategy for each community. That is, the contextual rationality held by the community appeared to overpower technocratic rationality. The Mentor experienced excitement at gaining this insight.

In sum, we saw several structures constraining the spread of innovations in the Chapter 12: risk aversion, constraining bureaucratic rationalities, limited time, energy, and resources. Facilitating spread required leaders capable of action when faced with something new and who provided the needed resources to support change. It required project champions capable of building needed power relations and novel bureaucratic rationalities that side-stepped constraints. It also required project champions with contextual and institutional rationality. These rationalities allowed champions to align their programme with useful trends in the environment (e.g. the Province's shift to primary care homes). They also allowed champions to understand the constraints stakeholders faced when trying to adopt new programmes and to work with those stakeholders to manoeuvre around those barriers.

This concludes the presentation of my results. I presented my results in thematic categories. In Chapter 7, I explored the values inherent in the Seniors Programme. Chapter 8 evaluated how the BC working group managed executive resistance. Chapter 9 highlighted how CEO1 bound the organization to the Seniors Programme. In Chapter 10, I explored how rationalities combined and conflicted. I assessed how individuals reified power in Chapter 11. Chapters 12 and 13 explored the intent to spread the Seniors Programme and structures constraining and enabling spread, respectively. In the remaining chapters, I discuss these results and address my research questions. Though this discussion, I develop conclusions and recommendations that contribute to the development of organizational wisdom.

Chapter 14

Discussion: Values, Rationality, and Power

In this and following chapters, I present my analysis of these results. At this point, I have several disparate threads and themes surfaced through my analysis. Over the following chapters, I will pull these threads together and link them to actionable recommendations for practitioners, educators, and researchers to develop the capacity of organizations to act wisely. Recall in Chapter 2 I presented a review of the literature on organizational wisdom. I pulled three themes out of that review: values guide wise action, knowledge is required but insufficient for wise action, and wisdom is action-oriented. Thus, my study focused on the constructs of values, rationality, and power. In this chapter, I start with a discussion of the impact of values on the life of the Seniors Programme and how my interviewees advanced their values and managed tensions between values. Then, I discuss how different rationalities impacted the Seniors Programme, considering examples of both enabling and constraining rationalities. I explore tensions between rationalities and ways my interviewees managed those tensions.

When considering power, recall that I applied a phronetic research approach that Flyvbjerg (2001) established to facilitate the development of institutions' practical wisdom. This methodology prescribed phronetic research questions, several of which focused on power. From this, I developed the following research questions:

- How did power affect the process of developing and implementing the Seniors Programme in the BC Health Authority?
- Did power wielded by stakeholders of the Seniors Programme result in organizational actions in keeping with the values of Canada's healthcare system?

I address the first research question at the end of this chapter and the second question in Chapter 15. This discussion leads to the final phronetic research question: 'What's to be done?' I address this in Chapter 16, and it is there that I draw all the threads from this study together to link my findings to the development of organizational wisdom. Finally, in Chapter 17, I pool this learning and propose a path forward to enact the ideas established in my discussion. With the path charted before us, I turn now to my discussion of values and their impact on the life of the Seniors Programme.

14.1. Values

Values guide wise action. They determine the ends we find worthy of achieving and the means we find acceptable to achieve them (Kalberg, 1980; Townley, 2008b; Weber, 1978). In this section, I discuss how values drove action during the Seniors Programme's life, providing examples of how they enabled and constrained action. I then focus on the relationship between values, rationality, and power, demonstrating that values need rationality and power to have an effect, but rationality and power need values to have direction. After that, I explore how values conflicted during the life of the Seniors Programme and the tactics my interviewees used to address these conflicts. Rather than provide an exhaustive list of the role every value played, which would be unwieldy, I will instead focus on illuminating examples demonstrating the points I wish to make. Let us now explore how values enabled and constrained action.

14.1.1. Values Enabled Action

The value dialogue was a structure enabling the action of collaboration and the collective reasoning that resulted from it. Let us first focus on CEO1. The value dialogue resonated strongly in him and was instrumental in leading him to collaborate with the Foundation and the NS Health Authority. In his own words:

> I think any health authority who becomes insular and inward-looking is going to have problems [...] Bringing these differences just adds strength. It adds strength to the form and structure of potential innovation. (CEO1, personal communication, 6 June 2017)

Individuals within the BC Health Authority shared this value. The Mentor, for example, exhibited a constant desire to refer issues to the Training Fellowship for discussion, such as the naming of the target patient population, creating their public name, and developing their vision statement.

Similarly, consider the effort the Training Fellowship put into crafting communications documents − thirteen drafts for a single-paged communication − to situate the Seniors Programme within a community of healthcare. Consider also the Foundation's mandate for spread, which explicitly identified collaboration as a key aim ('[The Foundation] − What We Do,' 2018). Moreover, recall CEO1's comments that the BC Health Authority had a culture of collective decision-making (personal communication, 6 June 2017). CEO1 operated in an environment that valued dialogue. It was a structure of the social system in which he worked in that the value emerged out of the actions of individuals yet was irreducible to any one agent's actions.

Was that structure enabling, however? To address this, imagine that rather than valuing dialogue, the healthcare system CEO1 worked in valued competition. How might his ability to bind his organization to collaboration have been affected if the healthcare system operated on the belief that only through pitting groups against each other could a health authority develop the best solution to its problems? Would the Foundation, an organization whose mandate was to facilitate collaboration, even exist in such a system? Instead, CEO1 operated in a system that, like him, valued dialogue. Within the ranks of his staff were individuals who also valued dialogue. Organizations such as the Foundation existed whose purpose was to assist in the formation of collaborations. Thus, the value of dialogue was a structure within healthcare organizations that enabled CEO1's ability to form a collaboration with organizations across the country to engage in collective reasoning and group action to address the problems of seniors' care.

14.1.2. Values Constrained Action

The value I will focus on is accountability and how it constrained the ability to develop and spread the Seniors Programme. To do this, I will first establish what members of the BC Health Authority were accountable to achieve. As described by the Province of British Columbia website (n.d.), the Ministry of Health set up healthcare regions in BC to administer care in specific geographic areas within the province. Managers and staff within the health authority were responsible for developing and implementing programmes and services that met the healthcare needs of residents within the region. To hold managers accountable, the Ministry of Health set performance objectives (Province of British Columbia, n.d.). In general, the Ministry of Health's objectives focused on supporting the health and well-being of BC citizens, delivering an effective and responsive system of healthcare to BC while achieving value for money spent. Collaboration and spread between regions and provinces were not the aims of the Ministry. When the BC Health Authority translated these objectives into performance targets, its focus was exclusively on metrics within its region (e.g. setting surgery wait time targets) (BC Health Authority, 2014, 2015). In short, the Ministry held staff and managers of the BC Health Authority accountable to objectives within their region.

Responses of my interviewees suggested many managers adopted the value of accountability towards the goals set out by the Ministry of Health. This value of accountability, thus, constrained the Training Fellowship's ability to collaborate and spread. We see this first surfacing as CEO1 described the lack of support he received from the Ministry for his desire to collaborate inter-provincially. We see this also with CEO2's focus on spreading the Seniors Programme within the BC Health Authority rather than nationally. In both these situations, those with authority, be it the Ministry or CEO2, did not oppose spread and collaboration. They simply did not prioritize it – they were not accountable to achieve it, and thus did not use their power to facilitate it.

There were, however, instances surfaced in my interviews where the value of accountability put up active barriers to collaboration and spread. One barrier was senior managers' focus on acute care and decongestion, both of which were consistent with the Ministry's objectives. The Mentor perceived this as a point of resistance to the Seniors Programme. The Senior Improvement Lead identified it as a cause of fatigue and stretched resources compromising managers' ability to adopt innovations. Thus, accountability erected barriers to collaboration and spread while discouraging senior leaders from exercising power to overcome them.

14.1.3.   Acting to Overcome Constraining Structures

Recall from Chapter 5, the Transformational Model of Social Action maintained that social structures shaped every action an individual takes, and those actions either reproduce or change those structures (Ackroyd & Fleetwood, 2000; Bhaskar, 1986; Giddens, 1976, 1984; Manicas, 1980; Pratten, 1993). Though the value of accountability constrained the BC working group's ability to collaborate and spread the Seniors Programme, they took actions to overcome them. Unable to find support in the Ministry of Health for collaboration, CEO1 partnered with the Foundation to access the resources the BC Health Authority needed to collaborate with other health authorities. The Site Director identified how the BC working group engaged in defining rationality by aligning the Seniors Programme with strategic objectives to gain managerial support. Other interviewees described how they activated other enabling structures such as CEO2's act of coercion through funding regions to adopt the Seniors Programme. The above suggested a vital component of the Seniors Programme's success were individuals who understood the enabling and constraining structures within their organizational context and then took effective action to reproduce the structures that enabled and overcame those that constrained.

Note the requirement of power for the above processes. To live the value of dialogue, CEO1 had to produce power relations with other organizations. To overcome managers' resistance, the BC working group aligned the Seniors Programme with VPs strategic objectives, an act of defining rationality. Power at turns enabled and constrained the Seniors Programme, and in each instance, it was the values of the wielder that guided those acts of power. Though values needed power to have an effect, power needed values to have direction.

14.2.   Rationality

Knowledge is required but insufficient for wise action. It is through rationality we determine how to achieve worthy ends (Townley, 2008b). Moreover, defining rationality is how power shapes preferences for action (Flyvbjerg, 1998). I have classified them as structures under the framework of critical realism, and thus I view them as capable of enabling and constraining action. In the following sections, I present examples of how rationality enabled action during the life of the Seniors Programme, as well as how it constrained. I will then consider the actions individuals took to reproduce and change those structures. As with my discussion of values above, I will focus my discussion on single examples, starting with an example of rationality enabling action.

14.2.1. Rationality-enabled Action

Bureaucratic rationality was a structure enabling the development and implementation of the Seniors Programme through the BC Health Authority's participation in the Training Programme. In Chapter 3, I presented five ways described by Townley (2008b) through which bureaucratic rationality enabled action, and each of these mechanisms was active in this example. (1) The Project Charter was a *document* that defined objects, activities, and people encompassed by the Training Programme. One of its significant tasks of definition was establishing that, through execution of the charter, the BC Health Authority committed to a collaboration with the Foundation and NS Health Authority to participate in the Training Programme. (2) The Project Charter established *boundaries* though defining the scope of the programme. (3) It codified *rules* of the collaboration, such as outlining requirements for terminating the agreement. (4) It identified *processes* through which the Training Fellowship would operate. (5) It specified *procedures and roles* for key personnel. In total, the Project Charter was a powerful act of bureaucratic rationality. It was through it that CEO1 established the structure of the Training Programme from which the fellowship then produced the Seniors Programme.

14.2.2. Rationality-constrained Action

Economic rationality, in conjunction with bureaucratic rationality, constrained the BC working group's ability to spread the Seniors Programme. From the perspective of economic rationality, recall the Site Director and MD Lead identified the lack of a billing framework for performing a CGA prevented physicians from adopting the Seniors Programme. Without appropriate remuneration, it made no financial sense for physicians to take the time required to complete this assessment. The bureaucratic rationality establishing how healthcare professionals delivered primary care supplemented this constraint. The healthcare system adopted procedures and roles that laid the responsibility for frailty assessments wholly on physicians. Processes prevented the collaboration between the primary care physician and other professionals that might otherwise have dispersed the responsibility of frailty assessment across several people. These rationalities combined to dissuade physicians from adopting the Seniors Programme, thereby constraining the BC working group's attempt to spread. Typically in the organizational wisdom literature, when they say knowledge is insufficient for wise action, they mean knowledge is often incomplete or flawed, necessitating the capacity for adaptation and improvisation (see, for example, Bierly et al., 2000; Chia & Holt, 2007; Weick, 2007). Here, though, we see another reason why knowledge may be insufficient, and that is because rationalities can define organizational structures that constrain a desired action. Knowing the Seniors Programme had benefit to elderly patients was insufficient to drive adoption because, regardless of its benefits, it did not make financial sense for physicians to implement it.

14.2.3. *Acting to Overcome Constraining Rationalities*

Throughout the life of the Seniors Programme, my interviewees took actions to overcome constraining structures of rationality. For example, they exercised their bureaucratic rationality to overcome the economic and bureaucratic constraints discouraging physicians from adopting the Seniors Programme. In response to those constraining structures, the BC working group took the documentation of the CGA and put it online. This action modified the procedures and processes physicians performed to assess frailty, effectively automating the assessment. These actions halved the time it took physicians to measure frailty, thereby mitigating the constraints that economic and bureaucratic rationality imposed on the programme's spread. As the above demonstrate, overcoming these constraints required the BC working group to possess deep insight into the rationalities guiding physician action combined with the creativity needed to modify these constraining structures to facilitate the desired outcome.

Exercising these rationalities required power, and I see three dynamics between power and rationality in this data. First, rationality required power for its implementation. For example, the bureaucratic rationality embodied in the Project Charter only had power because CEO1 had the authority to imbue it with power. Second, overcoming constraining rationalities required power. Developing the eCGA required power to obtain needed resources of personnel and funding, as well as the power to incorporate the eCGA in physician offices for use. Third, rationality – especially bureaucratic rationality – reified power. The authority of CEO1 to create the Seniors Programme was manifest through the Project Charter. Thus, whereas values guide power, rationality informs power how to achieve those ends while also being the means through which power manifests. I explore this concept in the next section where I discuss my first research question.

14.3. How Did Power Affect the Process of Developing and Implementing the Seniors Programme in the BC Health Authority?

Wisdom is action-oriented; to act, individuals must exercise power. Throughout this book, I have provided a detailed account of how individuals used power during the life of the Seniors Programme. Now I will step back and give a general commentary on the use of power. Throughout, my data showed that values guided individuals' action. They then applied various forms of rationality to determine how to achieve those ends. Combined, these formed structures that enabled or constrained action. It was power that gave these structures potency. To achieve a value, one must exercise power to overcome barriers. Likewise, one must exert power to ensure that it is their rationality that informs action, rather than another. Moreover, it is through rationality, especially bureaucratic rationality, that actors reified power.

I explore this further in the following sections. First, I consider values and their relationship with rationality and power. I review major value conflicts I observed in my data and how individuals addressed them. Then I turn to rationality, discussing first how bureaucratic rationality reified power. Following this, I discuss how individuals addressed rationality conflicts throughout the Seniors Programme's life.

14.3.1. Values Need Rationality and Power

What gives values the ability to enable or constrain action? They are only our beliefs, after all, little more than ephemeral thoughts and desires. As my results show, the BC Health Authority embedded values in webs of rationality and power, and it is this that gave values capacity to touch the world. Rationality and power answer the question of *how* the organization enabled or constrained action. Values answer the question of *what* actions the organization enabled or constrained. Without rationality and power, values have no effect. Without values, rationality and power have no direction. To demonstrate this point, I will focus on CEO1's actions to recruit the Mentor to the Training Fellowship.

Recall from Table 7.1 (page 81) that the prime value of public interest and instrumental values of innovation, dialogue, and effectiveness motivated CEO1's interest in the Seniors Programme. Recall also that CEO1 believed endeavours such as the Seniors Programme required project champions to succeed. Thus, a critical component of his intention to enact his values required the recruitment of 'disciples' to the cause. Recruiting disciples was itself an act of bureaucratic rationality (assigning roles and responsibilities). From his prior working relationship with the Mentor, CEO1 believed she had these qualities, and he attempted to recruit her to champion the programme. Though her values drew her to the programme, she was, however, busy in her current role in the BC Health Authority and declined his offer. CEO1 exercised his power in the organization, mediated through bureaucratic rationality, to arrange leave from her current position. The Mentor, however, had enough contextual rationality of the BC Health Authority to recognize the VPs did not support the Seniors Programme. She worried about the potential for political backlash if she became involved, especially if the programme failed. Informed by contextual rationality, both CEO1 and the Mentor recognized giving her a job title associated with the Seniors Programme would make her more of a target for VP backlash. CEO1 subsequently channelled his power through bureaucratic rationality to assign her to the programme without a job title. With reassuring actions such as this, the Mentor felt comfortable enough to accept his invitation, and the Seniors Programme got its first champion. In summary, without exercising rationality and power, CEO1 would have been bereft of a critical project champion needed to achieve his value of public interest. Likewise, it was the pursuit of these values that gave direction to CEO1's exercise of rationality and power.

One should also note that values were embedded in networks of power. Why was CEO1 able to advance a programme of public interest? Because he worked for the BC Health Authority, which had a mandate to pursue public interest

(BC Health Authority, 2014). Why did the BC Health Authority pursue public interest? Because the BC Ministry of Health established it to do so (Government of British Columbia, 2014). Why did the Ministry of Health do this? Because the Canada Health Act mandated it to do so (Government of Canada, 2014). What empowered the Canada Health Act to set this chain in motion? The will of the people manifest through the Government of Canada. Irrespective of CEO1's values, networks of power embedded the value of public interest in the BC Health Authority.

14.3.2. Value Conflict – Theatres of Battle

As discussed in Chapter 3, values may be incompatible, if not incommensurate with each other, creating challenges for individuals tasked with delivering them (De Graff et al., 2014; Kettl, 1993). As my above example of constraining values demonstrated, members of the BC working group encountered situations where the values guiding key stakeholders posed barriers to those the group were trying to realize through the Seniors Programme. I have identified two theatres of battle where stakeholder values conflicted with that of the Seniors Programme: differences in instrumental values, and differences in the timing of values. I describe these theatres of conflict below, providing examples of each. I then discuss how my interviewees sought to address these conflicts.

14.3.2.1. Theatre 1: Instrumental Values

Are values exclusively ends in themselves? The literature often describe them as such (see, for example, Kalberg, 1980; Townley, 2008b; Weber, 1978). Dahl and Lindblom (1953), however, challenged this notion.

> But because most 'ends' are themselves means in a lengthy chain
> of means-and-ends; because an end in one chain of means-ends
> may be a means in another chain of action; and because a means
> in one chain may be an end in another, sometimes the language
> of means-ends is slippery and cumbersome. (p. 26)

They subsequently distinguished between prime and instrumental values, the prime value being an end, the instrumental a means to an end. They were quick to point out, however, that real life is complicated enough to defy the simplicity of such nomenclature (they used the example of walking to a mailbox to mail a letter – is the walk purely instrumental if the individual enjoys a good walk?). Thus, even though applying differentiating nomenclature between the two types of values has utility in understanding the social process under investigation, one should remember these phenomena slide from one category to the other depending on the context and the individual.

Data from my interviews identified both prime and instrumental values. For example, many respondents did not appear to value innovation as an end. They were not interested in innovation for the sake of innovation. Instead, innovation was a means to achieve public interest (refer to Table 7.1, page 81, for a complete list of prime and instrumental values perceived in the Seniors Programme). My interviews revealed that differences in instrumental values led to value conflict, even when groups shared prime values. For example, both the BC working group and VPs of the BC Health Authority shared the prime value of public interest. The BC working group, however, relied on the instrumental value of innovation to achieve it (developing the Seniors Programme), whereas VPs relied on robustness (focusing on delivering acute care and decongestion). These different instrumental values led some VPs to erect barriers to the BC working group's efforts, such as preventing their staff from working on the programme.

14.3.2.2. Theatre 2: Temporal Dimensions of Values

Looking back at Figure 8.1 (page 93), we see that even when groups shared values, their timing may be a source of conflict. For example, the Seniors Programme focused on public interest, effectiveness, and sustainability in the long-term, whereas VPs focused on the same values in the short-term. The difference in time horizon created barriers to building support for the Seniors Programme among the VPs because the resources needed to achieve long-term values took away from the immediate needs facing managers. To further explain this, remember that structures do not work in isolation. Instead, they intertwine in complex ways. Here, even though they shared values, those values linked to conflicting bureaucratic rationalities (different boundaries of time) empowered through organizational means of coercion (incentives and punishments linked to achievements within a timeframe).

14.3.2.3. Addressing Value Conflicts

Recall that in Chapter 3 I presented several means through which public servants addressed value conflicts. These included firewalls, cycling, casuistry (Thacher & Rein, 2004), bias, hybridization, incrementalism (Stewart, 2006), and compromise (Oldenhof et al., 2014). Which of these did the BC working group use when managing value conflicts? To assess this, let us first identify the groups involved in value conflict with the Seniors Programme as well as the theatres of conflict. My interviews uncovered two broad groups with whom my interviewees experienced value conflicts. The first was with the VPs during the stage of assembling the Training Fellowship. You will recall from Chapter 8 not all of them supported the Seniors Programme and used their power within the organization to create roadblocks to its development. The second was healthcare directors in the community the BC working group encountered as they tried to spread the Seniors Programme through the BC Health Authority after the Training Fellowship. Recall that the 'urgency of the now' besieged these directors such that they lacked the energy or resources to commit to adopting the Seniors Programme. In both situations, the theatres of conflict were those described above: conflict over instrumental values and timing.

The BC working group demonstrated insight into the tensions leading to value conflict. To address these conflicts, they engaged in tactics of hybridization and incrementalism. Regarding hybridization, where individuals seek to reconcile conflicting values (Stewart, 2006), the BC working group employed two tactics to address the conflict in instrumental values (innovation versus robustness). First, they emphasized the shared prime value, public interest, by, for example, demonstrating the impact of the programme on senior health. Second, they aligned their innovative programme with the value of robustness as follows. Interviewees suggested healthcare managers knew current processes were unsustainable as the population aged (robustness was under threat), and they positioned the Seniors Programme as a solution (innovation used to remove the threat to robustness). Thus, even though differing instrumental values caused friction, they took action that reconciled these differences in the minds of managers, thereby creating support for the programme.

They combined the strategy of hybridization with incrementalism where officials emphasize one value over time (Stewart, 2006). For example, during the period they were assembling the Training Fellowship, CEO1 was a key driver of the Seniors Programme, and he engaged in incrementalism to address both different instrumental values and temporal conflicts. He did this through exercising his power to override VP concern and encourage their support for the Seniors Programme – that is, he emphasized innovation and a long-term view where otherwise robustness and short-termism would have dominated. Likewise, while the team focused on spreading the Seniors Programme after the Training Fellowship, they 'planted seeds' in managers' minds about the programme while they waited for the community to become ready to take on the change process. Meanwhile, CEO2 used his power to offer incentives and resources to communities adopting the Seniors Programme. Here, again, the BC working group emphasized innovation and long-termism in a realm where robustness and short-termism dominated, patiently waiting for communities to come on board.

In both situations, rather than directly challenge or attempt to override the other group's values, the BC working group used tactics to advance their values while preserving the other group's values. Why? Though members of the BC working group lacked the power to override the values of VPs and community managers, was this true of the CEO? Could he have not said 'This is the new direction' and driven adoption of the new values? I suggest four reasons this was not the case.

First, proponents of the Seniors Programme shared prime values with the VPs and community managers – it was instrumental values and timing over which conflict existed. Interview data indicated they recognized the importance of these instrumental values and time concerns in achieving the prime values. In effect, they agreed with the VPs and community managers. They were not enemies but instead focused on different faces of the same battle. They, therefore, sought an approach that maintained the VPs' instrumental values and time concerns. Second, the BC Ministry of Health gave the BC Health Authority its mandate and concomitant values. Not even the CEO could override the power structures the Ministry created to redirect the organization to new values. Third, CEO1 identified the BC Health Authority was a 'federal' organization, resulting in a collaborative rather than command-and-control organization. Again, not even the CEO could override these historical power structures to impose a new set of values. Fourth, the Seniors Programme was a tiny programme compared to the scale of activities the BC Health Authority performed. Though both CEO1 and CEO2 supported the programme, it would only occupy a small portion of their attention. They, therefore, delegated implementation to the BC working group. If CEOs lacked the power to alter organizational values radically, this was even more true of the members of the BC working group. Thus, they had to rely on approaches that advanced their values without compromising the values of the VPs and community managers. This concludes my discussion on the relationship between values and power. I now turn to explore the relation between rationality and power, considering first how bureaucratic rationality reified power.

14.3.3. *Bureaucratic Rationality Reified Power*

Earlier when discussing values and their relation to rationality and power, I said values answer *what* actions the organization enabled or constrained, whereas rationality and power answered *how* it enabled or constrained those actions. Rationality and power perform two separate roles when addressing 'how'. Rationality provides a framework for understanding the environment and determining actions. Power, on the one hand, shapes that framework and understanding while on the other hand gives the resultant actions force. Through values, actors give structures direction. Through rationality, they give them form. Through power, potency. The relation between rationality and power flows two ways: power shapes rationality, and rationality gives form and structure to power. In this section, I will focus my discussion here on how rationality – specifically bureaucratic rationality – gave form and structure to power in the Seniors Programme.

My interview data contained multiple examples of bureaucratic rationality giving form to power, the previous discussion of the Project Charter enabling development of the Seniors Programme being but one example. In that situation, CEO1 wanted his organization to commit to developing the Seniors Programme, he had enough power over the organization to accomplish this, and it was through his exercise of bureaucratic rationality that this power manifested to drive action. Other examples included the constraining nature of historical procedures, roles, process, and documentation in doctor's offices that restricted their ability to adopt the Seniors Programme. I also spoke of the BC working group's exercise of bureaucratic rationality to modify documents and processes (moving from paper CGAs to electronic). Additionally, I spoke of CEO2's modification of roles and boundaries (assigning nurses to participating physician offices to assist), and the Province's shift in procedures, roles, and processes (moving to a primary care home model of healthcare delivery) that enabled physician adoption of the Seniors Programme. What these examples show is bureaucratic rationality was one way that individuals reified power. It was a conduit through which one person's power translated into another's action. When the organization constructed effective bureaucratic rationalities, power flowed smoothly. For example, the Head Coach spoke at length about how it was a pleasure to work with the BC working group due to the clarity in processes, procedures, and roles. Ineffective bureaucratic rationalities constrained flows of power. Established procedures, roles, and processes in physician offices, for example, hampered the ability of doctors to adopt the Seniors Programme.

To reify power through bureaucratic rationality, one must first possess the power to do so. A janitor could not develop a project charter, sign it, and thus bind the organization in collaboration with others, but the CEO could. Likewise, CEO1 could execute the Project Charter, but CEO2 could not alter the fee codes and organizational structure of family practice to facilitate physician adoption of the Seniors Programme – the boundaries of his authority did not stretch that far. The power (or lack thereof) to enact bureaucratic rationalities are themselves governed by other bureaucratic rationalities. For example, the Project Charter assigned power to the Training Fellowship to develop the processes, documents, roles, and procedures they enacted with the BC Coaching Organization.

This finding is consistent with previous work. Smith (2001), for example, argued that it was through texts that organizations existed beyond particular times, places, and social interactions. She demonstrated that these texts coordinated the activity of personnel to create organizational action. As I further discussed in Chapter 3, Townley (2008b) identified bureaucratic rationality as a means of control. 'Bureaucracy allows the administration to be discharged precisely and unambiguously [...]' (Townley, 2008b, p. 49). In earlier work, Townley (1993) argued, 'Rationality is the idea that before something can be governed or managed, it must first be known' (p. 520). She demonstrated, for example, that the function of human resource management was to render individuals and activities knowable so that organizations might govern them. One can draw a connection between rendering individuals and activities knowable to her later discussion (2008b) of roles, procedures, and processes that she categorized as bureaucratic rationality. In addition to control, other rationalities gave actors an understanding of their environment and a plan of action. What happens, then, when rationalities conflict? I explore this next.

14.3.4. *When Rationalities Collide*

When I speak of conflicting rationalities in this context, I do not mean the process where people may disagree over, let us say, the interpretation of a set of data. Instead, I mean it to refer to those instances when different ways of knowing lead to different desired actions. For example, a scientific study may conclude that exercise is good for you (i.e. technocratic rationality), but the aches and pains in your joints tell you that to exercise would invite injury, worsening your health (i.e. body rationality). These conflicts can be pernicious because adherence to one way of knowing may lead an individual to invalidate another way of knowing. If two individuals subscribe to the same rationality, let us say technocratic, then they at least agree on the process of acquiring knowledge and determining action – you design an experiment, collect data, analyse it, and make conclusions. When individuals hold different rationalities, say technocratic versus body, then their ways of knowing are different − technocratic perform scientific experiments, body relies on subjective experience. When individuals cling too tightly to one form of rationality, they may not recognize the validity of the process another rationality uses to gain knowledge. What basis is there, then, for fruitful debate?

My data demonstrated that in addition to values, rationalities − different ways of knowing − were another domain of conflict. In the following sections, I highlight four areas of rationality conflict. These conflicts occurred when attempting to apply a standardized programme across diverse regions, naming the target population, applying a standardized intervention across diverse individual patients, and asking physicians to adopt the Seniors Programme. Through this discussion, I will show that technocratic rationality was always at odds with other rationalities. I will discuss reasons for this. Then I will conclude with an exploration of different means through which interviewees negotiated these conflicts.

14.3.4.1. Standardization versus Regional Differences

The Seniors Programme was an evidence-based programme. As such, it was a product of technocratic rationality. When considering what drew interviewees to the Seniors Programme, the idea of applying evidence to practice − that is, technocratic rationality − was a significant driver (see Table 7.1, page 81). As Townley (2008b) explained, technocratic rationality translates means-ends relations into reality assuming there exists one best means to achieve a particular end. Moreover, it assumes you can discover this one best means through the application of the scientific method. She categorized it as a form of disembedded rationality, which assumes there exists objective knowledge separate from contextual and individual differences.

During the Mentor's interview, she expressed the challenges they faced to this assumption (see, for example, Figure 10.2, page 129). Namely, differences in patient population between the BC and NS Health Authorities made applying a standardized, technocratic approach to both regions problematic. These differences implied the existence of contextual rationality. Contextual rationality assumes groups hold things in common that may differ from other groups, and so individuals can only determine what is rational from within that group. It is what Townley (2008b) classified as embedded rationality, which maintains that rationality is embedded in a perspective. Thus, technocratic and contextual rationalities conflicted in this instance. Interviewees wanted to apply the scientific method to discover how to prevent frailty, but differences between the regions thwarted their intentions of applying one best method.

14.3.4.2. Literature versus Group Preferences

My data showed technocratic and other rationalities conflicted again when the Training Fellowship developed the name 'pre-frail seniors with chronic conditions' to identify their target patient population (see Figure 10.4, page 135). The

Training Fellowship first went to the literature and sought expert opinion. I classified this as technocratic rationality. From the context of how my interviewees used the term 'literature,' I inferred it to mean the repository of documented scientific discoveries. 'Experts' were those individuals who had achieved some success publishing their scientific studies. This reliance on literature and those who engaged in scientific discovery were consistent with the precepts of technocratic rationality.

When the BC working group met with seniors groups to learn their preferences for their name, they discovered several rationalities arrayed against technocratic rationality. Many seniors did not perceive themselves as frail. This perception was an example of body rationality. As Townley (2008b) explained, body rationality assumes our senses and lived experience is a source of knowledge. She classified it as an embodied form of rationality, which maintains that it is through our bodies that we know the world. In addition to not perceiving themselves as frail, they also disliked the negative connotations of words like 'frail' or 'senior'. This preference demonstrated emotional rationality was also at play. Emotional rationality is another form of embodied rationality. Townley (2008b) described it as a response to social stimuli connecting what is felt with what is expressed. Seniors felt the words 'frail' and 'senior' were negative, and they had an emotional reaction in response to them. These body and emotional rationalities combined to create contextual rationality – within the senior demographic, words like 'frail' and 'seniors' were not appropriate. Despite what the literature might say, such terms were irrelevant and distasteful.

14.3.4.3. Standardization versus the Individual

The Head Coach presented another conflict between rationalities. Recall that what attracted the BC working group to the BC Coaching Organization was that it was 'evidence-based'. It employed the Stanford model of chronic disease management. Recall also that the Head Coach instructed her coaches to modify the model to the location and individual capacities of participating seniors. This instruction presented a conflict between technocratic rationality (the evidence-based Stanford model) and body rationality (the individual's physical capacity).

14.3.4.4. Evidence versus Economics and Structure

Despite the encouraging data of the Seniors Programme, lack of fee codes and organizational infrastructure posed barriers to physician adoption (see Figure 12.3(a,b), page 172). Using the absence of a fee code as a reason to not adopt the Seniors Programme was an example of economic rationality. Townley (2008b) described economic rationality as that used by individuals to maximize their utility. She also described it as instrumental rationality, a means to an end. This conflict implied that a primary end of a physician's office was its financial viability.

Unsupportive bureaucratic rationality exacerbated this conflict with economic rationality. Appropriate roles and procedures (e.g. the primary care home model of healthcare delivery) may have offset the economic costs to the physician of performing the CGA. Townley (2008b) argued that bureaucracies created processes and roles to achieve operational predictability. In this situation, this predictability compromised physicians' ability to adopt the Seniors Programme.

14.3.4.5. Why Was Technocratic Rationality the Source of So Much Conflict?

I want to explore this question before moving to a discussion of how my interviewees resolved these conflicts. The above sections summarize the major rationality conflicts I uncovered through my analysis. There existed a common combatant throughout these examples: technocratic rationality. Moreover, it was the sole defendant facing off against an array of rationalities in multiple instances. Why was it so often in conflict? Though it could be random chance that technocratic rationality was involved in every major conflict, I feel there may be more to it. Fleming and Spicer (2014) identified systematic faces of power that '[...] congealed into more enduring institutional structures' (p. 240). Examples of this include domination, where hegemonic ideologies shape people's preferences, and subjectification, where people gain a sense of identity within a social order. I suggest technocratic rationality was a dominant, hegemonic ideology of the Canadian healthcare system. That is, it was an element of systematic power structures.

To support this assertion, I refer to several strategic plans and missions of various organizations within the healthcare system. For example, The Royal College of Physicians and Surgeons of Canada, which oversees medical education and standards, sees as part of its mandate to ensure '[...] that patients receive care from specialists and aspiring specialists who are achieving the highest standard of *evidence-informed* professional competencies [...]' (*Better Education, Better Care: Strategic Plan 2018–2020*, p. 9, emphasis added). The BC Ministry of Health, responsible for the administration of healthcare in BC, stated quality occurs when, '[...] Care that is provided is *evidence-based*' (Government of British Columbia, 2014, p. 17, emphasis added). The BC Health Authority identified as priorities the pursuit of evidence-based primary prevention and health programmes and evidence-informed access to clinically effective pharmaceuticals (BC Health Authority, 2015).

The responses of my interviewees during our discussions suggested the healthcare system paid more than lip service to technocratic rationality. It was a dominant form of rationality. For example, the pursuit of technocratic rationality was a major draw for my interviewees to the Seniors Programme (see Table 7.1, page 81), and my interviewees referred to the concepts of evidence-based or evidence-informed practice and 'the literature' throughout our discussions. The focus on evidence (i.e. technocratic rationality) ran through Canada's healthcare system and was a major issue of interest to my interviewees. It was a dominant ideology.

The data I collected and discussed above, however, suggested technocratic rationality, with its claim to objective knowledge disembedded from any situation- or individual-specific parameter, was directly challenged by Canada's diversity in patient population (contextual and body rationalities) and healthcare administration (economic and bureaucratic rationalities). Some of my interviewees recognized this was a long-standing challenge. In the words of the Mentor:

> [...] [H]ow do we take what researchers have come up with and then implement that? That was the piece that I felt that there was an opportunity inside of the health care system, (personal communication, 19 May 2017)

As the MD Lead stated:

> [The Training Fellowship] was pitched to me as a way of learning more about research application and how to base interventions on what's in the literature and ensuring that we are evidence-based as we go forward with any interventions. (personal communication, 8 August 2017)

This interest in learning how to apply evidence to practice suggested a gap between evidence and practice. The rationality conflicts I discussed above are examples of this gap. I now turn to discuss how my interviewees addressed these conflicts.

14.3.4.6. Resolving Rationality Conflicts
Through the course of my interviews, I identified three broad strategies the BC working group used to address conflicting rationalities. The first two included *hybridization* and *bias*, terms that I have borrowed from the literature on value conflict (see Stewart, 2006). The third strategy I have called *striking exemplars*. I first consider hybridization, which is the act of trying to reconcile conflicting paradigms.

Hybridization. The BC working group used this approach when addressing the challenges in different patient populations between BC and NS, and again when the Head Coach modified the Stanford model to account for individuals' different physical capacities. When dealing with the differences in patient population between BC and NS, the Mentor identified that they developed a 'staged' approach. Likewise, the Head Coach explained how she adapted the Stanford model to the needs of the individual senior.

In both examples, technocratic rationality recommended an action that contextual and body rationalities opposed. Individuals modified the recommendations of technocratic rationality to the contextual and individual circumstances to reconcile this conflict. Remember, though, that a critical element of technocratic rationality is the assumption that there is one best way to achieve an end that we can know through science (Townley, 2008b). Modifying technocratic rationality to conform to contextual or body rationalities seemed to be an abandonment of technocratic rationality. Conversely, the different regions or individuals were not doing *whatever* they wanted and ignoring the research. Instead, technocratic rationality gave what one might call well-validated direction. Regions and individuals then plotted their course in pursuit of that direction.

Bias. With this strategy, individuals favour one rationality over others. The BC working group used this strategy when selecting the name for their target population. Technocratic rationality led to the name pre-frail seniors. The contextual, body, and emotional rationality of seniors resisted the use of the words 'frail' and 'seniors.' The BC working group ignored the seniors' rationalities.

Striking exemplars. This approach seeks to convince another to abandon their rationality and accept yours using a striking exemplar. The BC working group used this approach when convincing seniors that they could delay frailty through participation in the Seniors Programme. They did this using the combination of their shocking vision statement, 'Age well, die fit,' combined with the striking exemplar of Olga, the 90-year-old track star (see Figure 10.5, page 143). Seniors' body rationality informed them that frailty was a part of ageing. Technocratic rationality demonstrated this need not be true. Rather than present the evidence alone, coaches would tap into seniors' situational rationality by presenting Olga's story as a striking exemplar. Listeners to the story believed she was an example of technocratic rationality's truth claim. Seeing such a striking exemplar of what they perceived to be a consequence of technocratic rationality led them to abandon their body rationality in favour of technocratic.

14.3.4.7. Which Rationality Prevails?
As I showed in Table 7.1 (page 81), technocratic rationality was of great importance to the members of the BC working group. In the first example, however, technocratic rationality was subordinate to contextual and body rationalities, leading the BC working group to adulterate their technocratic intentions. In the second example, though, technocratic rationality prevailed over the body and emotional rationality of seniors when the BC working group named the target population. In the third example, technocratic rationality prevailed again, but rather than ignoring the rationality of seniors as was done when naming the target population, coaches manipulated them into accepting technocratic dogma. What determined which rationality prevailed in each circumstance?

Flyvbjerg (1998) answered this. 'Rationality is context-dependent, the context often being power' (p. 227). The group with the most power used the rationality that prevailed in each circumstance. We saw this in the example where the BC working group relied on the strategy of bias when naming the target population. Physicians implemented the Seniors Programme, and so the BC working group needed a name for the target population that physicians found meaningful. As I argued earlier, physicians were indoctrinated with technocratic rationality. Thus, the technocratic name prevailed.

When a clear power hierarchy did not exist, or technocratic rationality's supporting power structures were weak, the BC working group had to either reconcile (i.e. hybridization) or manipulate (i.e. striking exemplar). When attempting to apply a standardized approach to different regions, contextual differences precluded the ability to implement technocratic rationality. When attempting to apply a standardized approach to different individuals, the physical capacities of participants simply made it impossible to implement technocratic rationality. In both cases, the physical impossibility of uniformly applying technocratic rationality undermined its power. If the BC working group was to retain technocratic rationality in any capacity, it required modification. In the other example, when attempting to attract seniors to partake in the Seniors Programme, coaches lacked the power to coerce seniors' participation. Coaches had to convince seniors to participate voluntarily, and to do this they had to convince seniors their body rationality was wrong. They did this using a striking exemplar.

The above discussions highlight how power affected the implementation of the Seniors Programme in the BC Health Authority. Individuals used power to advance their values and to resolve conflicts between values. Individuals used power to implement forms of rationality to achieve those values. They also used power to define rationality to produce needed power relations that drove the desired action. We saw that people often used bureaucratic rationality to reify power. Finally, we also saw how power affected the resolution between conflicting rationalities. I now turn in the following chapter to consider my second research question: Did power wielded by stakeholders of the Seniors Programme result in organizational actions in keeping with the values of Canada's healthcare system?

Chapter 15

Was the Use of Power Consistent with the Values of Canada's Healthcare System?

My second research question, 'Did power wielded by stakeholders of the Seniors Program result in organizational actions in keeping with the values of Canada's healthcare system?' was perniciously tricky to answer. One might hope for the simplicity of saying, 'Program X was consistent with the healthcare system's values. Therefore, supporting it was in keeping with the healthcare system's values.' I, at least, had been hoping for such simplicity when developing my research questions. From the discussion above, however, I have shown that individuals may pursue the same prime value and yet conflict over instrumental values and timing. Thus, one might argue that supporting the Seniors Programme was as consistent with the values of Canada's healthcare system as resisting it. Therefore, I will not use the support of the Seniors Programme as a litmus test for the advancement of the healthcare system's values. Instead, I will evaluate the approach individuals took to advance the programme and assess whether that approach advanced the values of Canada's healthcare system. As a reminder, I have summarized the values embedded in the Canada Health Act in Table 3.2 (page 27). They include public interest, innovation, dialogue, equity, altruism, and neutrality. I will start by discussing how stakeholders approached values in the context of the Seniors Programme, followed by a similar assessment of their approach to rationality. This will lead to a discussion of how stakeholders worked with (or against) groups that did not support the Seniors Programme. I will consider how they used power to resolve these conflicts. I will build an argument for and against whether stakeholders used power in a way consistent with the values of the Canada Health Act, and then present my conclusions on the matter. With that course plotted, I now turn to discuss how stakeholders used power to advance their values.

15.1. Approach to Values

Proponents of the Seniors Programme exhibited keen insight into the nature of value conflicts within the BC Health Authority. When discussing sources of resistance with VPs, members of the BC working group expressed an understanding of the challenges VPs faced and how that translated into resistance (see Figure 8.1, page 94). More than this, they recognized the importance of the values the VPs pursued. Consequently, they did not seek to undermine or overpower VPs through political games. Instead, they exercised power to reconcile conflicts in a way that maintained the integrity of the VPs' pursuit of their values. The BC working group took the same approach when attempting to spread the programme after the Training Fellowship disbanded (Figure 12.3, page 172). They recognized the pressures healthcare managers faced, and they worked with those managers in a way that supported the values they pursued.

How is this consistent with the values of Canada's healthcare system? Canada's healthcare needs are diverse, spanning every disease and demographic imaginable. Canadians expect that its healthcare system serves the nation now and will continue doing so in the future. Delivering such a broad mandate requires the realization of many different values. Proponents of the Seniors Programme sought to advance it in a way that *added* to the healthcare system's ability to deliver on these commitments, rather than sacrificing its capacity elsewhere to advance the programme. They put time and effort meeting with executives to reconcile value conflicts. They chose to spread slower, waiting for communities' readiness to adopt the programme, rather than seek coercive power to subdue communities, which could have undermined their capacity to deliver healthcare elsewhere. This slower approach seemed likely to grow the healthcare system's ability to deliver on its values.

15.2.   Approach to Rationalities

Earlier, I established that technocratic rationality was a core way of knowing venerated by proponents of the Seniors Programme. Despite this emphasis, I feel it is important to note this was not the only way of knowing used during the Seniors Programme's life. In the following paragraphs, I will argue that the BC working group recognized the limits of technocratic rationality in their specific context. Though they promoted technocratic rationality heavily, in practice they blended multiple rationalities to inform action. Finally, rather than dismiss different rationalities held by others, they respected them. I will then discuss how these approaches contributed to the values of Canada's healthcare system.

Let us first consider the limits of technocratic rationality the BC working group perceived. Earlier, I discussed the conflict between technocratic and contextual rationalities regarding the implementation of the Seniors Programme between BC and NS. Differences in patient population prevented a standardized approach. In the Mentor's interview, she stated this was a significant struggle for the Training Fellowship. This implied they very much wanted a standardized, technocratic approach. Rather than force the issue, they ultimately relented, sacrificing some of the technocratic aspects of their study in the face of what they saw as contextual realities. The Senior Improvement Lead reinforced this idea when discussing spread. She stated differences between healthcare regions prevented the uniform application of programmes. Instead, regions needed to adopt programmes to their circumstances. The BC working group had an intuitive awareness of this tension. Many of them were drawn to the Training Programme to understand how to apply evidence to practice. Translating that into the language of my study, they wanted to understand what role technocratic rationality served in a vast, complex, and diverse healthcare system, and how they could support that role. How do we gain the benefits of technocratic rationality without sacrificing the knowledge gained either contextually or through individual experience? They realized technocratic rationality had limits; they pushed it as far as they felt they could, and then relented at those borders to allow other rationalities to share the stage.

The BC working group often blended multiple rationalities to inform action, not just in the design of their study, but in many of their internal activities. For example, the act of collective reasoning was commonly used to inform action. The Training Programme itself with its focus on collaboration was an exercise in collective reasoning. The Mentor facilitated collective reasoning during the development of the name for the target population, the public name for their programme, and their vision statement. Moreover, though they spent much time reviewing the literature when developing the programme, they put the books down and met with seniors groups to gain contextual rationality of their target population. Through these meetings, the BC working group not only learned seniors' preferences towards how to refer to them but also how to design an intervention with which seniors would comply. Recall it was through these meetings they learned to run the Seniors Programme through physician offices rather than as posters in a community centre. Though the evidence-based nature of the programme attracted CEO2, he was a leader who did not need years of data to make a decision — he exercised body rationality, intuition honed over a career in the industry. Throughout the life of the Seniors Programme, individuals blended multiple forms of rationality, creating a thick, rich understanding of the phenomena they sought to address. They did not allow their veneration of technocratic rationality to stop them from using the knowledge other rationalities provided.

Concomitant with the willingness to learn from other rationalities, the BC working group exhibited respect for the rationalities other stakeholders held. For example, I discussed earlier how the group used the Olga story as a striking exemplar to convince patients to participate in the Seniors Programme. They did not patronize their patients with a 'Doctor knows best' attitude. They instead respected the body rationality of their patients, accepted it as real, and sought to persuade them to a different way of thinking. Even when they discarded another group's rationality, as the Training Fellowship did when selecting the name 'pre-frail seniors' for their target patient, they did so grudgingly and with regret. In sum, though the BC working group honoured technocratic rationality, they exhibited deep respect for other ways of knowing.

Was the BC working group's willingness to limit and blend technocratic rationalities with others consistent with the values of the healthcare system? Drawing from many pools of rationality allowed the Training Fellowship to engage in collective reasoning. As Townley (2008b) argued, collective reasoning creates a reservoir of rationality from which many minds sharpen their arguments and sideline unreasonable positions, resulting in better decisions. My interviewees perceived that the Seniors Programme resulting from these processes held tremendous value. The preamble to the Canada Health Act acknowledges, 'that future improvements in health will require the cooperative partnership of governments, health professionals, voluntary organizations and individual Canadians' (Government of Canada, 2014), which implies an intention to tap into the diversity of knowledge within the healthcare system. The Training Fellowship's approach to rationality appeared to improve the robustness of the Seniors Programme's design and facilitated buy-in from multiple stakeholders. Their approach, therefore, seems to be one that grows the healthcare system's ability to deliver on its values.

15.3.   Building Bridges, Not Burning Them

Interview data from the Site Director and MD Lead suggested they were introducing the Seniors Programme to a healthcare community with incumbent senior-care programmes. When presenting themselves to this community, they paid exhaustive attention to ensuring they did so in a way that did not undermine or threaten the work of others (see Figure 8.4(c), page 109). From a political perspective, this minimized the chances of an incumbent group launching an attack on the nascent programme. More than that, though, interviewees expressed the sentiment they wanted to add to the existing community, not replace it. 'We wanted to make sure that we were aligning with everything that's out there and using the language that was going to blend rather than be in conflict' (MD Lead, personal communication, 8 August 2017). They appeared to respect the work ongoing in the community.

> They're all really well-meaning people, but they didn't know about each other, and so we needed to get them to really start working together and being in harmony for their community. (MD Lead, personal communication, 8 August 2017)

The BC working group wanted to add to ongoing efforts, not supplant them.

Is this in keeping with the values of Canada's healthcare system? Senior care is fiendishly challenging to manage. Seniors' health issues can become complicated, straining the ability of a community to support them. Fostering the health of seniors requires diverse resources. The MD Lead claimed many community programmes operated in isolation from each other. Presenting the Seniors Programme so these programmes saw it as an ally facilitated cooperation between all these necessary components of senior care. This approach seemed to advance the public interest and tightened the cooperation between healthcare workers and community organizations promoted by the Canada Health Act (Government of Canada, 2014).

15.4.   Using Power to Reconcile, Not Defeat

Above, I have described several conflicts of values and rationality and presented the approach my interviewees took in resolving those conflicts. In general, the approaches to resolving these conflicts consisted of strategies to reconcile (e.g. hybridization, bias) or persuade (e.g. striking exemplars). They avoided confronting or overpowering the position of others. It was possible this was because the BC working group lacked the organizational power to do so. Indeed, we did see individuals use coercive power when they were able. For example, we saw CEO1 overriding the resistance of his VPs. Likewise, the Training Fellowship overrode seniors' concerns with the name 'pre-frail seniors'.

Even though CEO1 overrode resistance in his organization, he recognized that resistance remained. Consequently, he recruited 'disciples', such as the Mentor, and protected them from the organization's politics so they could go out and coax the VPs onside. Even though the BC working group overroad seniors' concerns, it was after extensive consultation with them. Moreover, overriding these concerns was a source of lingering dissatisfaction. Overall, advocates of the Seniors Programme preferred to exercise power in a way that maintained stability across stakeholder groups.

Did this approach forward the values of Canada's healthcare system? Flyvbjerg (1998) argued rationality required stability to hold influence. '[...] [W]here power relations take the form of open, antagonistic confrontations, power-to-power relations dominate over knowledge-power and rationality-power relations' (p. 232). Had proponents of the Seniors Programme attempted to overpower the resistance of different groups, these groups might have marshalled their resources to defend themselves, regardless of the Seniors Programme's merits. 'In such confrontations, use of naked power tends to be more effective than any appeal to objectivity, facts, knowledge, or rationality [...]' (p. 232). In their politically complex environment, proponents of the Seniors Programme took pains to advance it in a way that maintained stability with their stakeholder groups, giving it the best chance of survival by avoiding power-on-power conflict. Given the healthcare system's value of health promotion and cooperation between healthcare professionals, avoiding conflict to allow the system to focus on delivery of these values seemed a sound strategy.

15.5. But …

Proponents of the Seniors Programme perceived real value in it for seniors' health. 'The outcome that we showed was that after the six-month intervention, the frailty scores decreased, which means that the patients actually became younger for having the six-month intervention' (MD Lead, personal communication, 8 August 2017). Moreover, they perceived the status quo as ineffective and unsustainable to which efforts like the Seniors Programme were the solution.

> [...] [I]f you keep on going as-is now and just wait for people to
> deteriorate and then land up in the hospital, it's not sustainable.
> But if we were to get a population that is healthier and better able
> to self-management and there's resources in the community to help
> them, that was what was going to save the day in the end for all of
> acute care. (MD Lead, personal communication, 8 August 2017)

If the intent of the Canada Health Act was the delivery of healthcare to the population, if the status quo was unsustainable, threatening the system's capacity to deliver on its values, and if the Seniors Programme offered a solution, would that not warrant use of coercive power to drive its adoption?

The tactics employed by proponents of the Seniors Programme carefully avoided stepping on toes. Spread was slow, piecemeal, and limited, and at the time of the writing of this book, its future remained clouded in uncertainty, national adoption a distant dream. If the status quo was unsustainable, then surely bold action was required to avoid calamity. The BC working group was not powerless – they had the support of the BC Health Authority's CEO, who had the power to drive action within his organization and influence it abroad. Was their strategy of caution wise?

One cannot answer objectively whether a course of action was wise – we cannot compare outcomes with what might have been. Let us look at what we know about the Seniors Programme, however, and the perceptions of those involved with it to see if we cannot tease out some idea of the wisdom of their actions. Let us first consider the actions of CEO1 and CEO2. They did act to drive the Seniors Programme. CEO1 bound the organization to the Training Programme and then recruited and protected project champions. CEO2 devoted funds to develop and spread the Seniors Programme. A CEO must choose where they focus their attention – fighting one battle takes away from their ability to fight others. Denis et al. (2001) argued that leaders needed to balance strategic coupling (between members of the leadership team), organizational coupling (between members of the leadership team and their organizational base), and environmental coupling (between members of the leadership team and the external environment) to move their agenda forward. Pushing too hard in one area, such as the Seniors Programme, may compromise their ability to make advances elsewhere. Rodriguez et al. (2007) explored the political web of relations in organizations, discussing how pulling back on coercive forces in one area may maintain relations needed to forward action on other fronts. Whatever the reasons, the CEOs involved in the Seniors Programme put as much effort as they were willing or able to give to drive the programme's adoption.

Moreover, we do not know the nature of other programmes focused on seniors' health within the BC Health Authority, let alone the rest of Canada. Proponents of the Seniors Programme perceived it had value, but how did that value compare to all other programmes? Perhaps other programmes were better. Perhaps one programme was better in one situation, a second programme in another. Perhaps the hierarchy of effectiveness among programmes was unclear.

Given that uncertainty, one could make an argument to advance with caution. A comment from the MD Lead highlighted a further advantage to their approach of building relations rather than trying to force change. 'Each relationship gave us the next little bit that we needed to move on' (MD Lead, personal communication, 8 August 2017). Each power relation produced built inroads to the next step. Each new relation deepened the pool of collective reasoning from which the BC working group could draw.

In the end, the healthcare system was complex enough to preclude simple answers. It is wisdom that individuals draw on to navigate complexity. Proponents of the Seniors Programme faced an immense problem — no less than the problem of old age itself, a challenge that has flummoxed humanity since time immemorial. They operated within an organization possessing labyrinthine complexity and then added to that challenge by collaborating with other organizations. In this milieu, advocates of the Seniors Programme exercised power with as much wisdom as they possessed. Though the spread of the programme was slower than they would have liked, developing a programme that meaningfully helped seniors, and then spreading it as far as they had in a few short years — often in addition to other managerial responsibilities — was a notable accomplishment. We can learn much from it. To tease out this learning, I now turn to the final question guiding phronetic research: What's to be done?

Chapter 16

What's to Be Done? Facilitating the Development of Organizational Wisdom

At this point, we still have many disparate threads that speak to different aspects of organizational wisdom as it was expressed over the life of the Seniors Programme. It is time to tie them together. By tying these threads together, I will pull out propositions that contribute to our current understanding of organizational wisdom. From these propositions, I will identify actionable recommendations to foster the development of organizational and managerial wisdom. Recall the three themes of organizational wisdom I provided at the end of Chapter 2. (1) Values guide wise action. In organizations, values of multiple stakeholders interact and conflict. Wisdom requires individuals to navigate this complex web of values and the power relations behind them. (2) Knowledge is required but insufficient for wise action. Knowledge informs us how to achieve an end, but knowledge is often flawed and incomplete. Moreover, different ways of knowing create conflict. Wisdom requires individuals to include different types of knowledge in their decision-making process and to expand their knowledge by learning from the insights of other stakeholders. (3) Wisdom is action-oriented. It requires individuals to exercise power to *do* the right thing. I have organized this chapter along these three themes. In Table 16.1, I have summarized my propositions and recommendations. Let us turn now to values.

16.1. Values Guide Wise Action

I want to start this section with a personal anecdote I experienced while developing this study. I was contacting organizations involved in the Seniors Programme to obtain permission to conduct interviews and gain access to project documents. At one point, I found myself introducing my study over the phone to a senior executive in one of these organizations. She found the concept of organizational wisdom interesting, but the moment I explained my intent to explore how values drove action I immediately sensed her withdrawal. I could feel her thumb hover over the end-call button as she explained they were a very business-minded organization tasked with the duty to improve the sustainability and efficacy of healthcare administration and was not confident my focus on values aligned with their needs. I quickly responded along the lines of, 'Ummm, think of values as objectives. Different groups in organizations have different objectives, and managers need to reconcile situations where their objectives

Table 16.1. Summary of Propositions and Recommendations.

Themes	Propositions	Recommendations
Values guide wise actions	(1) Values guide episodic uses of power.	(1) Incorporate value alignment in recruitment processes.
	(2) Values drive project champions, who then drive action.	
	(3) When personal values align with organizational values, synergies happen.	
	(4) Even when groups share values, value conflicts may occur along instrumental or temporal lines.	(2) Develop capacity to recognize and reconcile value conflicts in organizations.
	(5) Value conflicts can form a point of resistance to organizational action unless individuals address them.	
Knowledge is required but insufficient for wise action.	(6) Knowledge is required but insufficient for wise action.	(3) Blend rationalities.
		(4) Tap into the power of collective reasoning.
		(5) Experiment.
		(6) Have an 'appreciative inquiry' mindset.
	(7) Rationalities conflict and part of wisdom is recognizing which rationality has power in a specific context.	(7) Develop bureaucratic, institutional, and contextual rationalities through experience, self-reflectivity, and mentoring.
Wisdom is action-oriented	(8) Bureaucratic rationality translates power into action.	(8) Develop an organizational structure that facilitates the activities that lead to organizational wisdom.
	(9) Institutional and contextual rationality inform the effective use of bureaucratic rationalities.	
	(10) Facilitating organizational action is a group activity.	(10) Build teams capable of implementing the precepts of wise action.

Table 16.1. (*Continued*)

Themes	Propositions	Recommendations
		(11) Protect your team from the political dynamics of your organization.
	(12) Producing power relations and using them to advance your objectives is critical. Choose your partners thoughtfully.	(11) Develop effective negotiation skills that allow you to build needed power relations.
		(12) Avoid conflict when you can.
	(13) Defining rationality is a means to produce useful power relations.	

conflict.' I had her attention again. The thumb came off the end-call button with an, 'Oh, yes, that sounds interesting [...]'

This incident stuck with me. Despite a growing awareness of corporate social responsibility; despite the fact healthcare in Canada is socialized and not-for-profit; despite the fact healthcare organizations are built to provide a public good, here I was confronted with a senior manager of a healthcare organization who was so devoted to disembedded rationalities that she perceived 'values' a topic of little interest. I had to camouflage values in the lexicon of instrumental-rationality, masquerading them as glorified key performance indicators to which managers hold subordinates accountable, in order to retain her attention. If a healthcare organization has no interest in values, imagine how little regard for-profit businesses must hold them. As Weber (1978, p. 26) identified, those who adhere strongly to instrumental-rationality see value-rationality as irrational due to values' subjective nature. Yet profit maximization – the concept that serves as the foundation of managerial thought – is a value. So is a duty to share-holders, efficiency, customer service, innovation, valuing employees, and so on – values are woven into the fabric of our conceptualization of organizations. In organizational studies, however, they remain unacknowledged, unstudied, unproblematized, and seldom mentioned outside mandatory ethics courses. Power drives action, and we have libraries full of literature exploring power in the organization. How can we hope for organizational wisdom without the simi-lar depth of thought on the values that define the ends we empower those actions to achieve? Through the following propositions, I hope to establish the import-ance of values, and from the resulting recommendations, I hope to present ideas of how to incorporate values more explicitly into organizational action.

P1. Values guide episodic uses of power.

Throughout the life of the Seniors Programme, individuals exercised episodic power (i.e. coercion and manipulation) in the pursuit of values. Examples of this included CEO1 executing the Programme Charter to bind the BC Health Authority to the Training Programme in pursuit of the values of public interest and innovation. Similar values motivated his uses of power to entice the Mentor to join the programme. VPs engaged in acts of manipulation such as keeping the BC working group off meeting agendas and discouraging staff from joining the programme in pursuit of values such as robustness, effectiveness, and account-ability. Throughout this study, we never saw episodic power enacted for the sake of enacting power. Individuals always enacted episodic power in pursuit of one or more values. Less clear from this study is the relation between values and systematic power (e.g. domination and subjectification). Whether values are innate to individuals – something they are born with – or whether individuals adopt values through acts of domination and subjectification, or a combination thereof, cannot be answered by this study. Once those values were adopted, however, they directed individuals' subsequent use of episodic power.

P2. Values drive project champions, who then drive action.

CEO1, CEO2, and the Senior Improvement Lead spoke of the critical importance of project champions. Disciples who speak from the heart, passion-ately, without a script. During the life of the Seniors Programme, the Mentor, Site Director, and MD Lead filled this role. Wisdom requires passion to drive action, and one's values clarify goals and give courage to act (Bierly et al., 2000). With the project champions I mentioned, each of them was genuinely committed to deeply held values that motivated their actions. Their passion facilitated their ability to produce needed power relations to advance the pro-gramme and fuelled their creativity to overcome barriers.

P3. When personal values align with organizational values, synergies happen.

The prime values of the Seniors Programme included public interest, sustain-ability, and spread (see Table 7.2, page 87). Nearly everyone involved in the Seniors Programme held these same values. Reading the words of my intervie-wees, they each seemed to hold these values personally. That is, they were not pursuing public interest, for example, because it was a job requirement, but rather because it was a real value they held. These personally held values gave the drive to do the work required by the organization, often off the side of their desk, and a motivation to push through challenges.

Moreover, this facilitated the production of power relations needed to sup-port the programme within the organization. The BC working group's activities aligned with corporate goals and with the values of key stakeholder groups within the institution. This alignment gave a bridge to VPs who initially resisted the programme that the BC working group could use to bring them onside. Wisdom requires an environment that supports wise decisions (Conger &

Hooijberg, 2007). Facilitating alignment between personal and organizational values fosters this.

Recommendation 1: Incorporate value alignment in recruitment processes. Wisdom is doing the ethically practical within a social context (Flyvbjerg, 2001). For many organizations, that social context is the organization itself. Enacting the values of the organization, therefore, requires recruitment of employees willing to pursue those values. Before an organization can align employees' values with its own, however, the organization must first clearly know its values. Leaders within an organization can achieve this through developing a corporate culture that focuses on core values, principles, and balance of customer loyalty, employee morale, and long-term success, among other stakeholders (Bierly & Kolodinsky, 2007). DeNisi and Belsito (2007) then recommend designing the human resource system to balance the goals of the business with those of employees. They argue that though there may be trade-offs between the organization's and individuals' values, it is not a zero-sum game and areas of overlap can often be found. They recommended a recruitment process to facilitate the hiring of staff whose values align with the organization without sacrificing their skills. They described how many recruitment processes rank all candidates from most qualified to least. They note, however, that the differences in skills between, say, the first, second, and third candidates, are seldom significant. Thus, rather than ranking all candidates, form clusters of similarly skilled candidates instead. All the candidates in the top cluster have similar skill levels, and so employers can then choose the candidate from that cluster whose values most align with the organization's (Aguinis, 2004; DeNisi & Belsito, 2007).

P4. Even when groups share values, value conflicts may occur along instrumental or temporal lines.

We saw during the life of the Seniors Programme that even though different stakeholder groups shared prime values, conflicts occurred between instrumental values. Even when prime and instrumental values aligned, conflicts occurred between the time horizons within which different groups operated. Such conflicts may be unavoidable in an organization containing a certain amount of complexity. The organization tasks different departments with the pursuit of different values (e.g. reducing congestion in hospitals versus developing public health innovations). Different stakeholders may push the organization to achieve different ends (e.g. administering healthcare within a region versus spreading innovations nationally). The organization may face trade-offs in achieving goals along different time horizons (e.g. achieving long-term goals may take resources away from groups working to achieve short-term goals).

P5. Value conflicts can form a point of resistance to organizational action unless individuals address them.

Which acts people judge as wise are embedded in systems of power (McNamee, 1998; Pitsis & Clegg, 2007; Sampson, 1998). Different groups within a social system operate from different value positions, and these values may be incompatible or incommensurate (De Graff et al., 2014). If, as Flyvbjerg (2001) argued, wisdom is doing what is ethically practical in a social context, tension between values within a social context increases the difficulty of doing the ethically practical by creating points of resistance to action. We saw through the life of the Seniors Programme value conflicts between the BC working group and other stakeholders within the BC Health Authority. These conflicts created points of resistance towards the Seniors Programme. During the early stages of the Seniors Programme, conflicting values led VPs to resist the programme, manifest through withholding permission for their staff to participate and keeping the BC working group off meeting agendas. After the Training Fellowship ended, value conflicts slowed the Seniors Programme's spread throughout the region. Addressing these conflicts requires individuals who possess (1) a keen understanding of the various value positions within their operating environment, (2) strong interpersonal skills to reconcile these differences, and (3) enough power within their organization to execute the actions needed to resolve these resistance points.

Recommendation 2: Develop the capacity to recognize and reconcile value conflicts in organizations. Recall that wisdom is a social construct and that people embed wisdom in systems of power. As Flyvbjerg (2001) argued, there exists no objective basis for wisdom – instead, it is doing what is ethically practical within a social context. Part of wisdom is being able to read that social context to determine what is ethically practical. I believe this is linked to values. Values, too, are embedded in systems of power. If wisdom is the ethically practical, then that raises the question, 'Whose ethics?' The answer, of course, is, 'The ethics of whoever has power.' Large organizations distribute power across groups. Groups pursue different values, which then leads to tension. Those we consider wise can navigate this. They recognize the different values at play, and they can address value conflicts in pursuit of the ethically practical.

To develop this capacity, I will first highlight attitudes and approaches of leaders within organizations that facilitate the ability to recognize and reconcile value conflicts. Then, I will provide ideas for training programmes to achieve this. Bartunek and Trullen (2007) argued that organizations could act prudently when over-arching values guide their actions. In my study, we see the impact of this. The prime value of public interest was a significant driver of healthcare organizations, and we saw how this unifying prime value gave common ground over which different members of the organization could negotiate other value differences. Common prime values, however, may not be possible in organizations with significant diversity in operations, cultures, or locations. In these situations, Earley and Offermann (2007) advised corporations to develop some measure of commonality across the organization, be it common values despite local practices, or standard practices despite different values, and then to create conditions for positive inter-cultural experiences. When possible, look for opportunities to combine complimentary values to create synergies.

There will be times, however, when different values pursued by the organization unavoidably conflict. In these situations, leaders must learn to temporarily weaken some values to accommodate others (Schön, 1983). Leaders must develop the ability to balance short-term needs with long-term ones, and to balance their willingness to stand by their values with their ability to compromise and tolerate ambiguity (Conger & Hooijberg, 2007). Freeman et al. (2007) recommended implementing stakeholder theory of strategy management (Freeman, 2010). Applying stakeholder theory requires leaders to consider all stakeholders, identifying the values binding them together, and then identify appropriate action to achieve those values (Freeman et al., 2007). One may get the sense that reconciling value conflicts requires someone to compromise and forego their values. Bigelow (1992), for example, argued that wise decisions increase as leaders focus on long-term perspectives more than short-term. Likewise, Conger and Hooijberg (2007) argued organizations act wisely when leaders focus on the breadth of stakeholders rather than self-interest. Cropanzano et al. (2007), however, argued that wisdom need not mean forgoing self-interest in the short term, and indeed that self-interested behaviour may be a good thing. They argued that when approaching ethical questions, leaders should consider how self-interest is understood in that context (Holley, 1999), the extent to which others' needs should be considered (Blackburn, 2001), and when other motives beyond self-interest should guide behaviour (e.g. principlism, empathy-altruism, fairness, etc.) (Rachels & Rachels, 2015; Weaver, 2003).

The principle that comes from this recommendation seems to be the importance of balancing different value positions using one's judgement to determine the ideal balance. Lofty talk, but how do we develop this capacity? Conger and Hooijberg (2007) suggested that organizations and educational programmes can develop training scenarios and exercises identifying the types of dilemmas employees are likely to encounter, along with steps to help them reconcile these dilemmas. They further recommended leaders hold regular and open conversations about value dilemmas, the decision-making process used by senior managers, and incentive structures that reward desired behaviours.

16.2. Knowledge Is Required, But Insufficient for Wise Action

P6. Knowledge is required, but insufficient for wise action.

Knowledge informs action; it tells us how to achieve an end. The Training Fellowship dove into the literature to learn how to prevent frailty. They met with seniors groups to learn how best to get the elderly to participate in the Seniors Programme. The Training Programme itself was an embodiment of informing action with knowledge, asking how to apply evidence to practice? We also see bureaucratic rationality reifying power, creating systems that controlled and administered action.

This study also demonstrated that knowledge was insufficient. Even when one might genuinely 'know' what to do, the value conflicts I described above, or power structures I describe below, may constrain action. We saw this in examples where, despite knowing what the literature identified as effective ways to prevent frailty, different instrumental values led VPs to resist the programme, or fee structures discouraged physicians from adopting the programme. Aside from these structural constraints, how often do we truly 'know' the right action? Despite the literature telling the Training Fellowship how to prevent frailty, differences between regions created challenges in implementing that knowledge. Moreover, what of situations where knowledge is incomplete? The Training Fellowship struggled over what to call their target population because no one had authoritatively defined that population. The Seniors Programme was an innovation, and innovations by their nature exist beyond the bounds of current knowledge. What is the role of knowledge when knowledge is incomplete or flawed?

Weick (1998) said wisdom was an attitude that balanced confidence with doubt. You must be confident enough to act, but you must realize the fallibility of your knowledge. You must have faith in your ability to improvise (Weick, 1998). Chia and Holt (2007), conversely, argued there are times when knowledge is a hindrance – do not fret your lack of knowledge because ignorance is a blessing! Progress, they maintained, requires unlearning what you know, becoming ignorant of constraints and unlearning orthodoxy so that you might envision genuinely innovative paths forward. Wisdom requires enough knowledge to inform action while recognizing knowledge's limits. Wisdom requires the ability to operate in realms where knowledge is incomplete or flawed and to see beyond the bounds of knowledge to create new paths forward.

Recommendation 3: Blend rationalities. As with my previous discussions on rationality, when I recommend blending rationalities, I mean to blend different ways of knowing. Wisdom requires perception, which is the ability to perceive and interpret the specific situation you are in, noting what is similar to past experience and what is new (McVea & Freeman, 2005; Nussbaum, 1990; Sherman, 1989; Wiggins, 1975). Cultivating this perception requires the full utilization of emotional, imaginative, and moral capacities (Freeman et al., 2007) – that is, blended rationality. The Training Fellowship used this strategy to good effect throughout the life of the Seniors Programme. Technocratic rationality informed them how to prevent frailty, for example, while contextual rationality informed them how to apply that strategy to different regions. Likewise, technocratic rationality informed coaches how to assist participating seniors to manage and improve their frailty, while body rationality informed them how to adapt that to each individual's physical capacity. Knowledge is often incomplete or flawed. By combining different rationalities, an element one rationality is blind to may be revealed through another. Wise action requires a depth of understanding of a specific situation (Flyvbjerg, 2001). Blending rationalities create that depth of understanding.

Recommendation 4: Tap into the power of collective reasoning. Recall that collective reasoning is a form of deliberative democracy where individuals forward ideas for debate, creating a shared pool of rationality where participants improve good arguments and discard weak ones (Townley, 2008b). The experiences of those involved in the Seniors Programme highlighted two reasons to engage in collective reasoning: enhanced decision-making ability and development of power relations. Throughout the life of the Seniors Programme, individuals engaged in collective reasoning extensively. Indeed, the Training Programme was an act of collective reasoning. Collective reasoning led to the creation of the Seniors Programme, the development of the strategy of how to apply standardized approaches to regions with contextual differences, the creation of a compelling vision statement that led seniors to participate in the Seniors Programme, and much more. Also, collective reasoning facilitated the formation of power relations that supported the advancement of the Seniors Programme. Collaboration with the Foundation, for example, gave the BC working group the support it needed to convince CEO2 to become the new champion for the programme.

I will present two frameworks of how to improve the quality of collective reasoning in organizations. The authors of these frameworks did not explicitly link them to collective reasoning, but they are nonetheless useful for groups seeking to enhance this ability. The first framework by De Meyer (2007) covered structural elements of forming a group that effectively engages in collective reasoning. The second framework by Vaill (2007) identified the actions and attitudes of individuals that enhance a group's deliberation of issues. Turning first to structural elements, De Meyer (2007) provided a five-point framework for effectively tapping into the power of collective reasoning. The BC working group adhered to many of these points.

(1) *Create credibility.* The BC working group achieved this by, for example, adhering firmly to technocratic rationality, which was the dominant rationality endorsed by their organization. This credibility fostered the development of trust between groups and individuals and served as the basis for establishing needed power relations.

(2) *Stimulate diversity.* The Mentor identified building a diverse team was essential to her when recruiting members. The BC working group ultimately contained diversity, its members including front-line physicians and administrators from different areas of the organization. This diversity provided multiple perspectives and skill sets. For example, the MD Lead, a physician, understood how doctors addressed frailty in their offices whereas the Site Director, an administrator, understood how to build power relations to secure needed resources in the organization. Wise people understand that we create our realities through our interpretations of events. They are then able to reconsider their interpretations in light of others' (Gioia, 2007).

(3) *Invest in communication.* In the Seniors Programme, this included internal communications between the Training Fellowship and external communication with other stakeholders. Internally, the Training Fellowship met often. This created a sense of team among the members and allowed for frequent deliberation over the many challenges they faced. Externally, the Training Fellowship took great pains crafting communications with other stakeholders – recall the thirteen drafts of a single page communication they spent months developing. This care defined rationality in stakeholders' minds that benefited the advancement of the Seniors Programme.

(4) *Develop an extended network.* Recall the Senior Improvement Lead dubbed the Site Director the 'queen of building connections.' The Mentor, likewise, met extensively with VPs of the BC Health Authority and initiated contact with the BC Coaching Organization. These networks provided pools of perspectives the team could draw from to troubleshoot problems (e.g. the Site Director built connections with experts who developed the eCGA). Also, they built power relations that supported the programme through troubled times (e.g. consider the role VP support had in keeping the Seniors Programme alive during CEO turnover).

(5) *Provide appropriate tools for communication.* The BC working group met in person at least monthly, and sometimes weekly. They teleconferenced with the NS working group as often and arranged to meet in person at least yearly. Employing the appropriate tools for communication facilitated the rich discussions needed to engage in collective reasoning.

These above five points can then be leveraged to access wisdom through sensing (gathering information about users globally), melding (identifying opportunities to innovate and gather/integrate knowledge to exploit), and deploying (rolling out innovations globally) (De Meyer, 2007).

The quality of a group's deliberation over topics of discussion is important because choosing the right action cannot always be systematized. Proper deliberation encompasses all concerns, good ends, all possible actions, and the ability to respond to situational needs (Freeman et al., 2007). Vaill's (2007) framework for developing process wisdom is instructive with regards to getting the most value out of collective reasoning processes. His framework has seven points.

(1) *Understand how you use your power within a group to disempower others.* When debating, we like to think the power of our argument carries the day. In groups with power asymmetries (e.g. a VP versus front-line workers), the power one person has may shut down the debate. Understanding this dynamic is essential in determining how to avoid it so the free flow of ideas may reign.

(2) *Identify the possibilities possible when working as a team, and act to develop the team* (Bradford, 2002). We see several examples of the Training Fellowship developing itself as a team. As a team, they engaged in literature reviews, focus groups, and expert interviews to develop team expertise in

frailty prevention. The Mentor explicitly used several of these activities to build a sense of team: naming the target population, creating a programme name, developing a vision statement. If collective reasoning involves individuals adding to a pool of rationality, then these development activities deepen and enrich that pool.

(3) *Step back from daily pressures to get a broader view of the problem.* This can be hard to achieve but is worth the effort. As the MD Lead explained:

> It's like everybody is so inundated with the demand and congestion, and when you can lift them out of that for just even a few minutes as you talk about prevention [...] people listen and they actually take it up. (personal communication, August 8, 2017)

(4) *Help group members to think of their situation in a new light.* Creating diverse teams may facilitate this, as diversity brings different perspectives to the table. Blending rationality as per my recommendation above also facilitates this. Initially, the Training Fellowship applied technocratic rationality when designing the Seniors Programme. It was not, however, until they sought contextual rationality through meeting with seniors groups that they learned that running the Seniors Programme through physician offices was the best way to encourage seniors to participate in the programme.

(5) *Accept that you cannot control everything.* The BC working group recognized that due to a variety of constraints, they could not spread the Seniors Programme through the BC Health Authority, let alone the rest of Canada, at the pace they wanted. They, instead, did what they had the power to do to keep the programme moving forward. I believe this attitude was vital because it allowed the team to maintain motivation in the face of constraints. It also gave them a practical perspective of the challenges they faced, which directed problem-solving efforts to those areas they could control.

(6) *Recognize that wisdom has a spiritual aspect of meanings and values.* Wisdom is required to manage complexity. Values are what gives direction to those navigating complex environments. Though my interviewees never explicitly said common values united them, they all shared a passion for improving the health of seniors (i.e. public interest). This gave the group cohesion and direction as they slogged through the labyrinth of structures within their organizations.

(7) *Adopt a learner attitude.* This segues into my next recommendation of experimentation. We see the BC working group exemplifying a learner attitude. They performed the Seniors Programme, which itself was an experiment. They got feedback from doctors — the frailty assessment took too long. They adapted, developing an eCGA. They, then, slowly rolled out the Seniors Programme with the eCGA, gaining more feedback and adjusting as required.

Recommendation 5: Experiment. Complex environments where knowledge is often limited (if not flawed) require wisdom. Thus, almost by definition, the knowledge individuals have is insufficient for those situations. Moreover, as I have described earlier, there are often trade-offs between values. Managers aspiring to wisdom need to act in a way that recognizes the values foregone (Nussbaum, 1990). Experimental action, trying different solutions and adapting, can deepen our understanding of trade-offs and help find the path forward when in unknown territory (De Meyer, 2007; Romme, 2003; van Aken, 2004).

The action-reflection cycle is an essential component of experimentation. Freeman et al. (2007) recommended managers adopt the attitude that all action is subject to change – act, reflect on incoming results, reflect on the values appropriate for that context, and then adjust action as needed. Examples of this approach existed throughout the life of the Seniors Programme. Participation in the Training Programme was an act of experimental action aimed at determining how to apply evidence to practice. The Training Fellowship experimented by designing its programme to apply a standardized approach that each region could then modify. They assessed results – not just of the study, but from physicians and other stakeholders as well – made modifications, and then advanced.

Recommendation 6: Have an 'appreciative inquiry' mindset. Adler (2007) proposed appreciative inquiry was a practical approach to experimental action that led to organizational wisdom. Rather than limiting organizational attention to areas of dysfunction, it is a positive approach that focuses on what is working so that organizations can learn from and strengthen processes that lead to desired outcomes (Adler, 2007; Pitsis & Clegg, 2007). To apply appreciative inquiry, Adler (2007), had eight recommendations.

First, develop insight through reflection. Adler (2007) argued people focus too much on action, too little on reflection. We saw this tension during the development of the Seniors Programme: the Mentor wanted the group to reflect on its vision, the group wanted to dive into the work. Reflection, however, is one of three competencies of great leaders (the other two being leveraging and framing) (Gardner, 2011). Adler (2007) recommended that at the start and end of each day, leaders should think about what they are trying to achieve, how they are doing it, and identifying changes to make.

Second, Adler (2007) advised us to be aware of the interrelated structure of the social world. Actions impact others, and with each act you give something, and you receive something. Consider your action's impact on others (what you give) and on yourself (what you receive). Throughout the Seniors Programme's life, we see this attitude. For example, in exchange for VP support, the programme offered solutions to their long-term problems. This attitude facilitated the development of needed power relations. It also prevented conflict (recall how carefully the BC working group introduced itself to the healthcare community so as not to antagonize incumbent groups).

Third, Adler (2007) recommended partnering with individuals and groups with relevant expertise. There are many examples of this during the Seniors Programme: the BC working group met with experts, physicians, IT personnel, and so on. Such partnering provides insights into seemingly paradoxical facts that are the conundrums wisdom is tasked to resolve. For example, Olga was a

90-year-old track star. This is a paradox! Ninety-year-old people do not participate in track and field, let alone become stars in it. Through this exhaustive collaboration with many different experts, blending many different rationalities, the
Seniors Programme sheds light on just how such a paradox can occur.

Fourth, Adler (2007) emphasized focusing on developing good questions.
Examples of the questions asked throughout the life of the Seniors Programme
included: 'How do we prevent frailty?', 'How do we apply evidence to practice?',
'How do we apply a standardized approach across different regions and individuals?', among others. These are big questions, compelling questions. These
questions change organizations, maybe even societies. These questions may also
be unanswerable. Appreciative inquiry does not shy away from unanswerable
questions. It embraces them. In environments of ambiguity and uncertainty –
those environments that demand wisdom – '[...] good questions often guide us
much more powerfully than do their hoped-for answers' (Adler, 2007, p. 437). It
is the pursuit of answers to good questions that gives them power, for it is
through this pursuit we create change.

Fifth, Adler (2007) recommended engaging with the public. The reason for
this is the limitation of disembedded rationalities (e.g. technocratic, economic,
and bureaucratic) to address localized issues. That is, she argued that situational
and contextual rationalities were essential additions to disembedded rationalities, which harkens back to my recommendation to blend rationalities. Again,
we see the Training Fellowship applied this approach through their consultation
with seniors groups. Through these meetings, they learned seniors' preferences
regarding what to call them (which the fellowship chose to ignore) as well as
learning that implementing the Seniors Programme through physician offices
would improve chances of recruiting participants (which they adopted).

Sixth, Adler (2007) recommended building structures to support changes.
I discuss this further below in recommendation eight. Here, though, I will identify two unique characteristics of the structures Adler recommended. First, she
discussed developing metaphors to describe your new structure. For example, a
common metaphor for the organization is the machine metaphor. We associate
certain structural features with this metaphor, and if we want to move away
from that structure, we need to develop new metaphors, envisioning the organization, say, as an organism or a family. In the Seniors Programme, the Olga
story was a powerful metaphor used to motivate action. Second, Adler (2007)
cautioned against maximizing rules to guide action but instead advised organizations to develop minimum specifications. Rules impede flexibility, and when
operating in environments of uncertainty, actors need the flexibility to adapt and
change to circumstances. Minimum specifications give them a guiding light of
what they are to achieve, while a paucity of rules gives them the flexibility to
figure out how to achieve it. We saw this approach between the BC working
group and the BC Coaching Organization. The BC working group provided
minimum specifications of what coaches had to do, and the coaches then used
their discretion to implement the programme.

Seventh, Adler (2007) promoted a method to embrace 'wicked problems'.
These are complex challenges that cannot be reduced to constituent parts

(Zimmerman, Lindberg, & Plsek, 1998). *How do we spread healthcare innovations across Canada?* is an example of a 'wicked problem' that, at the writing of this book, stymied the Training Fellowship. The approach Adler (2007) recommended involved meeting with experts and the public, as mentioned above, to discuss the challenges of the wicked problem, identifying what makes the challenge so difficult. The role of the listener is to ask 'wicked questions'. Wicked questions challenge underlying assumptions and orthodoxy and point out contradictory assumptions. Articulating these assumptions can reveal patterns of thought and differences, which may then lead to creative ideas to address pernicious challenges (Zimmerman et al., 1998).

Finally, Adler (2007) recommended identifying spectacular examples of success: positive deviants. Though studying failures have value in teaching us what to avoid, studying failure, ultimately, teaches us how to fail. Study of positive deviants, conversely, leads to an understanding of what led to success. Through that, individuals may replicate or adapt those actions elsewhere. Olga, the 90-year-old track star, was a positive deviant. Study of her yielded insights into the connection between physical activity, nutrition, sleep, and overall mental well-being to the age-old search for the fountain of youth.

P7. Rationalities conflict and part of wisdom is recognizing which rationality has power in a specific context.

In wisdom literature, when they say knowledge is not enough, they usually say it to mean that knowledge is flawed or incomplete, and so one must proceed carefully, experimentally, and with the awareness that what you 'know' may be wrong. The experience of the Seniors Programme highlighted another reason why knowledge is insufficient – rationalities conflict with each other. 'What' you know depends on 'how' you know. Through technocratic rationality, the BC working group 'knew' how to prevent frailty, but due to the economic rationality of physicians who cannot bill for frailty assessments, doctors 'knew' they could not implement the programme. Progress requires an awareness of which rationality has power in each situation.

16.3.   Wisdom Is Action-oriented

P8. Bureaucratic rationality translates power into action.

Bureaucratic rationality mediates organizational action. We saw several examples of this through the Seniors Programme's life. Executing the Project Charter bound the BC Health Authority to the Training Programme and led CEO2 to attend the Ottawa symposium where he chose to become the programme's new executive champion. Developing new processes and documentation, such as creating the eCGA and providing more physician support through restructuring the delivery of primary care, facilitated the spread of the Seniors Programme. Clear processes and procedures allowed the BC Coaching Organization to implement the Seniors Programme seamlessly. If you wish for the organization to take action, one way to achieve this is through changing, creating, or removing the bureaucratic rationalities practiced by the firm.

P9. Institutional and contextual rationality inform the effective use of bureaucratic rationalities.

We considered earlier how bureaucratic rationality reified power in organizations. You may recall my comment that effective application of bureaucratic rationality allows power to flow, ineffective application constrains it. I want to add two more rationalities to this discussion: institutional (knowing what is rational within a sphere of human activity) and contextual (knowing what is rational within a culture). These rationalities inform the practitioner of how best to exercise bureaucratic rationality within their industry (institutional rationality) and their organization (contextual rationality). If effective bureaucratic rationality allows power to flow, then it is institutional and contextual rationalities that inform the individual of how to create an effective bureaucratic rationality in their social setting.

Throughout the life of the Seniors Programme, several individuals demonstrated a firm grasp of bureaucratic, institutional, and contextual rationalities within the BC Health Authority. CEO1 and the Mentor recognized the power the Project Charter would have to bind the organization to development of the Seniors Programme. The Site Director exhibited skill at recruiting personnel with the abilities to develop an eCGA compatible with physician EMR systems and securing funding to finance the development and implementation of the eCGA. The BC working group developed effective procedures to facilitate the smooth implementation of the Seniors Programme by the BC Coaching Organization. The team overcame many challenges to the Seniors Programme because *they knew how their organization worked.*

Recommendation 7: Develop bureaucratic, institutional, and contextual rationalities through experience, self-reflectivity, and mentoring. Institutional and contextual rationality develop through career training and socialization within organizations (Stinchcombe, 1990; Van Maanen & Barley, 1982), and it is through this an individual learns the bureaucratic rationality within their specific environment. These rationalities are developed, in other words, over time, through experience and exposure to one's operating environment. This does not mean, however, that the only thing we can do to develop this is to start an individual off along a career path, wait twenty years, and then hope they learned something useful along the way. Though experience is a great (but slow) teacher, we can supplement its teachings with self-reflectivity exercises and mentoring. Let us consider the role of experience first. *Experience* gives a repertoire of cases individuals can pull from when they encounter new situations (Schön, 1983). To facilitate this, encourage coworkers, subordinates, and yourself to seek out as many unique cases and opportunities as possible (Bartunek & Trullen, 2007). To magnify the benefits of experience, combine it with *self-reflectivity* exercises where, with every major decision you make, you take time afterwards to question your assumptions, preferences, and values to gain awareness of your own mental frameworks. Based on that assessment, combined with the results of your decision, you can revise and change your future actions (Fowers, 2003; Freeman et al., 2007; Johnstone, 1983). This learning can then be further enhanced through *mentoring* (Dewey, 1998). Organizations should select mentors based on their previous success, and should focus their efforts on overseeing the mentee's self-reflectivity exercises in order to help organize the mentee's experience (Baltes & Kunzmann, 2004; Dewey, 1998).

Recommendation 8: Develop an organizational structure that facilitates the activities that lead to organizational wisdom. Since organizations mediate action through bureaucratic structures, leaders may consider structuring their organizations in a way that facilitates the types of actions leading to organizational wisdom. Kotter and Heskett (1992) identified key attributes that an effective organizational structure should facilitate, including adaptability, innovation, problem prevention, confidence in problem-solving abilities, trusting, risk-taking, enthusiasm, honesty and integrity, flexibility, and having a long-term view. Beckhard (1969) and Burke (1994, 2007) identified structural elements that facilitate actions contributing to organizational wisdom. They identify that organizations need to develop goals and plans focused on three key constituents: customers, employees, and owners (Kotter & Heskett, 1992). Organizations need to create structures that facilitate the desired action, rather than having action driven by structures.[1] To achieve this, they recommended that organizations push decision-making to areas that are the source of information and expertise, and to base reward systems on performance. They recommended organizations put energy into developing open lines of communication. They encouraged leaders to manage conflict to maintain stability and to respect differences within their organizations for their innovative potential. They advised leaders to view their organization as an open system and to value integrity and interdependence (Beckhard, 1969; Burke, 1994, 2007).

In order to achieve the above elements, Bierly and Kolodinsky (2007) argued that organizations need to develop the infrastructure (especially IT infrastructure) and culture that allows for the accumulation and sharing of organizational knowledge. Organizations must first develop intellectual capital, and then build systems of organizational learning where individuals teach each other in communities of practice. They advised leaders to encourage the development of norms that put knowledge into practice and devote resources to the development of IT systems that allow the seamless transfer of knowledge among staff and strategic decision makers (Bierly & Kolodinsky, 2007). To create an adaptive workforce capable of improvisation, DeNisi and Belsito (2007), recommended that

---

[1]For example, Beckhard (1969) and Burke (1994, 2007) both might take issue that structures such as existing fee frameworks constrained physicians from performing frailty assessments.

organizations develop quality training programmes that focus on general, rather than firm-specific, training. Then, tie compensation to the skills and knowledge the employee has, rather than the tasks the employee performs (Murray & Gerhart, 1998), and incorporate employee input into appraisal systems (DeNisi & Belsito, 2007).

P10. Facilitating organizational action is a group activity.

In organizational contexts, action is group mediated. Thus, if organizations are to act wisely, they require teams that act wisely. For teams to act wisely, they must use values to guide action, possess knowledge, though they can still act despite its limitations, and have the power to make things happen. In the Seniors Programme, CEO1 formed a team to pursue the values of public interest and innovation, focused on delaying frailty. This group possessed considerable knowledge and enhanced that knowledge through research, community outreach, and collective reasoning. When they ran past the limits of knowledge, they experimented, learning more along the way. They further demonstrated a capacity to accomplish needed tasks within their organization, developing needed power relations to support their activities as required.

Recommendation 9: Build teams capable of implementing the precepts of wise action. I have identified three themes of organizational wisdom: values guide action, knowledge is required but insufficient, and wisdom is action-oriented. Since organizational action is group-mediated, the organization needs to develop the capacity to build teams that operate along these precepts. Developing teams with these capacities does not happen by accident − it requires purposeful managerial action. Managerial action combined with member attributes creates norms. If the appropriate norms develop, they lead to wise actions over the short- and long-term. (Nielsen et al., 2007).

Nielsen et al. (2007) developed guidelines for managers seeking to develop teams capable of wise action. They identified when creating teams that managers imbue that team with specific qualities to make it a real 'team'. They must establish clear boundaries including the scope of activities, expectations, available resources, and lifespan. Members of the team must be interdependent, share responsibilities, and tasked with pursuing a common outcome. When teams have multiple common outcomes, the manager should specify priorities among those goals. Membership should be stable, and each member should have a role within the group. These structures allow teams to discuss individual issues and tensions openly. We see many of these attributes in place in the BC working group and Training Fellowship. The Project Charter identified the group's goal and the scope and lifespan of the team. Membership was identified and remained unchanged throughout the programme.

Nielsen et al. (2007) recommended managers carefully select team members with the following criteria in mind. Select members based on their possession of requisite knowledge, skills, and abilities for the job at hand. Also, members should possess self-awareness about their strengths, weaknesses, and how they operate in group situations, especially when under pressure. Since operating in a group often requires managing tensions between members, and the group itself will engage in collective reasoning and creating needed power relations with other groups, managers should select members with strong communication skills.

In addition to these characteristics specified by Nielsen et al. (2007), I will add one more from my observation of the Seniors Programme. Members of the group should possess the authority within the organization to act. Many members of the BC working group held director-level positions in the BC Health Authority. They, therefore, had an established network of power relations within the organization that combined with their authority to make things happen. They had resources within their departments they could access to assist with administrative tasks such as arranging meetings, planning focus groups with seniors, developing project documentation, and so on. They could also approach leaders of other departments as peers to request needed resources, as the Site Director did when recruiting IT expertise to develop the eCGA. This example is not to imply that all teams must consist of senior managers, but rather teams must possess the level of authority needed to carry out the actions the manager established the group to achieve. Since wisdom requires action, teams must possess the power to act. There are situations, however, that may limit a manager's ability to recruit team members with authority needed to execute the manager's vision – say, for example, if the manager themselves lacks the authority to take the actions they desire. In this case, teams must possess the capacity to build power relations with the relevant authority in the organization.

More on that later. For now, let us turn back to the recommendations of Nielsen et al. (2007). They further suggested that the manager should focus on developing effective norms within the team. These norms include the ability to discuss individual and team issues openly. These may include tensions within the team, such as conflicting priorities, disagreements within the group, the impact that external constituents have on the team's objectives, and so on.

Nielsen et al. (2007) further recommended that managers need to support their team. This support not only includes providing needed information systems and physical facilities, but also relevant training as well as appropriate measurement, feedback, and reward systems. Managers should provide proper coaching to members and provide facilitators when needed to help the team resolve stumbling blocks. Importantly, after all this, the manager must remain willing to disband the team if it is unable to perform.

Recommendation 10: Protect your team from the political dynamics of your organization. The experience of the Seniors Programme highlighted the importance of protecting teams from the politics of your organization. Without this, CEO1 could not have recruited the Mentor, his first project champion. The BC working group pursued an innovative change, which exposed it to certain risks. High on the Mentor's mind was the risk of failure. She argued that groups need to take risks to be innovative. Experiments, no matter how well thought out, have a risk of failure. Other risks include upsetting political balances within the organization. If power networks within the organization perceive the group's activities as a potential threat, they may act to undermine that group. Either of these dangers may negatively impact an individual's career prospects and reputation within the organization. This fear may discourage needed action and distract people's attention from the job at hand. Rather than allowing values to guide their action, people allow fear and self-preservation to dominate.

The actions of CEO1 provide four examples of how he protected the team developing the Seniors Programme. First, he communicated to the organization that he wanted this project to happen. In his own words, you need '[...] a leader who says, "I actually believe in this and I want to see the outcome. I think this could make a difference. I'm nailing my colours to the mast on this [...]"' (CEO1, personal communication, June 6, 2017). His signing of the Project Charter was a public declaration of his commitment to the Seniors Programme. Even then, power structures within the organization may still threaten your team. Thus, a second tactic CEO1 used to protect his team was to establish it outside of the typical hierarchy of the organization, creating in effect a skunkworks (see Bower, 1997; Fosfuri & Rønde, 2009, for examples of skunkworks used to mitigate organizational resistance). The BC working group was not physically separate from the organization, as many skunkworks are, but through the structures of the Training Programme, they operated outside standard reporting lines, answering directly to CEO1.

Third, CEO1 made creative use of bureaucratic rationalities to protect team members. A notable example was not giving the Mentor a job title within the Seniors Programme, an act the Mentor believed reduced her visibility for political attack. Finally, CEO1 along with the Mentor recruited team members who possessed political savvy within the organization. They recruited team members from high-level management positions. These people understood their organization, knew where political pitfalls lay, and had experience managing such dangers. For example, the BC working group understood the political landscape of the seniors' healthcare community. Their understanding informed the actions they took when they introduced the Seniors Programme and sought to integrate it into that community.

P11. Producing power relations and using them to advance your objectives is critical. Choose your partners thoughtfully.

Throughout the life of the Seniors Programme, groups produced power relations that became invaluable to advancing the programme. CEO1 brought his organization into collaboration with the Foundation and the NS Health Authority. These alliances gave access to valuable expertise. Recall, also, that the Foundation's endorsement of the Seniors Programme encouraged CEO2 to become the programme's new executive champion. The Mentor met extensively with VPs in the BC Health Authority to gain their support. These relations provided powerful voices within the organization that helped the programme survive as CEOs turned over. The Site Director and MD Lead continuously built connections with managers in the community. These connections facilitated the spread of the Seniors Programme as communities became ready to take on this innovation. We consistently saw individuals building power relations with multiple stakeholders, and then using those relations to advance the programme.

P12. Defining rationality is a means to produce useful power relations.

A method individuals frequently used to produce power relations was exercising the episodic power tactic of defining rationality. The Mentor and Site Director spoke of aligning the Seniors Programme with the strategic objectives of the potential partner − i.e. defining rationality to show value alignment. The Mentor discussed sharing results to show the programme was successful, noting that people want to align themselves with winners. That is, she defined rationality to show the project was a winner. In each case, prospective partners used preferred modes of rationality. For example, when assessing value alignment, VPs used their judgement (body rationality). When assessing programme success, they looked at the study's results (technocratic rationality). These and other examples show one way to build power relations is to understand the values and rationalities held by the prospective group, and then to demonstrate how your programme facilitates advancement of those values using the preferred rationality of the target partner.

Recommendation 11: Develop effective negotiation skills that allow you to build power relations. Developing power relations involves elements of negotiation − you are, after all, asking for their support in exchange for a means for them to achieve their own goals. Lewicki (2007) developed negotiating precepts consistent with organizational wisdom. He argued that wise negotiators resist utilitarian reasoning and act with the best standards of honesty, though they acknowledge the need for 'less-than-complete candour' (p. 113). Also, though wise negotiators focus on developing strong relations of trust, they recognize the need to 'trust but verify' (p. 113). Importantly, wise negotiators understand the norms of the community they are in and negotiate by those norms. In short, they negotiate with good intent while remaining realistic about the nature of the environment in which they negotiate. Lewicki (2007) identified several principles for those who wish to negotiate in a manner consistent with organizational wisdom. These include

- learn to recognize negotiating opportunities;
- understand multiple negotiating strategies are available − one strategy does not work in all situations;
- prepare thoroughly for the negotiation ahead of time;
- gain familiarity with cognitive biases undermining negotiations;[2]
- understand positive interpersonal relationships are critical to successful deals;

---

[2]Lewicki (2007) identified five biases that undermine negotiations: irrational escalation of commitment, belief in a mythical fixed pie, anchoring and adjustment, availability of information, and overconfidence.

- listen as much as you talk, if not more;
- understand the context-dependent nature of negotiations;
- know how to use power properly;
- realize there are cultural differences to negotiations;
- cultivate a reputation for integrity; and
- learn from experience.

Recommendation 12: Avoid conflict when you can. When in conflict, groups marshal their power as they gear up to defend themselves and defeat forces opposing them. Rational thought is a victim of this dynamic as groups opt instead for tools of brute power (Flyvbjerg, 1998). Though I did not observe open conflicts in my data, I hypothesize that values may, too, fall victim to conflict as groups replace them with an instinct for self-preservation and a will to dominate. Unfortunately, in organizational contexts, the diversity of functions and values pursued by different groups creates fertile soil for conflict. The challenge, then, becomes how to advance your goals against those who might oppose you without escalating that tension to open clashes.

I provide recommendations for organizations and individuals to walk this tightrope. I organize these recommendations into three levels. First, I explore organizational structures that reduce the chance of conflict. Then, I will consider the actions leaders of organizations might take to advance goals while minimizing conflict. Finally, I will consider individual tactics and approaches to advancing goals without conflict. There are times, however, when conflict happens despite our best efforts. I close this section with recommendations of how to recover when this happens.

Thacher and Rein (2004) described a means of structuring an organization to reduce the chance of conflict they called firewalls. With firewalls, the organization assigns responsibility to achieve different values to different groups who then achieve their goals separate from other groups. Combined with this, developing structures and cultures that promote open communication as recommended earlier provides a forum for groups to meet to discuss differences and, hopefully, de-escalate tension when groups inevitably clash. Beyond organizational design, there exist actions leaders can take to reduce conflict. For example, they can signal what values they want the organization to pursue. Thacher and Rein (2004) described the tactic of cycling where leaders support one value over others until resistance builds, leading to a change. Stewart (2006) identified tactics of bias and incrementalism. Bias occurs when leaders cease support for one set of values, and incrementalism is the process of slowly emphasizing one value over time.

Thus far, the tactics I have identified are implemented by those with authority to determine which groups do what and to signal what values the organization wants its members to pursue. There are tactics individuals within groups may implement when engaged with other groups possessing conflicting values to reduce conflict. These include casuistry (Thacher & Rein, 2004), where managers rely on their experience with similar conflicts to resolve them, hybridization

(Stewart, 2006), where individuals seek to reconcile conflicting values with each other, and compromise (Oldenhof et al., 2014), where each side gives something up to achieve a workable solution. Avoiding conflict requires acts of power. The experience of the BC working group suggested using tactics of manipulation rather than coercion were effective ways to apply hybridization or compromise while minimizing the risk of conflict. The tactic of manipulation I observed most often was defining rationality by, for example, showing how the Seniors Programme was a means for the other group to achieve their own goals. Applying the principles of wise negotiation as outlined in the previous recommendation also facilitates the individual's ability to engage other groups in a way that minimizes conflict.

Alas, sometimes conflicts happen, either because tensions escalate out of control, or because they are unavoidable. We see this in the very early stages of the Seniors Programme's life. Even though some VPs were not in agreement, CEO1 overrode their concerns and committed the organization to the Training Programme. Overriding their disagreement was a straight act of coercion: power trumped persuasion. Sometimes, the wise thing to do is to act despite opposition. Frost (2003) argued that in these situations individuals need to circle back afterwards to mend whatever damage their coercive act may have caused, lest resentment fester to lay the groundwork for future conflicts. There are times when it may not be possible for the person who performed the coercive act to mend broken relations effectively. Perhaps trust no longer exists; perhaps the individual is a busy executive and does not have the time to recuperate the relation. In these situations, Frost (2003) recommended a separate individual should engage the aggrieved group to mend relations. We saw CEO1 employ this tactic. Yes, he did override VP opposition to the programme. He then recruited the Mentor who very quickly went on an extensive campaign of meeting with the VPs to foster their support.

In this chapter, I have summarized the key learnings of my study. From the propositions I derived from my data, I developed recommendations that individuals and organizations may use to facilitate the development of organizational wisdom. What does the road ahead look like for the study of organizational wisdom? Despite wisdom's importance, it is underrepresented in scholarly work and ignored in education systems. In the next chapter, I close this book with my thoughts on how we can rectify that.

Chapter 17

Wisdom's Future

I believe we can grow wiser. Wisdom, however, is action oriented. Based on the propositions and recommendations presented in the previous chapter, I have identified actions that, if we implement them, will further our capacity to develop organizations capable of wise action. I describe those actions in this chapter. First, I summarize where this study leaves us, presenting an overview of its contributions to the field. I then make a call to educators. I do not limit the term 'educator' to mean a teacher in front of a class, though it certainly includes them. Rather, I mean educators of all types: teachers, trainers, mentors, coaches, and so on. If you, in any capacity, take others under your wing to 'show them the ropes', there are actions you can take to develop within them the capacity to act wisely, and I describe those below. My final call is for scholars. The research on organizational wisdom is underdeveloped. I hope this study serves as a model for how we might tackle this amorphous subject. Later in this chapter, I outline suggested avenues for future research to expand our understanding of this topic. I then close this book with some brief thoughts.

17.1. This Study's Contribution: Where Are We at Now?

I have performed a single, embedded case study of the development of a programme aimed at preventing frailty in seniors within a Canadian health authority. I have modelled this study on a phronetic research (PR) approach developed by Flyvbjerg (2001). Though the intention of PR is to facilitate society's capacity for value-rationality, the specific values studied in the works of Flyvbjerg have never been explicitly labelled, nor has the consequence of value interactions been assessed (see, for example, Flyvbjerg, 1998, 2006a, 2008, 2009; Flyvbjerg et al., 2009; Flyvbjerg, Glenting, & Rønnest, 2004). I have addressed this in this study by putting values on equal footing with rationality and power. By doing this, I demonstrated the capacity of values to drive action. This study also demonstrated that the dynamics between values in an organization are complex. For example, even when groups shared prime values, different instrumental values and timelines led to resistance. This study also demonstrated a connection between values and power. In this research setting, I did not observe people exercising power for the sake of it. Instead, values guided the use of episodic power. People used power to achieve their prime values, or they used it to stymie others whose values conflicted. Values gave power direction.

Though Flyvbjerg studied the relation between power and rationality (see, for example, Flyvbjerg, 1998, 2008; Flyvbjerg et al., 2009), I added an evaluation of how different ways of knowing influenced action. Doing so allowed me to demonstrate that differences in rationalities could also create conflicts that individuals must resolve. It, however, also demonstrated the power of blending rationalities to yield practical solutions to difficult problems. Additionally, by explicitly identifying relations between power and different rationalities, I demonstrated the vital role bureaucratic rationality has in translating power into action. Bureaucratic rationality reified power in the organization, turning will into action. In this research setting, institutional and contextual rationality informed the creation of bureaucratic rationality. Whereas effective bureaucratic rationalities facilitated action, ineffective ones impeded it.

This study adds to the burgeoning field of PR. Previous researchers applying a PR approach focused on governmental or societal levels of analysis (see, for example, Basu, 2012; Eubanks, 2012; Flyvbjerg, 1998; Griggs & Howarth, 2012; Olsen et al., 2012; Sandercock & Attili, 2012). I performed this study at the level of the organization, which established that we could successfully apply PR to this level of analysis. Moreover, it demonstrated that by applying PR to this level of analysis we could uncover practical means to enhance the value-rationality of organizations.

What can I say about this study's contribution to organizational wisdom? I feel I must be careful pronouncing the actions of the organization as wise or foolish for two reasons. First, wisdom is a social construct embedded in systems of power, so who am I to judge an organization as wise or not? Second, we will never know what might have been had people made different choices. How, then, can one make a claim about an organization's wisdom? To address this conundrum, I pulled three themes out of the literature on organizational wisdom that highlighted the roles of values, rationality, and power. I combined this with PR's perspective that *phronesis* was doing the ethically practical within a social context (Flyvbjerg, 2001). I, thus, set the organization's stated values as a litmus test for wise action and explored whether people acted consistently with those values, and if not, why.

Through this approach, I observed people exhibiting keen insight into the values that other groups held within their organization. Individuals demonstrated an understanding of how values led to resistance, but more than that, they demonstrated that by emphasizing where values overlapped and using episodic power in a way that maintained stability, they could turn those resistance points into networks of support. I observed people with a strong preference for technocratic rationality but who also recognized and respected the different ways of knowing that other groups used. They used multiple rationalities to overcome challenges. They also recognized which rationality had power in a given context, and they adapted to it rather than fought it.

The consequences of their actions resulted in the development and spread of the Seniors Programme, an intervention that demonstrably delayed, if not reversed, frailty. Though spread was slower and more localized than the BC working group had hoped, it had several notable accomplishments. By comparison to the scale of the BC Health Authority, the Seniors Programme was a tiny project driven by only a handful of people off the side of their desk. This tiny programme, however, received the endorsement of not one, but two CEOs, survived political turmoil as executives turned over, and overcame a lack of support among VPs. It acquired the enthusiastic support of the Foundation, a not-for-profit keen on spreading it nationally. At the time I wrote this book, the programme was still alive and making inroads throughout the BC Health Authority. Regardless of whether you or I consider these individuals wise, their actions told us a lot about how to facilitate value-rational organizational action. So, where do we go from here? I explore this in the following sections, beginning first with a call to educators. After this, I discuss the limitations of my study and identify future streams of research in my call to scholars.

17.2. A Call to Educators, Trainers, Mentors, and Coaches: Implementing Pedagogy that Creates a Foundation for Wise Action

In the previous chapter, I have identified several propositions my research led me to, along with actionable recommendations for individuals within organizations at all levels of authority that will facilitate the development of organizational wisdom. It is my sincere hope this will make a meaningful contribution to the development of organizations that act wisely. To create a wise society, we need wise organizations. To create wise organizations, however, we need wise individuals, and therein lies a question, a 'wicked question' in the parlance of appreciative inquiry described by Adler (2007). Can we teach wisdom?

There exist compelling reasons why the answer may be no. We require wisdom in complex situations, and it is challenging to develop texts to teach wisdom as complexity may defy our ability to name and record (Weick, 2007). Moreover, wisdom is hard to acquire; it is cumulative, gained through experience in the 'real world' rather than the classroom — it is a process, a journey never completed (Kessler & Bailey, 2007b). Remember also that people embed wisdom in systems of power, and so those acts people consider wise depends on the social context (McNamee, 1998; Pitsis & Clegg, 2007; Sampson, 1998). What right, then, does the teacher possess to pronounce which recommendations their students develop are wise and which are not? In addition to these challenges, I would add two more. First, we draw on wisdom in situations where knowledge is lacking or flawed. In the absence of knowledge, what, then, is there for the teacher to teach? Can the teacher be said to 'know' what the wise action is any better than the student? Second, wisdom is action oriented. It is a choice to let your values guide you to 'do the right thing' in the heat of the moment. As a teacher, I can teach my students how to make decisions. I can have them write reports to defend their position, and I might think their rationale is robust. Can I teach them, however, to find the courage to enact that decision outside the safety of the learning environment? I believe the answer is no. I do not believe we can teach wisdom per se.

There is still, however, a powerful role for educators in the development of wisdom. Values guide those exhibiting wisdom, they possess knowledge but can operate in its absence, and they take action. In the above propositions and recommendations I have made from this study, there are several skills and capabilities individuals use to achieve each of those elements. We can teach those skills and capabilities. We can teach students to recognize values and arm them with tactics to address value conflicts. We can give them the knowledge of their discipline, and we can develop the critical thinking skills that will allow them to reason their way through situations where knowledge is insufficient. We can develop their interpersonal skills and emotional intelligence that they can then use in their interactions with others. We can teach them tactics of power they can use to create action in their organization. Perhaps 'developing wisdom' is a more apt phrase than 'teaching wisdom', for though we may not be able to teach wisdom, we can create fertile soil in which it can flourish.

In the following sections, I outline challenges to developing wisdom under our current approach to education. I then list several ways in which educators may develop organizational and managerial wisdom. Then, I conclude with pedagogical tools educators may find useful in this endeavour. When I speak of education, I am biased by my background. I teach undergraduate business courses, and so I approach my discussion on education from that level. Despite that focus, there is no reason why educators cannot adopt the following precepts to any level of education across any discipline.

17.2.1. Challenges to Developing Wisdom under Our Current Approach to Education

Fukami (2007) identified several aspects of our current education system making the teaching of wisdom problematic. Education focuses on giving knowledge, defining excellence as intellectual performance (Martin & Pisón, 2005). It gives students information but seldom helps them learn what to do with that information (Fukami, 2007). It teaches rules, rather than developing the situational recognition that helps individuals understand when to follow the rules, and when to ignore them (Dreyfus & Dreyfus, 1986; Halverson, 2004). Fukami (2007) identified several reasons for this, including: teaching is not respected; we focus on teaching rather than student learning; we focus on quantity over quality; we create competitive classrooms; we ignore the whole student and their experiences; we ignore tacit knowledge; the rise of professional schools and accreditation shifts the emphasis away from teaching to academic scholarship. Pitsis and Clegg (2007) spoke explicitly about management education, arguing that in these programmes teachers have theoretical knowledge while students have experience. Wisdom resides in neither. Only through dialogue with both can wisdom surface. Business schools, however, venerate theory as legitimized through publications: 'powerful words' in 'powerful places' (p. 405). Pitsis and Clegg (2007) further argued that those who question are sidelined. Management education fetishizes methodological control. Business educators pretend they can control the uncontrollable in their studies or ignore it and explain it away. A school of management premised on authority and right and wrong only prepare students to work in a world of the same (Pitsis & Clegg, 2007).

If we wish to cultivate wisdom in our society, educators need to adjust their teaching approaches. Educators need to understand that teachers do not have a privileged role as purveyors of knowledge. Rather, they are one of many interpreters of wisdom. For managers, academia provides, at best, popular tools constituting their ability (Pitsis & Clegg, 2007). Learners for their part must gain not just knowledge but also a growing sense of self-awareness and humility (Conger & Hooijberg, 2007). Fukami (2007) specified four elements that would facilitate the teaching of wisdom: (1) promoting the scholarship of teaching and learning, (2) good pedagogy linking theory to practice, which I will discuss later, (3) serving as role models linking theory to practice, and (4) emphasizing the role of values that underlie choices. In the following section, I will outline several practices for developing wisdom, and in the section after that, I will provide pedagogical tools educators can add to their lessons.

17.2.2. Ways to Develop Organizational and Managerial Wisdom

Recall the three themes of wisdom I have identified: values guide wise action, knowledge is required but insufficient, and wisdom is action oriented. If we are to develop wisdom, then it is these attributes educators must imbue in their students. Kessler and Bailey (2007b) identified five best practices to develop organizational and managerial wisdom: focusing on attitude, awareness, ability, application, and design. I have cross-referenced these five practices with the three themes of wisdom in Table 17.1. I will summarize each of these five practices, describing how they relate to the themes of wisdom. This will give educators an overview of elements to include in their instruction to develop wisdom.

The first practice recommended by Kessler and Bailey (2007a, 2007b) is *focus on attitude*. The goal here is to develop the mindset need to practice wisdom. This mindset includes the acceptance that values guide action, that practitioners require knowledge though they accept they may have to act in its absence, and that they take action. Educators develop students' capacity to engage in dialogue, impressing on them the idea that organizational action is relational and that different groups may have different yet equally valid definitions of wisdom (McNamee, 1998; Sampson, 1998). Educators imbue their students with aesthetic regard where they seek to pursue personal values and interests, shape sharing and productive relations, and develop and design well-functioning groups and organizations (Kessler & Bailey, 2007b). Fostering a wisdom-developing attitude requires the development of students' emotional and social intelligence, which educators can facilitate (see, for example, Boyatzis, 2007).

Second, *focus on awareness*. The goal here is for educators to give practitioners a broader sense of their own identity, of what they bring to a dialogue (Kessler & Bailey, 2007b). Elements of awareness include understanding important aspects of yourself, such as spirituality, values, motivating interests, ideals, and the practice of self-talk (Goleman, Boyatzis, & McKee, 2013; Kessler & Bailey, 2007b). Developing students' emotional intelligence gives practitioners

Table 17.1. A Framework for Educators to Develop Organizational and Managerial Wisdom.

Focus On[a]	Values Guide Action	Knowledge Is Required but Insufficient	Wisdom Is Action Oriented
Attitude (dialog, acceptance, aesthetic regard, recognition, vision)	✓	✓	✓
Awareness (spirituality, values, interests, ideals, self-talk)	✓✓✓		
Ability (competency, critical thinking, experience, broad education/specific training, use of knowledge resources)		✓✓	✓
Application (coaching, action/reflection, mentorship, creating change, experimentation)		✓	✓✓
Design (develop appropriate systems, team support, stakeholder relations, cultural sensitivity, positive power dynamics)			✓✓✓

[a]*Source*: Kessler and Bailey (2007a, 2007b).

insight into whom they want to be and how others perceive them (Boyatzis, 2007). Through developing positive self-talk, practitioners gain competencies in self-appraisal, self-regulation, and perceptual control (Nicholson, 2007). Here is where the educator can discuss the role of values in organizational action, assist students in understanding their guiding values, and in helping them understand how values are embedded in systems of power.

The third practice Kessler and Bailey (2007b) identified for the teaching of organizational and managerial wisdom is *focus on ability*. The goal here is developing the general competency of practitioners. General competency arms students not only with the knowledge they need to act but also with the awareness of the limits of their knowledge and the capacity to improvise when they must operate beyond those limits. To achieve this, educators teach the needed competencies for the field. In addition to this, though, they develop students' critical thinking capacity and provide them with relevant hands-on experience so that they learn how to use their knowledge resources effectively. To facilitate students' capacity to improvise, they provide a broad education in addition to specific job training. Educators should make students aware of the fallacies of thinking that undermine wise action (egocentrism, omnipotence, omniscience, invulnerability, unrealistic optimism) (Jordan & Sternberg, 2007). Here, I would add educators can introduce practitioners to the different types of rationality people use to gain knowledge and how that impacts organizational actions. Different disciplines favour different forms of rationality, and educators can provide value by highlighting such biases and leading practitioners in evaluations of the blind-spots to which that bias makes them susceptible.

Fourth, Kessler and Bailey (2007b) recommended *focusing on application*. The goal here is to provide practitioners with an understanding of how things work in practice. Educators achieve this goal through acts of coaching, action/ reflection cycles, mentorship, creating change, and experimentation. To facilitate this, educators can develop in their students the ability to engage in dialogical thinking (seeing an issue from multiple viewpoints) and dialectical thinking (recognizing that what constitutes a good answer changes over time) with the aim of gaining skill in weighing multiple factors to achieve a common good (Jordan & Sternberg, 2007). The educator should facilitate within their students the awareness that textbooks seldom have the answers that matter and the capacity to exercise their judgement in applying, ignoring, or creating rules.

Finally, Kessler and Bailey (2007b) recommended educators *focus on design* to facilitate the development of organizational and managerial wisdom. The goal here is to arm practitioners with the tools they need to design operating environments in which wisdom can grow. This includes understanding how to develop appropriate systems, team support, stakeholder relationships, cultural sensitivity, and positive power dynamics. Here, educators can teach practitioners about tactics of organizational power they can use to make things happen. Educators can achieve this through demonstrating how power is manifest through bureaucratic rationality. Cultural training can further arm practitioners with an understanding of how different cultures view wisdom, and appropriate means to exercise power in those cultures (Earley & Offermann, 2007). The above five practices inform what educators should instill in their students to develop organizational and managerial wisdom. What pedagogical tools help educators deliver this content? I address that question next.

17.2.3. Pedagogical Tools to Develop Organizational and Managerial Wisdom

Developing wisdom requires pedagogies that link knowing to doing (Fukami, 2007). The best way to learn how to do something is to do it — that is, through experience. Through experience, we gain the ability to acquire meaning from the environment, integrate and assess that meaning, and then arrive at appropriate actions (Bierly et al., 2000). Experience gives the practitioner a repertoire of cases they can pull from when they encounter new situations (Schön, 1983). Though experience is necessary, it is not sufficient for wisdom, for some experiences shut down growth whereas others are fonts of insight (Dewey, 1998). It is the educator's role to guide practitioners towards experiences laden with insight.

If experience is something practitioners gain as they go through life, does the educator have any role in providing this? The answer is yes; the educator can assist the practitioner in framing their experiences in a way that promotes growth. As discussed by Nicholson (2007), educators can provide opportunities for practitioners to observe and imitate other practitioners and add commentary on decisions made. They can lead the practitioner to participate in smart questioning, analysing, theorizing, intuiting, and testing of different actions. If a student is of an age or developmental level where they lack sufficient real-world experience, educators can design experiential learning activities where students make decisions on the spot under emotional pressure similar to how they would in real circumstances (Statler, Roos, & Victor, 2006). Likewise, educators can make arrangements for internships or develop practical assignments that require students to work with industry partners on some problem and then link these to self-reflectivity exercises where practitioners review their decision-making process and assess whether they acted for the right reason (Fowers, 2003). Such activities put students into situations where they start acquiring the experience they will need to develop their wisdom (Schön, 1983; Talbot, 2004).

Combining experience with mentoring helps practitioners organize their experiences so they can pull out valuable learning and insights more readily (Dewey, 1998). To effectively mentor, educators pair practitioners with leaders who have already developed wisdom of their own (Baltes & Kunzmann, 2004; Freeman et al., 2007). A good mentor will challenge mentees on how they perceived their decision-making environment, how they deliberated on the problems they faced, help them reflect on whether the reasons why they chose an option were the right ones, and assess how effective their choices were (Freeman et al., 2007). It may not be feasible to establish effective mentoring relations in all classroom settings, though, depending on the ratio of student to instructor. Even then, educators remain in an influential position to facilitate mentoring through their network of past students and alumni. An instructor might open their network to their class and arrange meetings between current and past students on an as-requested basis. Moreover, educators are in a position to act as role models (Jordan & Sternberg, 2007), putting into practice the three themes of wisdom: values, knowledge, action.

Regarding class assignments, case studies, especially those focusing on ethical concerns, are useful tools to develop wisdom and leadership skills (Bartunek & Trullen, 2007; Conger & Hooijberg, 2007). Cases can simulate the dilemmas decision-makers face. They also simulate situations where the knowledge students would like to have to make their decision is either missing or incomplete. Freeman et al. (2007), however, identified that a drawback of cases is they may not impose the demand to resolve tensions among stakeholders because they are not real. They argued that an appreciation of the arts could help fill this gap as this can increase imagination, empathy, and connectedness. The presentation and discussion of stories accompanied by guiding principles, for example, can add to practitioners' repertoire of cases, and can also convey some of the emotional tension characters experienced (McCloskey, 2007; Oliver & Roos, 2005). Also, cooperative learning, an approach where students are organized into small groups to work together in the class (Cooper, Robinson, & McKinney, 1994; Johnson, Johnson, & Smith, 1991), develops students' ability to work in teams and engage in collective reasoning. Martin and Pisón (2005) demonstrated that students are more likely to adopt a mastery orientation in cooperative rather than a competitive classroom environment.

Recall that elements of organizational and managerial wisdom often require groups to engage and build power relations with other groups. In a sufficiently complex organization, these groups may consist of individuals with different educational backgrounds and, subsequently, different rationalities and values. An example might be a department of physicians in a hospital, trained in technocratic rationality to pursue public interest, having to secure the support of the finance department whose members are trained in economic rationality to pursue effectiveness. Encountering seemingly intelligent and successful people with radically different ways of knowing who pursue radically different ends can be flummoxing. Developing an interdisciplinary curriculum and team-teaching can be an effective means to introduce students to other practitioners of a different background. As Fukami et al. (1996) explained, this brings students of multiple disciplines to courses that are team-taught by teachers of multiple disciplines. It gives students a much more realistic preparation for the work world where they will have to work with others of diverse background.

If wisdom is something we wish organizations to possess, then we must foster wisdom's development in our workforce. Implementing all the ideas I presented above in a pre-existing educational programme may not be feasible. Every educator, however, can adopt one or two of the above ideas and incorporate them into their curriculum. Educational programmes go through periodic reviews, and these are opportunities for educators to incorporate these ideas more holistically in their programme. If every educator, regardless of their discipline, adopted one or two of these ideas, if every programme considered how they might incorporate these ideas, imagine the capacity of the practitioners we produce to tackle the complex, value-laden, wicked challenges of our world.

17.3. A Call to Scholars: Further Developing Our Understanding of How to Facilitate Organizational Wisdom

Wisdom is neglected in scholarly work, especially in organizational studies (Cooperrider & Srivastva, 1998; Kessler & Bailey, 2007b). Perhaps that is because it is so hard and nebulous to define — it is one of those things we know when we see it but cannot objectively 'stick a pin in it' to define as an object of study. Perhaps it is because it is socially constructed — one person's sage is another's reckless fool. Perhaps it is because we pursue instrumental-rationality to the point that values seem soft and irrelevant to the hard-nosed, bottom-line pursuit of organizations.

We do know wisdom when we see it, however. It does have a social reality. We honour it and feel graced when in the presence of someone we believe has it. For thousands of years, scholars across many cultures have reflected on what it means to be wise. Wisdom is not a passing management fad. From the diverse literature on the topic of organizational wisdom, themes emerged: values guide wise action, knowledge is essential but insufficient for wise action, and wisdom is action oriented. I believe we can study organizational wisdom, and I believe we can foster it more purposefully than what we are. It is to that end I hope this study contributes.

There is, of course, much work to be done to develop a discipline of organizational wisdom. This investigation had its limitations. I will now highlight areas of future study to which my research points to address the gaps I could not fill. My research suggested values are a crucial topic of future research. My research setting was in the public sector, and I was fortunate that other groups had laid the groundwork for the study of values in this context. This leads to the following avenue of research:

- How do values in the private sector differ from the public sector? Are the same values in play? An excellent first step to this type of research might be to create a taxonomy of corporate values in the same vein as what Beck Jørgensen and Bozeman (2007) did in the public sector.

In this research setting, my interviewees expressed a perception that the individuals they interacted with shared their prime values despite differing instrumental values and time frames. Everyone was ultimately on the same side. They used these shared prime values to overcome resistance and gain support for the Seniors Programme. I was not, however, able to observe interactions between groups with conflicting prime values. This opens the following train of research.

- What happens in organizations where groups or individuals have different prime values? How does one manage conflicting prime values in a way that preserves the value-rationality of the organization?

In my research setting, individuals managed to avoid open confrontation with other groups. Flyvbjerg (1998) demonstrated that maintaining stability was crucial to engaging rationality, for in open conflict rationality is supplanted with raw acts of power. I hypothesized the same was true of values, though lacked the data to show it due to the stellar job individuals in my research setting did at avoiding conflict. This leaves the door open to another avenue of research.

- What impact does open conflict between groups have on values? Does the will to survive and defeat the enemy replace values? Do values require stability to guide action?

My study did not focus on systematic power such as acts of domination and subjectification. It was designed to observe episodic acts of power, and indeed I saw many examples of the exercise of episodic power to further values. Many of the values I observed were embedded in the structures of the Canada Health Act as well as in the various organizations involved in the Seniors Programme. During my interviews, however, I always felt I was speaking to people who honestly held those values. That is, they did not pursue those values because it was their job, but rather because it was who they were. This leads to the following avenues of research.

- In an organizational context, where do values come from? Do managers and employees internalize the values of the corporation or their profession through domination and subjectification? Alternatively, are they born with their values and then create organizations and pursue professions that embody those intrinsic values? Perhaps it is combinations thereof? What is the relation between systematic power and values in organizations?

Moving away from values to address organizational wisdom in general, I note that the members of the BC working group who created the Seniors Programme were what one might call 'upper-middle management'. They were mostly senior managers and directors within the BC Health Authority. They, therefore, had greater political savvy and networks than lower-level managers or front-line workers, though they were not yet at the pinnacle of authority in their organization. This opens other roads for future studies.

- How might organizational wisdom manifest at the highest levels of authority in an organization? At the VP and C-suite level, individuals possess significant authority to exercise episodic power as well as extensive experience. They, however, are far removed from the front-line where the work of the organization happens. Their knowledge of what is happening is, therefore, filtered through layers of summary reporting. They are also much more likely to interface with influential external stakeholders who seek to exercise power over and through the organization. How might organizational wisdom differ at this level from others?
- Likewise, how might organizational wisdom manifest at the lowest levels of authority? Here, employees and managers have direct contact with the operations of the organization, giving them real-time, unfiltered knowledge of what is happening. Their authority to act, however, is limited and their networks of power under-developed. How does organizational wisdom differ at such a level compared to others?

Though the interviewees I spoke to were managers in the BC Health Authority, and thus immersed in what Vaill (1998) called the 'permanent white water' of organizational life, the Seniors Programme itself was not a mission-critical endeavour. It was a side project, a training exercise, an experiment. To play on Vaill's nautical metaphor, it was an eddy along the banks of the otherwise permanent white water. If it failed utterly, the BC Health Authority would continue as it always had with most of its members unaware the programme ever existed. This raises the following question.

- How does organizational wisdom operate under pressure? This could include studying wisdom in the context of a mission-critical function. It may also include studying wisdom in an organization that is experiencing distress.

17.4.   In Closing ...

Wisdom is the quality we draw on in situations of complexity and uncertainty. We see wisdom in those who are guided by values that we venerate. It requires knowledge bred from study, experience, and dialogue with multiple rationalities. Wise practitioners are capable of improvisation and experimental action when they operate beyond the limits of knowledge. Critically, wisdom is an action. It is not a 'knowing'; it is a 'doing'. And so now as I end this book, I turn my attention to you, the reader. I have studied organizational wisdom in practice, surfacing many propositions of organizational wisdom and concomitant recommendations for action. I have summarized means to develop wisdom in ourselves and the students we teach, whether those students sit in your class or work beside you. I have identified further branches of research into the phenomena of organizational wisdom. From all this, do you see something you can add to your daily practice? What actions can you incorporate into your role to further develop your wisdom as well as that of others?

Appendix

A.1. Appendix: Interview Questions

Question 1. Why was it important for you to become involved in the Seniors Programme/Training Fellowship?

Prompts

- In what ways did these programmes align with the principles and beliefs of your organization/department?
- In what ways, if any, did your organization support your involvement? Why were they willing to support your involvement?
- How does participation in the Seniors Programme project add value to your organization? To the public? To you?
- How does participation in in the Training Programme add value to your organization? To the public? To you?

Question 2. The Seniors Programme project involved collaboration between BC Health Authority, NS Health Authority, private providers of long-term care, community organizations, and the Foundation. Can you give me an example of a major challenge you experienced collaborating with so many groups?

Prompts

- How did you overcome this challenge?
- During the planning stages of Seniors Programme, the team put in significant time and effort meeting with different community groups, meeting with thought leaders, and attending conferences. Why?
- Did each of these groups involved in the programme have similar or different reasons for participating?
- How were they different? Or how were they the same?
- How did the people involved manage these differences?

Question 3. Given the differences in areas served by BC Health Authority and NS Health Authority, and the resulting differences in trial design, what was the reasoning justifying the collaboration with NS Health Authority?

Prompts

- Can you give an example of a significant benefit of the collaboration between the two health authorities? If not, can you provide an example of what prevented any benefits from being realized?
- What actions did the team take to ensure the benefit was realized in the project's outcome?
- What was the reasoning behind the differences in trial design between BC Health Authority and NS Health Authority?

Question 4. Could you explain the process the team used to select the BC Coaching Organization as your community partner?

Prompts

- Why did the team select the BC Coaching Organization rather than some of the other groups you met with?

Question 5. How important was it for the Seniors Programme/Training Programme project to be seen as innovative? Can you give an example demonstrating the importance of being innovative?

Prompts

- To whom did you need to appear innovative?
- Was appearing innovative equally important to each stakeholder in Training Programme/Seniors Programme?
- If the importance of innovation was different between stakeholder groups, how was this difference addressed?
- How did you demonstrate to your stakeholders that you were being innovative?
- Was Seniors Programme innovative? In what ways was it (or wasn't it)?

Question 6. How important was it that the Seniors Programme/Training Programme project create widespread and lasting change (i.e. spread)?

Prompts

- Were all stakeholders equally interested in spread? Can you give examples demonstrating this?
- If the importance of spread was different between stakeholder groups, how was this difference addressed?
- Do you have an example demonstrating how important spread was to a successful Seniors Programme/Training Programme project?
- Do you believe the practices tested in the Seniors Programme project should be spread across the region? Why or why not?

- What are the challenges to spread of practices tested in Seniors Programme?
- Can you give an example demonstrating how BC Health Authority is willing and able (or not) to spread Seniors Programme?

Question 7. In the early stages of developing the trial, there was some discussion on use of terminology when identifying your target population for inclusion in the study: e.g. healthy, not frail, non-frail, not-yet-frail, pre-frail, frail. The team seemed to settle on 'pre-frail' in some documents, 'non-frail' in others. Could you describe the process the team used to arrive at the classification you finally did?

Prompts

- Why was choosing the classification so important?
- The Steering Committee seemed intent on a non-frail target population. Why? How did this influence the name the team went forward with?
- Why did you pick the name you did?

Question 8. (Provide interviewee with printout of name options they considered). The project team spent time the first couple of meetings coming up with the name (for the Seniors Programme). During that process, several other alternative names were discussed, listed in this handout. Could you explain how the official name was chosen? How did the Steering Committee, executive management, the Foundation, and/or NS Health Authority contribute to this decision-making process?

Prompts

- (Redacted to maintain confidentiality)

Question 9. (Provide interviewee with printout of vision options they considered). The project team spent time over several months in the beginning coming up with the vision for Seniors Programme: 'Age well, die fit'. During that process, several other alternative names were discussed, listed in this handout. Could you explain how this vision was chosen? How did the Steering Committee, executive management, the Foundation, and/or NS Health Authority contribute to this decision-making process?

Prompts

- Why 'Age well' and not other choices, such as 'Healthy aging' or 'Proactively delaying frailty' or other?
- Why 'die fit' and not other choices such as 'end well'
- Why did the team move away from sentiments such as 'every senior counts', or 'one senior at a time' or 'every senior matters'?

Question 10. At the time of the Seniors Programme, potential barriers to the successful implementation of the project included executive leadership of BC

Health Authority's focus on acute care and decongestion. Could you give an example of how these barriers posed challenges to the Seniors Programme project? How did the Seniors Programme team overcome them?

Prompts

- How serious a challenge was executive leadership's focus on acute care and decongestion?

Question 11. At times, significant amount of effort went into preparing communication documents. For example, a 'one-pager' communication sheet underwent over thirteen drafts. In meeting minutes, it was documented that it was important to align Seniors Programme key messages with documents such as the BC Health Authority Healthy Aging Profile, BC Ministry of Health documents, BC Health Authority strategic plans, BC Action Plan for Seniors, and so on. Why was such effort and attention spent on crafting documents used to communicate Seniors Programme messages to internal and external stakeholders?

Prompts

- What are some of potential impacts of a poorly crafted communications document?
- What might happen if Seniors Programme key messages were not aligned with other BC Health Authority reports and plans?

Question 12. As the Seniors Programme project was coming to a close, the Steering Committee was interested in the team developing a business case for the final Training Programme report. Why did they want a business case? What does developing a business case mean?

Prompts

- What was the business case used for?
- How did the team do this?
- Was creating a business case part of the considerations when initially designing the trial?
- Was the Seniors Programme trial design appropriate to generate data to create a business case?
- Are there any particular metrics a study's findings must achieve to be considered a successful business case?

Question 13. How was the Seniors Programme project evaluated? How would key stakeholders know whether the project had been a success?

Prompts

- Who developed the evaluation plan?
- How do you feel about the Foundation's evaluation strategy?

- Did each stakeholder group agree with the evaluation plan presented by the Foundation? How were objections addressed?
- The evaluation plan seemed to be developed near the end of the Seniors Programme project. Why do you believe it was developed near the end of the project rather than the beginning?

Question 14. The final Training Programme report seemed to have a lot feedback – some meeting minutes document the sentiment among team members that the Foundation was changing requirements mid-stream. In your opinion, how was the final Training Programme report received by key stakeholder groups? Was their response fair?

Prompts

- What was the Foundation's response to the final report?
- What was executive leadership's response to the final report?
- What was the medical community's response to the final report?

Question 15. At one point, the minutes of a meeting record the Training Programme coach assigned to the team as stating the Seniors Programme project was 'evidence informed' rather than 'evidence based'. During another meeting, the coach stated Seniors Programme was a quality improvement initiative, not a research project. Could you explain what these statements means?

Prompts

- What is the difference between evidence 'informed' versus evidence 'based'?
- How do quality improvement initiatives differ from research projects?
- The Seniors Programme project has many hallmarks of an evidence-based research study designed to collect data showing an intervention had an impact on participants' health. How would you reconcile that with the coach's comments?
- As an 'evidence informed' 'quality improvement initiative', what conclusions can and cannot be drawn from the Seniors Programme project?

Question 16. The Seniors Programme study used a number of tools to assess frailty: Montreal Cognitive Assessment (MoCA), Time Up and Go (TUG), Functional Reach, Community Comprehensive Geriatric Assessment (CGA), Functional Assessment Staging (FAST), and Patient Activation Measure (PAM). Could you explain the process the team used to choose appropriate assessment methods?

Prompts

- It seemed the assessment tools weren't finalized until almost right before patient enrolment began. Why was this?
- How did the team choose criteria by which it judged assessment methods?

- What was the role of your literature review in this decision? What was the role of consultation with experts? Your personal experience and training?
- Why were other assessment tools, such as or the Resident Assessment Instrument (RAI) not used?
- The project ended up using several assessment tools. Why so many? Why not one or two tools to simplify?

Question 17. Physicians and the project manager were remunerated for their involvement in Seniors Programme, but not team members, BC Coaching Organization volunteers, or patients. Could you explain why physicians and the project manager received payment for their involvement, but not others?

Prompts

- Why were patients not paid for their participation in the study?
- Why were BC Coaching Organization coaches not paid for their role in Seniors Programme?
- Why were members of the Seniors Programme working group not paid for their role in Seniors Programme?
- How was the rate of remuneration for physicians determined?

Question 18. In what ways was support by executive leadership at BC Health Authority, say, at the CEO and VP level, important to the Training Programme/ Seniors Programme project? Can you give an example of how you obtained and maintained that support?

Prompts

- In what ways did executive leadership show their support (or fail to show their support) for the Training Programme/Seniors Programme project?
- Participation in the Training Programme programme seemed, at times, to be very labour and time intensive (preparation of reports; travel; etc.). What was executive leadership's motivation to support this effort?

Question 19. During implementation of Seniors Programme, BC Health Authority had three CEOs in succession. Can you provide some examples of how this turnover in executive leadership impacted the ongoing Seniors Programme?

Prompts

- How did the project team respond to this uncertainty in executive leadership?
- Did this turnover make it easier or harder to manage and maintain ongoing activities of the Seniors Programme? How? Can you provide examples?

Question 20. Thanks for your time! Is there anything else you'd like to share about your experience with the Training Programme/Seniors Programme project?

References

BC Health Authority. (2014). *2014/15–2016/17 service plan*. Surrey, Canada.

BC Health Authority. (2015). *2015/16–2017/18 service plan*. Surrey, Canada.

[The Foundation]-[NS Health Authority]-[BC Health Authority] Collaborative. (2013). [The Foundation]-[NS Health Authority]-[BC Health Authority] Collaborative project to improve senior care: Project charter.

The Foundation. (2015). Proactively delaying frailty in not-yet frail seniors: An interprovincial collaborative. Retrieved from http://www.cfhi-fcass.ca/WhatWeDo/EducationandTraining/EXTRA/2014-extra-competition-results/Project3. Accessed on July 30, 2015.

The Foundation. (2018). What we do. Retrieved from https://www.cfhi-fcass.ca/WhatWeDo.aspx. Accessed on August 2, 2018.

The Seniors Program. (2014). *Project intervention summary*.

About BC Health Authority. (2018). Retrieved from https://www.fraserhealth.ca/about-us/about-fraser-health/#.W2HpGtJKjD5. Accessed on August 1, 2018.

About Us. (2018). Retrieved from https://www.cfhi-fcass.ca/AboutUs.aspx. Accessed on May 22, 2018.

Ackroyd, S. (2000). Connecting organisations and societies: A realist analysis of structures. In S. Ackroyd & S. Fleetwood (Eds.), *Realist perspectives on management and organisations* (pp. 87–108). New York, NY: Routledge.

Ackroyd, S., & Fleetwood, S. (2000). Realism in contemporary organisation and management studies. In S. Ackroyd & S. Fleetwood (Eds.), *Realist perspectives on management and organisations* (pp. 3–25). New York, NY: Routledge.

Adler, N. J. (2007). Organizational metaphysics—Global wisdom and the audacity of hope. In E. H. Kessler & J. R. Bailey (Eds.), *Handbook of organizational and managerial wisdom* (pp. 423–458). Thousand Oaks, CA: Sage Publications.

Aguinis, H. (Ed.). (2004). *Test-score banding in human resource selection: Legal, technical, and societal issues*. New York, NY: Praeger Publishers.

Alexander, E. R. (1979). The design of alternatives in organizational contexts: A pilot study. *Administrative Science Quarterly*, 24(3), 382–404.

Alvesson, M. (1987). *Organization theory and technocratic consciousness: Rationality, ideology and quality of work*. New York, NY: De Gruyter.

Ardelt, M. (2000). Intellectual versus wisdom-related knowledge: The case for a different kind of learning in the later years of life. *Educational Gerontology*, 26(8), 771–789.

Ardelt, M. (2004). Wisdom as expert knowledge system: A critical review of a contemporary operationalization of an ancient concept. *Human Development*, 47(5), 257–285.

Arrow, K. J. (1992). Rationality of self and others in an economic system. In M. Zey (Ed.), *Decision making: Alternatives to rational choice models* (pp. 63–77). Thousand Oaks, CA: Sage Publications.

Astley, W. G., & Sachdeva, P. S. (1984). Structural sources of intraorganizational power: A theoretical synthesis. *The Academy of Management Review*, *9*(1), 104–113.

Badaracco, J. L. (1997). *Defining moments: When managers must choose between right and right*. Boston, MA: Harvard University Press.

Baltes, P. B., & Kunzmann, U. (2004). The two faces of wisdom: Wisdom as a general theory of knowledge and judgment about excellence in mind and virtue vs. wisdom as everyday realization in people and products. *Human Development*, *47*(5), 290–299.

Baltes, P. B., & Staudinger, U. M. (2000). Wisdom: A metaheuristic (pragmatic) to orchestrate mind and virtue toward excellence. *American Psychologist*, *55*(1), 122–136.

Barker, J. (1993). Tightening the iron cage: Concertive control in self-managing work teams. *Administrative Science Quarterly*, *38*(3), 408–437.

Barnard, C. I. (1962). Mind in everyday affairs. In *The functions of the executive* (pp. 301–322). Cambridge, MA: Harvard University Press.

Barry, B., Fulmer, I. S., & Long, A. (2000). Ethically marginal bargaining tactics: Sanction, efficacy, and performance. In *Annual meeting of the academy of management*. Toronto, Canada.

Bartunek, J. M. (2007). Academic-practitioner collaboration need not require joint or relevant research: Toward a relational scholarship of integration. *Academy of Management Journal*, *50*(6), 1323–1333.

Bartunek, J. M., & Trullen, J. (2007). Individual ethics—The virtue of prudence. In E. H. Kessler & J. R. Bailey (Eds.), *Handbook of organizational and managerial wisdom* (pp. 91–108). Thousand Oaks, CA: Sage Publications.

Basu, R. (2012). Spatial phronesis: A case study in geosurveillance. In B. Flyvbjerg, T. Landman, & S. Schram (Eds.), *Real social science: Applied phronesis* (pp. 264–284). Cambridge: Cambridge University Press.

BC Working Group. (2014, May 8). Minutes: [Seniors Group] Project – [BC] Working Group Planning Meeting 2014-05-08.

BC Working Group. (2015, March 26). [Seniors Program] Project – [BC] Working Group Meeting 2015-03-26.

Beck Jørgensen, T., & Bozeman, B. (2007). Public values: An inventory. *Administration & Society*, *39*, 354–381.

Beck Jørgensen, T., & Sørensen, D.-L. (2013). Codes of good governance: National or global values? *Public Integrity*, *15*(1), 71–96.

Beckhard, R. (1969). *Organization development: Strategies and models*. Reading, MA: Addison-Wesley Publishing.

Bedford, L., Clarke, B., Chu, L., Friesen, K., Garm, A., MacPherson, C., & Park, G. (2015). *Intervention project final report: [The Seniors Program] project—Proactively delaying frailty in pre-frail seniors*.

Better Education, Better Care: Strategic Plan 2018–2020. (n.d.). Ottawa, ON.

Beyer, J. M., & Nino, D. (1998). Facing the future: Backing courage with wisdom. In S. Srivastva & D. L. Cooperrider (Eds.), *Organizational wisdom and executive courage* (pp. 65–97). San Francisco, CA: The New Lexington Press.

Bhaskar, R. (1978). *A realist theory of science*. New York, NY: Harvester Press.

Bhaskar, R. (1986). *Scientific realism and human emancipation*. London: Verso.

Bierly, III, P. E., Kessler, E. H., & Christensen, E. W. (2000). Organizational learning, knowledge and wisdom. *Journal of Organizational Change Management*, *13*(6), 595—618.

Bierly, III, P. E., & Kolodinsky, R. W. (2007). Strategic logic—Toward a wisdom-based approach to strategic management. In E. H. Kessler & J. R. Bailey (Eds.), *Handbook of organizational and managerial wisdom* (pp. 61—88). Thousand Oaks, CA: Sage Publications.

Bigelow, J. (1992). Developing managerial wisdom. *Journal of Management Inquiry*, *1*(2), 143—153.

Birren, J. E., & Fisher, L. M. (1990). The elements of wisdom: Overview and integration. In R. J. Sternberg (Ed.), *Wisdom: Its nature, origins, and development* (pp. 317—322). New York, NY: Cambridge University Press.

Blackburn, S. (2001). *Being good: A short introduction to ethics*. New York, NY: Oxford University Press.

Boltanski, L., & Thévenot, L. (1991). *De la Justification: Les Économies de la Grandeur [Of Justification: Economies of size]*. Paris: Les Editions Gallimard.

Bower, J. L. (1997, October). Teradyne: The Aurora project. *Harvard Business Review*.

Bowie, N. E. (1999). *Business ethics: A Kantian perspective*. Oxford: Blackwell Publishing.

Boyatzis, R. E. (2007). Interpersonal aesthetics—Emotional and social intelligence competencies are wisdom in practice. In E. H. Kessler & J. R. Bailey (Eds.), *Handbook of organizational and managerial wisdom* (pp. 223—242). Thousand Oaks, CA: Sage Publications.

Bradford, D. L. (2002). The challenge of a team. In A. R. Cohen (Ed.), *The portable MBA in management* (3rd ed.). New York, NY: John Wiley.

Bucher, R., & Stelling, J. (1969). Characteristics of professional organizations. *Journal of Health and Social Behavior*, *10*(1), 3—15.

Burke, W. W. (1994). *Organization development: A process of learning and changing* (2nd ed.). Reading, MA: Addison-Wesley Publishing.

Burke, W. W. (2007). Organizational aesthetics—Aesthetics and wisdom in the practice of organization development. In E. H. Kessler & J. R. Bailey (Eds.), *Handbook of organizational and managerial wisdom* (pp. 243—259). Thousand Oaks, CA: Sage Publications.

Burt, R. S. (1995). *Structural holes: The social structure of competition*. Cambridge: Cambridge University Press.

Camerer, C., & Thaler, R. H. (1995). Anomalies: Ultimatums, dictators and manners. *The Journal of Economic Perspectives*, *9*(2), 209—219.

Cameron, K. S., Freeman, S. J., & Mishra, A. K. (1993). Downsizing and redesigning organizations. In G. P. Huber & W. H. Glick (Eds.), *Organizational change and redesign: Ideas and insights for improving performance* (pp. 19—65). New York, NY: Oxford University Press.

Carter, N., Klein, R., & Doey, P. (1992). *How organizations measure success*. London: Routledge.

Chase, S. E. (2005). Narrative inquiry: Multiple lenses, approaches, voices. In N. K. Denzin & Y. S. Lincoln (Eds.), *Handbook of qualitative research* (pp. 651—679). Thousand Oaks, CA: Sage Publications.

Chia, R., & Holt, R. (2007). Wisdom as learned ignorance—Integrating East-West perspectives. In E. H. Kessler & J. R. Bailey (Eds.), *Handbook of organizational and managerial wisdom* (pp. 505–526). Thousand Oaks, CA: Sage Publications.

Chong, L. M. A., & Thomas, D. C. (1997). Leadership perceptions in cross-cultural context: Pakeha and Pacific Islanders in New Zealand. *The Leadership Quarterly*, *8*(3), 275–293.

Cicmil, S. (2006). Understanding project management practice through interpretive and critical research perspectives. *Project Management Journal*, *37*(2), 27–37.

Clegg, S. R. (2009). Doing power work. In D. A. Buchanan & A. Bryman (Eds.), *The Sage handbook of organizational research methods* (pp. 143–159). Thousand Oaks, CA: Sage Publications.

Clegg, S. R., & Pitsis, T. S. (2012). Phronesis, projects and power research. In B. Flyvbjerg, T. Landman, & S. Schram (Eds.), *Real social science: Applied phronesis* (pp. 66–91). Cambridge: Cambridge University Press.

Collins, J. C., & Porras, J. I. (1997). *Built to last: Successful habits of visionary companies*. New York, NY: HarperBusiness.

Conference Board of Canada. (2012). Health. Retrieved from http://www.conferenceboard.ca/HCP/Details/Health.aspx

Conger, J., & Hooijberg, R. (2007). Organizational ethics—Acting wisely while facing ethical dilemmas in leadership. In E. H. Kessler & J. R. Bailey (Eds.), *Handbook of organizational and managerial wisdom* (pp. 133–150). Thousand Oaks, CA: Sage Publications.

Cooper, J. L., Robinson, P., & McKinney, M. (1994). Cooperative learning in the classroom. In D. F. Halpern (Ed.), *Changing college classrooms: New teaching and learning strategies for an increasingly complex world* (pp. 74–92). San Francisco, CA: Jossey-Bass.

Cooperrider, D. L., & Srivastva, S. (1998). An invitation to organizational wisdom and executive courage. In S. Srivastva & D. L. Cooperrider (Eds.), *Organizational wisdom and executive courage* (pp. 1–22). San Francisco, CA: The New Lexington Press.

Coopey, J., Keegan, O., & Emler, N. (1998). Managers' innovations and the structuration of organizations. *Journal of Management Studies*, *35*(3), 263–284.

Costello, N. (2000). Routines, strategy and change in high-technology small firms. In S. Ackroyd & S. Fleetwood (Eds.), *Realist perspectives on management a* (pp. 161–180). New York, NY: Routledge.

Covey, S. R. (1990). *Principle centered leadership*. New York, NY: Simon & Shuster.

Cropanzano, R., Stein, J., & Goldman, B. M. (2007). Individual aesthetics—Self-interest. In E. H. Kessler & J. R. Bailey (Eds.), *Handbook of organizational and managerial wisdom* (pp. 181–221). Thousand Oaks, CA: Sage Publications.

Crossley, N. (1998). Emotion and communicative action. In S. J. Williams & G. Bendelow (Eds.), *Emotions in social life: Critical themes and contempory issues* (pp. 17–38). New York, NY: Taylor & Francis e-Library.

Crozier, M. (1964). *The bureaucratic phenomena*. Chicago, IL: Chicago University Press.

Dahl, R. A., & Lindblom, C. E. (1953). *Politics, economics, and welfare*. Chicago, IL: The University of Chicago Press.

De Graaf, G., & Van Exel, J. (2009). Using Q methodology in administrative ethics. *Public Integrity*, *11*(1), 63–78.

de Graaf, J. (2004). Time for bread and roses. Retrieved from http://www.alternet. org/story/20786/time_for_bread_and_roses. Accessed on December 26, 2016.

De Graff, G., Huberts, L., & Smulders, R. (2014). Coping with public value conflicts. *Administration & Society*, 1−27.

De Meyer, A. (2007). Strategic epistemology—Innovation and organizational wisdom. In E. H. Kessler & J. R. Bailey (Eds.), *Handbook of organizational and managerial wisdom* (pp. 357−374). Thousand Oaks, CA: Sage Publications.

Denis, J.-L., Dompierre, G., Langley, A., & Rouleau, L. (2011). Escalating indecision: Between reification and strategic smbiguity. *Organization Science*, *22*(1), 225−244.

Denis, J.-L., Hébert, Y., Langley, A., Lozeau, D., & Trottier, L.-H. (2002). Explaining diffusion patterns for complex health care innovations. *Health Care Management Review*, *27*(3), 60−73.

Denis, J.-L., Lamothe, L., & Langley, A. (2001). The dynamics of collective leadership and strategic change in pluralistic organizations. *Academy of Management Journal*, *44*(4), 809−837.

Denis, J.-L., Langley, A., & Rouleau, L. (2006). The power of numbers in strategizing. *Strategic Organization*, *4*(4), 349−377.

DeNisi, A. S., & Belsito, C. A. (2007). Strategic aesthetics—Wisdom and human resources management. In E. H. Kessler & J. R. Bailey (Eds.), *Handbook of organizational and managerial wisdom* (pp. 261−273). Thousand Oaks, CA: Sage Publications.

Dewey, J. (1998). *Experience and education* (60th Anniv). Indianapolis, IN: Kappa Delta Pi.

DiMaggio, P. J., & Powell, W. W. (1983). The iron cage revisited: Institutional isomorphism and collective rationality in organizational fields. *American Sociological Review*, *48*(2), 147−160.

Dreyfus, H. L. (1990). What is moral maturity? A phenomenological account of the development of ethical expertise. Retrieved from http://conium.org/~hdreyfus/rtf/ Moral_Maturity_8_90.rtf. Accessed on December 26, 2016.

Dreyfus, H. L., & Dreyfus, S. E. (1986). *Mind over machine: The power of human intuition and expertise in the Era of the computer*. New York, NY: Free Press.

Durand, R., & Calori, R. (2006). Sameness, otherness? Enriching organizational change theories with philosophical considerations on the same and the other. *Academy of Management Review*, *31*(1), 93−114.

Earley, P. C., & Ang, S. (2003). *Cultural intelligence: Individual interactions across cultures*. Palo Alto, CA: Stanford University Press.

Earley, P. C., & Offermann, L. R. (2007). Interpersonal epistemology—Wisdom, culture, and organizations. In E. H. Kessler & J. R. Bailey (Eds.), *Handbook of organizational and managerial wisdom* (pp. 295−325). Thousand Oaks, CA: Sage Publications.

Eisenberg, N., & Miller, P. A. (1987). The relation of empathy to prosocial and related behaviors. *Psychological Bulletin*, *101*(1), 91−119.

Eriksson, P., & Kovalainen, A. (2008). *Qualitative methods in business research*. Thousand Oaks, CA: Sage Publications.

Eubanks, V. (2012). Feminist phronesis and technologies of citizenship. In B. Flyvbjerg, T. Landman, & S. Schram (Eds.), *Real social science: applied phronesis* (pp. 228−245). Cambridge: Cambridge University Press.

Feldman, M. S., Sködberg, K., Brown, R. N., & Homer, D. (2004). Making sense of stories: A rhetorical approach to narrative analysis. *Journal of Public Administration Research & Theory, 14*(2), 147−170.

Fenton, C., & Langley, A. (2011). Strategy as practice and the narrative turn. *Organization Studies, 2*(6), 1171−1196.

Ferguson, K. E. (1994). On bringing more theory, more voices and more politics to the study of organization. *Organization, 1*(1), 81−99.

Fleming, P., & Spicer, A. (2014). Power in management and organization science. *The Academy of Management Annals, 8*(1), 237−298.

Flyvbjerg, B. (1998). *Rationality and power: Democracy in practice*. Chicago, IL: The University of Chicago Press.

Flyvbjerg, B. (2001). *Making social science matter: Why social inquiry fails and how it can succeed again*. New York, NY: Cambridge University Press.

Flyvbjerg, B. (2002). Bringing power to planning research: One researcher's praxis story. *Journal of Planning Education and Research, 21*(4), 353−366.

Flyvbjerg, B. (2004). Phronetic planning research: Theoretical and methodological reflections. *Planning Theory and Practice, 5*(3), 283−306.

Flyvbjerg, B. (2006a). From nobel prize to project management: Getting risks right. *Project Management Journal, 37*(3), 5−15.

Flyvbjerg, B. (2006b). Making organization research matter: Power, values and phronesis. In S. R. Clegg, C. Hardy, T. B. Lawrence, & W. R. Nord (Eds.), *The SAGE handbook of organizational studies* (2nd ed., pp. 370−387). Thousand Oaks, CA: Sage.

Flyvbjerg, B. (2008). Curbing optimism bias and strategic misrepresentation in planning: Reference class forecasting in practice. *European Planning Studies, 16*(1), 3−21.

Flyvbjerg, B. (2009). Survival of the unfittest: Why the worst infrastructure gets built, and what we can do about it. *Oxford Review of Economic Policy, 25*(3), 344−367.

Flyvbjerg, B. (2012). Why mass media matter and how to work with them: Phronesis and megaprojects. In B. Flyvbjerg, T. Landman, & S. Schram (Eds.), *Real social science: Applied phronesis* (pp. 95−121). Cambridge: Cambridge University Press.

Flyvbjerg, B., Bruzelius, N., & Rothengatter, W. (2003). *Megaprojects and risk: An anatomy of ambition*. Cambridge: Cambridge University Press.

Flyvbjerg, B., Garbuio, M., & Lovallo, D. (2009). Delusion and deception in large infrastructure projects: Two models for explaining and preventing executive disaster. *California Management Review, 51*(2), 170−193.

Flyvbjerg, B., Glenting, C., & Rønnest, A. K. (2004). *Procedures for dealing with optimism bias in transport planning*. London: The British Department for Transport.

Flyvbjerg, B., Landman, T., & Schram, S. (2012). Introduction: New directions in social science. In B. Flyvbjerg, T. Landman, & S. Schram (Eds.), *Real social science: Applied phronesis* (pp. 1−12). Cambridge: Cambridge University Press.

Fosfuri, A., & Rønde, T. (2009). Leveraging resistance to change and the skunk works model of innovation. *Journal of Economic Behavior & Organization, 72*(1), 274−289.

Foucault, M. (1977). *Discipline and punish: The birth of the prison*. Toronto: Random House.

Fowers, B. J. (2003). Reason and human finitude in praise of practical wisdom. *American Behavioral Scientist, 47*(4), 415–426.

Freeman, R. E. (2010). *Strategic management: A stakeholder approach.* New York, NY: Cambridge University Press.

Freeman, R. E., Dunham, L., & McVea, J. (2007). Strategic ethics—Strategy, wisdom, and stakeholder theory: A pragmatic and entrepreneurial view of stakeholder strategy. In E. H. Kessler & J. R. Bailey (Eds.), *Handbook of organizational and managerial wisdom* (pp. 151–177). Thousand Oaks, CA: Sage Publications.

Friedland, R., & Alford, R. (1991). Bringing society back in: Symbols, practices and institutional contradictions. In W. W. Powell & P. J. DiMaggio (Eds.), *The new institutionalism in organizational analysis* (pp. 232–263). Chicago, IL: The University of Chicago Press.

Frost, P. J. (2003). *Toxic emotions at work: How compassionate managers handle pain and conflict.* Boston, MA: Harvard Business School Press.

Fukami, C. V. (2007). Strategic metaphysics – Can wisdom be taught. In E. H. Kessler & J. R. Bailey (Eds.), *Handbook of organizational and managerial wisdom* (pp. 459–473). Thousand Oaks, CA: Sage Publications.

Fukami, C. V., Clouse, M. L., Howard, C. T., McGowan, R. P., Mullins, J. W., Silver, W. S., ... Wittmer, D. P. (1996). The road less traveled: The joys and sorrows of team teaching. *Journal of Management Education, 20*(4), 409–410.

Gardner, H. (2011). *Leading minds: An anatomy of leadership* (Reprint ed.). New York, NY: Basic Books.

Giacalone, R. A., & Jurkiewicz, C. L. (2003). *Handbook of workplace spirituality and organizational performance.* Armonk, NY: M. E. Sharpe.

Giddens, A. (1976). *New rules of sociological method.* London: Hutchinson.

Giddens, A. (1982). *Profiles and critiques in social theory.* Berkeley, CA: University of California Press.

Giddens, A. (1984). *The constitution of society.* Cambridge: Polity Press.

Gioia, D. A. (2006). On weick: An appreciation. *Organization Studies, 27*(11), 1709–1721.

Gioia, D. A. (2007). Individual epistemology—interpretive wisdom. In E. H. Kessler & J. R. Bailey (Eds.), *Handbook of organizational and managerial wisdom* (pp. 276–294). Thousand Oaks, CA: Sage Publications.

Goleman, D., Boyatzis, R. E., & McKee, A. (2013). *Primal leadership: Unleashing the power of emotional intelligence.* Boston, MA: Harvard Business Review Press.

Gordon, R., Kornberger, M., & Clegg, S. R. (2009). Power, rationality and legitimacy in public organizations. *Public Administration, 87*(1), 15–34.

Gouldner, A. (1970). *The coming crisis of western sociology.* New York, NY: Basic Books.

Government of British Columbia. (2014). *Setting priorities for the B. C. health system.* Victoria, Canada.

Government of Canada. (2014, July 26). Canada Health Act: R.S.C., 1985, c. C-6. Retrieved from http://laws-lois.justice.gc.ca/eng/acts/C-6/page-1.html

Grandy, G. (2011). Chapter 13: Power and organizational life. In A. J. Mills, J. C. H. Mills, J. Bratton, & C. Forshaw (Eds.), *Organizational behaviour in a global context* (pp. 389–422). North York: University of Toronto Press.

Grant, R. M. (1996a). Prospering in dynamically-competitive environments: Organizational capability as knowledge integration. *Organization Science, 7*(4), 375–387.

Grant, R. M. (1996b). Toward a knowledge-based theory of the firm. *Strategic Management Journal, 17*(S2), 109–122.

Grant, R. M. (2005). *Contempory strategic analysis.* Malden, MA: Blackwell Publishing.

Grierson, B. (2014). *What makes Olga run: The mystery of the 90-something track star, and what she can teach us about living longer, happier lives.* Vintage Canada.

Griggs, S., & Howarth, D. (2012). Phronesis and critical policy analysis: Heathrow's "third runway" and the politics of sustainable aviation in the United Kingdom. In B. Flyvbjerg, T. Landman, & S. Schram (Eds.), *Real social science: Applied phronesis* (pp. 167–203). Cambridge: Cambridge University Press.

Güth, W., Schmittberger, R., & Schwarze, B. (1982). An experimental analysis of ultimatum bargaining. *Journal of Economic Behavior & Organization, 3*(4), 367–388.

Hackman, J. R. (2002). *Leading teams: Setting the stage for great performances.* Boston, MA: Harvard Business Review Press.

Halverson, R. (2004). Accessing, documenting, and communicating practical wisdom: The phronesis of school leadership practice. *American Journal of Education, 111*(1), 90–121.

Hamel, G., & Prahalad, C. K. (1994). *Competing for the future.* Boston, MA: Harvard Business School Press.

Hamilton, L. (2012). Purity in danger: Power, negotiation and ontology in medical practice. *International Journal of Organizational Analysis, 20*(1), 95–106.

Hardin, G. (1968). The tragedy of the commons. *Science, 162*(3859), 1243–1248.

Hardy, C., & Clegg, S. R. (1996). Chapter 3.7: Some dare call it power. In S. R. Clegg, C. Hardy, & W. R. Nord (Eds.), *Handbook of organization studies* (pp. 622–641). London: Sage Publications.

Hariman, R. (Ed.). (2003). *Prudence: Classical virtue, postmodern practice.* University Park, PA: The Pennsylvania State University Press.

Harre, R. (1988). Modes of explanation. In D. J. Hilton (Ed.), *Contemporary science and natural explanation: Commonsense conceptions of causality* (pp. 129–144). New York, NY: New York University Press.

Harre, R., & Madden, E. H. (1975). *Causal powers.* Oxford: Blackwell Publishing.

Harre, R., & Secord, P. F. (1972). *The explanation of social behaviour.* Oxford: Rowman & Littlefield.

Henrich, J., Boyd, R., Bowles, S., Camerer, C., Fehr, E., Gintis, H., & McElreath, R. (2001). In search of homo economicus: Behavioral experiments in 15 small-scale societies. *The American Economic Review, 91*(2), 73–78.

Hickson, D. J., Hinings, C. R., Lee, C. A., Schneck, R. E., & Pennings, J. M. (1971). A strategic contingencies' theory of intraorganizational power. *Administrative Science Quarterly, 16*(2), 216–229.

Holley, D. (1999). *Self-interest and beyond.* St. Paul, MN: Paragon House.

Holliday, S. G., & Chandler, M. J. (1986). Wisdom: Explorations in adult competence. *Contributions to Human Development, 17*, i–ix.

Holmes, J. G., Miller, D. T., & Lerner, M. J. (2002). Committing altruism under the cloak of self-interest: The exchange fiction. *Journal of Experimental Social Psychology*, *38*(2), 144−151.

Holmqvist, M., & Maravalias, C. (2011). *Managing healthy organizations: Worksite health promotion and the new self-management paradigm*. London: Routledge.

House, R. (1968). Leadership training: Some dysfunctional consequences. *Administrative Science Quarterly*, *12*(4), 556−571.

Janis, I. L. (1972). *Victims of groupthink; A psychological study of foreign-policy decisions and fiascoes*. Boston, MA: Houghton Mifflin.

Johnson, D. W., Johnson, R. T., & Smith, K. A. (1991). *Active learning: Cooperation in the college classroom*. Edina, MN: Interaction Book.

Johnstone, C. L. (1983). Dewey, ethics, and rhetoric: Toward a contemporary conception of practical wisdom. *Philosophy and Rhetoric*, *16*(3), 185−207.

Jordan, J., & Sternberg, R. J. (2007). Individual logic−wisdom in organizations: A balance theory analysis. In E. H. Kessler & J. R. Bailey (Eds.), *Handbook of organizational and managerial wisdom* (pp. 3−19). Thousand Oaks, CA: Sage Publications.

Kahneman, D., Knetsch, J. L., & Thaler, R. H. (1986). Fairness and the assumptions of economics. *The Journal of Business*, *59*(4), S285−S300.

Kalberg, S. (1980). Max Weber's types of rationality: Cornerstones for the analysis of rationalization processes in history. *American Journal of Sociology*, *85*(5), 1145−1179.

Katzenbach, J. R., & Smith, D. K. (2015). *The wisdom of teams: Creating the high-performance organization* (2nd ed.). Boston, MA: Harvard Business Review Press.

Kessler, E. H., & Bailey, J. R. (Eds.). (2007a). *Handbook of organizational and managerial wisdom*. Thousand Oaks, CA: Sage Publications.

Kessler, E. H., & Bailey, J. R. (2007b). Introduction − Understanding, applying, and developing organizational and managerial wisdom. In E. H. Kessler & J. R. Bailey (Eds.), *Handbook of organizational and managerial wisdom* (pp. xv−lxxiv). Thousand Oaks, CA: Sage Publications.

Kettl, D. F. (1993). *Sharing power: Public governance and private markets*. Washington, DC: Brookings Institution Press.

Knights, D., & Morgan, G. (1991). Strategic discourse and subjectivity: Towards a critical analysis of corporate strategy in organizations. *Organization Studies*, *12*(3), 251−273.

Kodeih, F., & Greenwood, R. (2013). Responding to institutional complexity: The role of identity. *Organization Studies*, *35*(1), 7−39.

Kornberger, M., & Clegg, S. (2011). Strategy as performative practice: The case of Sydney 2030. *Strategic Organization*, *9*(2), 136−162.

Kotter, J. P., & Heskett, J. L. (1992). *Corporate culture and performance*. New York, NY: The Free Press.

Kunda, G. (1992). *Engineering culture: Control and commitment in a high-tech corporation*. Philadelphia, PA: Temple University Press.

Landman, T. (2012). Phronesis and narrative analysis. In B. Flyvbjerg, T. Landman, & S. Schram (Eds.), *Real social science: Applied phronesis* (pp. 27−47). Cambridge: Cambridge University Press.

Langley, A., & Denis, J.-L. (2011). Beyond evidence: The micropolitics of improvement. *BMJ Quality & Safety, 20*(Suppl 1), i43–i46.

Lawrence, P. R. (2007). Orgainzational logic – Institutionalizing wisdom in organizations. In E. H. Kessler & J. R. Bailey (Eds.), *Handbook of organizational and managerial wisdom* (pp. 43–60). Thousand Oaks, CA: Sage Publications.

Lawrence, P. R., & Nohira, N. (2002). *Driven: How human nature shapes our choices.* San Francisco, CA: Jossey-Bass.

Lawrence, T. B., & Suddaby, R. (2006). Institutions and institutional work. In S. R. Clegg, C. Hardy, T. B. Lawrence, & W. R. Nord (Eds.), *Handbook of organization studies* (2nd ed., pp. 215–254). London: Sage.

Lennick, D., & Kiel, F. (2008). *Moral intelligence: Enhancing business performance and leadership success.* Upper Saddle River, NJ: Wharton School Publishing.

Levitt, H. M. (1999). The development of wisdom: An analysis of tibetan buddhist experience. *Journal of Humanistic Psychology, 39*(2), 86–105.

Lewicki, R. J. (2007). Interpersonal ethics–the wise negotiator. In E. H. Kessler & J. R. Bailey (Eds.), *Handbook of organizational and managerial wisdom* (pp. 109–132). Thousand Oaks, CA: Sage Publications.

Lewicki, R. J., & Robinson, R. J. (1998). A factor-analytic study of negotiator ethics. *Journal of Business Ethics, 18*, 211–228.

Lewis, M. M. (1996, June 17). Snobs and yobs: How British banking produced nick leeson. *The New Yorker*, p. 97.

Lukes, S. (2005). *Power: A radical view* (2nd ed.). New York, NY: Palgrave Macmillan.

Manicas, P. (1980). The concept of social structure. *Journal for the Theory of Social Behaviour, 10*(2), 65–82.

Martin, M. K., & Pisón, R. M. de. (2005). From knowledge to wisdom: A new challenge to the educational milieu with implications for religious education. *Religious Education, 100*(2), 157–173.

Marwell, G., & Ames, R. E. (1981). Economists free ride, does anyone else?: Experiments on the provision of public goods, IV. *Journal of Public Economics, 15*(3), 295–310.

Mathieson, K., & Miree, C. A. (2003). Illuminating the invisible: IT and self-discovery in the workplace. In *Handbook of workplace spirituality and organizational performance* (pp. 461–474). Armonk, NY: M. E. Sharpe.

McCloskey, D. N. (2007). *The bourgeois virtues: Ethics for an age of commerce.* Chicago, IL: The University of Chicago Press.

McCracken, G. (1988). *The long interview.* Newbury Park, CA: Sage Publications.

McNamee, S. (1998). Reinscribing organizational wisdom and courage: The relationally engaged organization. In S. Srivastva & D. L. Cooperrider (Eds.), *Organizational wisdom and executive courage1* (pp. 101–117). San Francisco, CA: The New Lexington Press.

McVea, J. F., & Freeman, R. E. (2005). A names-and-faces approach to stakeholder management: How focusing on stakeholders as individuals can bring ethics and entrepreneurial strategy together. *Journal of Management Inquiry, 14*(1), 57–69.

Mechanic, D. (1962). Sources of power of lower participants in complex organizations. *American Science Quarterly, 7*(3), 349–364.

Merton, R. K. (Ed.). (1968). *Social theory and social structure.* New York, NY: Simon and Shuster.

Meyer, J. W., & Rowan, B. (1977). Institutional organizations: Formal structure as myth and ceremony. *American Jounal of Sociology, 83*(2), 340–363.

Meyer, M. (2002). *Rethinking performance measurement*. Cambridge: Cambridge University Press.

Murray, B., & Gerhart, B. (1998). An empirical analysis of a skill-based pay program and plant performance outcomes. *Academy of Management Journal, 41*(1), 68–78.

National Audit Office. (2001). *Measuring the performance of government departments*. London. Retrieved from https://www.nao.org.uk/report/measuring-the-performance-of-government-departments/

Nicholson, N. (2007). Individual metaphysics–the getting of wisdom: Self-conduct, personal identity, and wisdom across the life span. In E. H. Kessler & J. R. Bailey (Eds.), *Handbook of organizational and managerial wisdom* (pp. 377–397). Thousand Oaks, CA: Sage Publications.

Nielsen, T. M., Edmondson, A. C., & Sundstrom, E. (2007). Interpersonal logic— Team wisdom: Definition, dynamics, and applications. In E. H. Kessler & J. R. Bailey (Eds.), *Handbook of organizational and managerial wisdom* (pp. 21–42). Thousand Oaks, CA: Sage Publications.

Nonaka, I. (1994). A dynamic theory of organizational knowledge creation. *Organization Science, 5*(1), 14–37.

Nussbaum, M. C. (1990). *Love's knowledge: Essays on philosophy and literature*. Oxford: Oxford University Press.

OECD Health Data 2014. (2014). Retrieved from http://www.oecd.org/health/healthdata

Offermann, L. R., Kennedy, J. K., & Wirtz, P. W. (1994). Implicit leadership theories: Content, structure, and generalizability. *The Leadership Quarterly, 5*(1), 43–58.

Offermann, L. R., & Phan, L. U. (2002). Culturally intelligent leadership for a diverse world. In R. E. Riggio, S. E. Murphy, & J. Pirozzolo (Eds.), *Multiple intelligences and leaderships* (pp. 187–214). Mahwah, NJ: Lawrence Erlbaum.

Oldenhof, L., Postma, J., & Putters, K. (2014). On justification work: How compromising enables public managers to deal with conflicting values. *Public Administration Review, 74*(1), 52–63.

Oliver, D., & Roos, J. (2005). Decision-making in high-velocity environments: The importance of guiding principles. *Organization Studies, 26*(6), 889–913.

Olsen, T. D., Payne, L. A., & Reiter, A. G. (2012). Amnesty in the age of accountability: Brazil in comparative context. In B. Flyvbjerg, T. Landman, & S. Schram (Eds.), *Real social science: Applied phronesis* (pp. 204–227). Cambridge: Cambridge University Press.

Orwoll, L., & Perlmutter, M. (1990). The study of wise persons: Integrating a personality perspective. In R. J. Sternberg (Ed.), *Wisdom: Its nature, origins, and development* (pp. 160–177). Cambridge: Cambridge University Press.

Ostrom, E. (1998). A behavioral approach to the rational choice theory of collective action. *American Political Science Review, 92*(01), 1–22.

Park, G. H., Garm, A., Friesen, K., & Chu, L. (2015). Delaying proactively the frailty/Retrasar Proactivamente la Fragilidad. *International Journal of Integrated Care, 15*(8).

Paton, B. (2003). *Managing and measuring social enterprises*. London: Sage Publishing.

Peck, J. (2000). Structuring the labour market: A segmentation approach. In S. Ackroyd & S. Fleetwood (Eds.), *Realist perspectives on management and organisations* (pp. 220–244). New York, NY: Routledge.

Pentland, B. T. (1999). Building process theory with narrative: From description to explanation. *Academy of Management Review*, *24*(4), 711–724.

Perrow, C. (1986). Economic theories of organization. *Theory and Society*, *15*(1/2), 11–45.

Peterson, C., & Seligman, M. E. P. (2004). *Character strengths and virtues: A handbook and classification*. Washington, DC: American Psychological Association.

Pfeffer, J., & Salanick, G. R. (1974). Organizational decision making as a political process: The case of a university budget. *Administrative Science Quarterly*, *19*(2), 135–151.

Phillips, N., & Oswick, C. (2012). Organizational discourse: Domains, debates and directions. *Academy of Managment Annals*, *6*, 435–481.

Phillips, R. A. (1997). Stakeholder theory and a principle of fairness. *Business Ethics Quarterly*, *7*(1), 51–66.

Pitsis, T. S., & Clegg, S. R. (2007). Interpersonal metaphysics – "We live in a political world": The paradox of managerial wisdom. In E. H. Kessler & J. R. Bailey (Eds.), *Handbook of organizational and managerial wisdom* (pp. 399–422). Thousand Oaks, CA: Sage Publications.

Polanyi, M. (1966). *The tacit dimension*. London: Routledge & Kegan Paul.

Porter, S. (1993). Critical realist ethnography: The case of racism and professionalism in a medical setting. *Sociology*, *27*(4), 591–609.

Pratten, S. (1993). Structure, agency and Marx's analysis of the labour process. *Review of Political Economy*, *5*(4), 403–426.

Province of British Columbia. (n.d.). Health authorities – province of British Columbia. Retrieved from https://www2.gov.bc.ca/gov/content/health/about-bc-s-health-care-system/partners/health-authorities. Accessed on August 17, 2018.

Rachels, J., & Rachels, S. (2015). *The elements of moral philosophy* (8th ed.). New York, NY: McGraw-Hill Education.

Reay, T., & Hinings, C. R. (2009). Managing the rivalry of competing institutional logics. *Organization Studies*, *30*(6), 629–652.

Reed, M. (1997). In praise of duality and dualism: Rethinking agency and structure in organisational analysis. *Organization Studies*, *18*(1), 21–42.

Rockwood, K., Song, X., MacKnight, C., Bergman, H., Hogan, D. B., McDowell, I., & Mitnitski, A. (2005). A global clinical measure of fitness and frailty in elderly people. *Canadian Medical Association Journal*, *173*(5), 489–495.

Rodriguez, C., Langley, A., Beland, F., & Denis, J.-L. (2007). Governance, power, and mandated collaboration in an interorganizational network. *Administration & Society*, *39*(2), 150–193.

Romme, A. G. L. (2003). Making a difference: Organization as design. *Organization Science*, *14*(5), 558–573.

Rubery, J. (1994). The British production regime: A societal-specific system? *Economy and Society*, *23*(3), 335–354.

Salovey, P., & Mayer, J. D. (1990). Emotional intelligence. *Imagination, Cognition and Personality*, *9*(3), 185–211.

Sampson, E. E. (1998). The political organization of wisdom and courage. In S. Srivastva & D. L. Cooperrider (Eds.), *Organizational wisdom and executive courage* (pp. 118–133). San Francisco, CA: The New Lexington Press.

Sandercock, L., & Attili, G. (2012). Unsettling a settler society: Film, phronesis and collaborative planning in small-town Canada. In B. Flyvbjerg, T. Landman, & S. Schram (Eds.), *Real social science: Applied phronesis* (pp. 137–166). Cambridge: Cambridge University Press.

Sayer, A. (1992). *Method in social science: A realist approach.* New York, NY: Routledge.

Schön, D. A. (1983). *The reflective practitioner: How professionals think in action.* New York, NY: Basic Books.

Schram, S. (2012). Phronetic social science: An idea whose time has come. In B. Flyvbjerg, T. Landman, & S. Schram (Eds.), *Real social science: Applied phronesis* (pp. 15–26). Cambridge: Cambridge University Press.

Scott, W. R. (1982). Managing professional work: Three models of control for health organization. *Health Services Research, 17*(3), 213–240.

Selden, S. C., Brewer, G. A., & Brudney, J. L. (1999). Reconciling competingvalues in public administration: Understanding the administrative role concept. *Administration & Society, 31*, 171–204.

Self-Management Resource Center. (2018). Chronic Disease Self-Management (CDSMP). Retrieved from https://www.selfmanagementresource.com/programs/small-group/chronic-disease-self-management/. Accessed on August 4, 2018.

Sewell, G., & Wilkinson, B. (1992). Someone to watch over me: Surveillance, discipline and the just-in-time labour process. *Sociology, 26*(2), 271–289.

Shdaimah, C., & Stahl, R. (2012). Power and conflict in collaborative research. In B. Flyvbjerg, T. Landman, & S. Schram (Eds.), *Real social science: Applied phronesis* (pp. 122–136). Cambridge: Cambridge University Press.

Sherman, N. (1989). *The fabric of character: Aristotle's theory of virtue.* Oxford: Oxford University Press.

Siggelkow, N. (2007). Persuasion with case studies. *Academy of Management Journal, 50*(1), 20–24.

Simmons, W. P. (2012). Making the teaching of social justice matter. In B. Flyvbjerg, T. Landman, & S. Schram (Eds.), *Real social science: Applied phronesis* (pp. 246–263). Cambridge: Cambridge University Press.

Simon, H. A. (1959). Theories of decision-making in economics and behavioral science. *The American Economic Review, 49*(3), 253–283.

Simons, T., & Ingram, P. (1997). Organization and ideology: Kibbutzim and Hired labor: 1951–1965. *Administrative Science Quarterly, 42*(4), 784–813.

Simpson, J. (2012). *Chronic condition: Why Canada's health-care system needs to be dragged into the 21st century.* Toronto: Penguin Canada.

Slaznick, P. (1949). *TVA and the grassroots.* Berkeley, CA: University of California Press.

Smith, D. E. (2001). Texts and the ontology of organizations and institutions. *Studies in Cultures, 7*(2), 159–198.

Smith, P. (1993). Outcome related performance indicators and organizational control in the public sector. *British Journal of Management, 4*(3), 135–152.

Spender, J. C. (1996). Making knowledge the basis of a dynamic theory of the firm. *Strategic Management Journal, 17*(S2), 45–62.

Statler, M., & Roos, J. (2006). Reframing strategic preparedness: An essay on practical wisdom. *International Journal of Management Concepts and Philosophy*, *2*(2), 99—117.

Statler, M., Roos, J., & Victor, B. (2006). Illustrating the need for practical wisdom. *International Journal of Management Concepts and Philosophy*, *2*(1), 1—30.

Sternberg, R. J. (Ed.). (1990). *Wisdom: Its nature, origins, and development.* New York, NY: Cambridge University Press.

Sternberg, R. J. (1998). A balance theory of wisdom. *Review of General Psychology*, *2*(4), 347—365.

Sternberg, R. J. (Ed.). (2002). *Why smart people can be so stupid.* New Haven, CT: Yale University Press.

Sternberg, R. J. (2003a). WICS: A model of leadership in organizations. *Academy of Management Learning & Education*, *2*(4), 386—401.

Sternberg, R. J. (2003b). *Wisdom, intelligence, and creativity synthesized.* New York, NY: Cambridge University Press.

Sternberg, R. J. (2005a). Foolishness. In R. J. Sternberg & J. Jordan (Eds.), *A handbook of wisdom: Psychological perspectives* (pp. 331—352). New York, NY: Cambridge University Press.

Sternberg, R. J. (2005b). WICS: A model of positive educational leadership comprising wisdom, intelligence, and creativity synthesized. *Educational Psychology Review*, *17*(3), 191—262.

Stewart, J. (2006). Value conflict and policy change. *Review of Policy Research*, *23*, 183—195.

Stinchcombe, A. L. (1990). Reason and rationality. In K. S. Cook & M. Levi (Eds.), *The limits of rationality* (pp. 285—323). Chicago, IL: The University of Chicago Press.

Talbot, M. (2004). Good wine may need to mature: A critique of accelerated higher specialist training. Evidence from cognitive neuroscience. *Medical Education*, *38*(4), 399—408.

Thacher, D., & Rein, R. (2004). Managing value conflict in public policy. *Governance*, *17*, 457—486.

The College of Family Physicians of Canada. (2018). The patient's medical home. Retrieved from https://patientsmedicalhome.ca/. Accessed on July 24, 2018.

Townley, B. (1993). Foucault, power/knowledge and its relevance for human resource management. *Academy of Management Review*, *18*(3), 518—545.

Townley, B. (2008a). Performance measurement systems and the criminal justice system: Rationales and rationalities. In J. Hartley, C. Skelcher, C. Donaldson, & M. Wallace (Eds.), *Managing improvement in public service delivery: Progress and challenges.* Cambridge: Cambridge University Press.

Townley, B. (2008b). *Reason's neglect: Rationality and organizing.* New York, NY: Oxford University Press.

Training Fellowship. (2014a, August 1). Minutes: [Seniors Group] project team meeting 2014-08-01.

Training Fellowship. (2014b, September 19). Minutes: [Seniors Group] project team meeting 2014-09-19.

Tsoukas, H. (1989). The validity of idiographic research explanations. *Academy of Management Review*, *14*(4), 551—561.

Tsoukas, H. (1994). What is management? An outline of a metatheory. *British Journal of Management, 5*(4), 289–301.

Tsui, A. S., & O'Reilly, C. A. (1989). Beyond simple demographic effects: The importance of relational demography in superior-subordinate dyads. *Academy of Management Journal, 32*(2), 402–423.

Tucker, A. W. (1983). The mathematics of tucker: A sampler. *The Two Year College Mathematics Journal, 14*(3), 228–232.

Turillo, C. J., Folger, R., Lavelle, J. J., Umphress, E. E., & Gee, J. O. (2002). Is virtue its own reward? self-sacrificial decisions for the sake of fairness. *Organizational Behavior and Human Decision Processes, 89*(1), 839–865.

Vaill, P. B. (1998). The unspeakable texture of process wisdom. In S. Srivastva & D. L. Cooperrider (Eds.), *Organizational wisdom and executive courage* (pp. 25–39). San Francisco, CA: The New Lexington Press.

Vaill, P. B. (2007). Organizational epistemology–interpersonal relations in organizations and the emergence of wisdom. In E. H. Kessler & J. R. Bailey (Eds.), *Handbook of organizational and managerial wisdom* (pp. 327–355). Thousand Oaks, CA: Sage Publications.

van Aken, J. E. (2004). Management research based on the paradigm of the design sciences: The quest for field-tested and grounded technological rules. *Journal of Management Studies, 41*(2), 219–246.

van Dijk, E., & Tenbrunsel, A. (2005). The battle between self-interest and fairness: Evidence from ultimatum, dictator, and delta games. In S. W. Gilliland, D. D. Steiner, D. P. Skarlicki, & K. van den Bos (Eds.), *What motivates fairness in organizations* (pp. 31–48). Greenwich, CT: Information Age.

Van Maanen, J., & Barley, S. R. (1982). *Occupational communities: Culture and control in organizations*. Fort Belvoir, VA: Defense Technical Information Center.

Vaughan, D. (1990). Autonomy, interdependence, and social control: NASA and the space shuttle challenger. *Administrative Science Quarterly, 35*(2), 225.

Weaver, R. M. (2003). *Ideas have consequences* (Expanded ed.). Chicago, IL: The University of Chicago Press.

Weber, M. (1978). *Economy and society*. In G. Roth & C. Wittich (Eds.). Berkeley, CA: University of California Press.

Weick, K. E. (1998). The attitude of wisdom: Ambivalence as the ultimate compromise. In S. Srivastva & D. L. Cooperrider (Eds.), *Organizational wisdom and executive courage* (pp. 40–64). San Francisco, CA: The New Lexington Press.

Weick, K. E. (2001). *Making sense of the organization*. Malden, MA: Blackwell Publishing.

Weick, K. E. (2007). Forward. In E. H. Kessler & J. R. Bailey (Eds.), *Handbook of organizational and managerial wisdom* (pp. ix–xiii). Thousand Oaks, CA: Sage Publications.

Whittington, R. (1989). *Corporate strategies in recovery and recession: Social structure and strategic choice*. London: Unwin Hyman.

Whittington, R. (1992). Putting giddens into action: Social systems and managerial agency. *Journal of Management Studies, 29*(6), 693–712.

Wiggins, D. (1975). Deliberation and practical reason. *Proceedings of the Aristotelian Society, 76*(1975–1976), 29–51.

Wilkins, A. L. (1989). *Developing corporate character: How to successfully change an organization without destroying it.* San Francisco, CA: Jossey-Bass.

Willmott, R. (1997). Structure, culture and agency: Rejecting the current orthodoxy of organisation theory. *Journal for the Theory of Social Behaviour, 27*(1), 93–123.

Yin, R. K. (2014). *Case study research: Design and methods* (5th ed.). Thousand Oaks, CA: Sage Publications.

Zimmerman, B., Lindberg, C., & Plsek, P. E. (1998). *Edgeware: Insights from complexity science for health care leaders.* Irving, TX: VHA.

Index

www.ingramcontent.com/pod-product-compliance
Lightning Source LLC
Jackson TN
JSHW011916131224
75386JS00004B/220